The Option Offense
For Winning Basketball

Dedication

To the unsung—those teachers of the most exciting and greatest of all American sports, who for reasons known only to them, remain deep in the "bushes" of basketball, with only the permanently instilled awe and respect they get from the young men whose lives they touched early as testimony to their importance.

The Option Offense
For Winning Basketball

A.L. "Lee" Walker

Parker Publishing Company, Inc.
West Nyack, New York

Library of Congress Cataloging in Publication Data

Walker, A L
   The option   offense for winning basketball.

   Includes index.
   1. Basketball coaching. I. Title.
GV885.3.W34   796.32'3'077   77-6404
ISBN 0-13-638361-0

Printed in the United States of America

Providing the Coach
With a Complete Offense

This book presents a basketball offense which functions readily against either the man-man defense or the variety of zone formations. It furnishes drills and ideas that make the offense successful. It is a reference for the new coach who is looking for an offensive plan, and also for the experienced coach who is looking for a change.

Since the offense is workable against any defensive plan without major adjustment or improvisation, it should be called a multiple offense. The multiplicity derives mainly from the feature of *option*. In the philosophy of option in basketball, if something doesn't work, something else will if the optional sequences are followed; and there need be no breakdown in continuity and tempo. Tempo is important. It dictates the game!

Four major tactical qualities provide the foundation for this offensive plan: (1) purposeful movement of the ball, (2) purposeful movement of players, (3) floor balance, and (4) patience in shot selection. The plan is also based on a positive premise that an offense of five men working as a team with purpose and plan can overwhelm and outmaneuver any defense and that the ultimate in offense is achieved when a player takes a good, high-percentage shot at the end of a pass from his teammate.

The Option Offense consists of three series: Red, White, and Blue—all signalled and keyed by a play-maker as the ball is being brought down-court. Each of them (Red, White, and Blue) has a built-in, integral phase called Mixmaster. Emphasizing simplicity and attention to basic fundamentals, all three series feature purposeful movement in primary and secondary routes, including those of Mixmaster, during which options unfold and are discarded until one provides the prime attempt at a field goal.

While the material in this book emphasizes the disciplined approach towards offense, with planned movements and routes, the individualistic aspect is not discouraged at all. When installing your offense (Chapter 1), you stress that the patterned offense does not dictate and rule at the expense of individual basketball spontaneity; instead, every player is encouraged to take advantage of an opening that occurs during the sequence of the patterns.

The Option Offense is applicable to all levels of competition. Probably the only difference to be noted in its usage would be the quality of performance and execution at different levels. Certain parts of this offense have been, and are being, accepted and utilized by teams wherever basketball is played; but the totality is my own doing. The basic concepts and ideas presented in this book have roots in my coaching of Army teams in the 1950's, although changes and modifications have been made since that time.

The Option Offense requires drills that uniquely demand perfection in basic fundamentals, the coaching of which has captivated and dominated my own interest and effort. Chapters 7 and 12 are particularly devoted to this important part of a basketball program.

Special plays are in Chapter 8. It will be noted that individuals set up in special play positions in conformity with the way they set up in the regular offense. The idea, again, is simplicity. Each player at each of the five positions has a special play. Also included is one out-of-bounds under-basket play with options and a side-court pass-in procedure. All of these add dimension to the offense because there are times and situations in a game when a "sure-fire" field goal is needed.

Although the book is essentially one of offense, there must be discussions and material pertaining to defense. Chapters 5, 6, and 10 are very worth-while and provocative in showing what to expect from present-day defenses in response to the Option Offense, because illustrations and specific examples are included. Within the Option Offense is a well-tested plan for meeting pressure defenses; it is detailed in Chapter 10.

A highlight must be noted in Chapter 13, "Preparing the Offense for the Game." In a rehearsal the day before, you run two five-man teams through all of the previously practiced options that may occur. The "starting five" is at one end of the court, the "second five" at the other. You take the teams through the offense in an intensive review. Organized and executed as intended, it helps you to summarize and prepare for the game.

The material in Chapter 9, "Coordinating a Fast Break Plan into the Option Offense," offers a change of pace to the reader, in that verbatim instructions are being issued directly to the players in a fast break practice session. The mechanics of defensive rebounding, the outlet pass, filling the lanes, penetration, and convergence on the basket are dealt with in this personal manner.

The Option Offense, some years in the making, is a sound one which contains *floor balance* at all times, gives full play to continuous movement, and looks for scoring options. It will be successful if you will combine these inherent characteristics with your teaching of aggressiveness, basic fundamentals, and physical conditioning.

I hope this book describes and interprets the Option Offense to the extent that reader-coaches, both new and experienced, will gain useful ideas and, at the same time, be encouraged to adopt it as a promising offensive system.

A.L. "Lee" Walker

Acknowledgements

I must give credit to two people for their help in the preparation of this book. Mr. John L. Griffith, publisher of *Athletic Journal*, may have, unknowingly, furnished the initial spark and motivation when he accepted two articles from me for publication. I was flattered, because I have always had such a high regard for the quality and professionalism of *Athletic Journal*. More important, his communications to me carried a tone of encouragement to the extent that I felt qualified to expand my effort. Again, he may not realize this at all.

The second person knows little about the intricacies of basketball and has done little writing beyond that required of the manager of a household. But I would never, ever, have finished what I set out to do without her understanding and tolerance. The past couple of years have not been easy. Without the help of my wife, Lucia, they would have been impossible.

A.L. "Lee" Walker

Table of Contents

12. Directing Special Drills *(Cont.)*

Front-Wheel Drive (217) . . . Basics at Start of Blue Series
(218) . . . Shoot in the Triangle (220) . . . Quick Release
(220) . . . Shoot and Retrieve (221) . . . Triangle Passing
(222) . . . Double-Post Drill (222) . . . Work for the Good
Shot (223) . . . 4-on-4, Count the Passes (223) . . . Three
Passes to Number Three (224) . . . Example of Penetration
by a Pro (225) . . . Penetration, Red Series (226) . . .
Down the Middle and Pass Out (227) . . . Move or Run a
Lap (227) . . . Fast Break (228) . . . Fast Break, Pass to
the Trailer (229) . . . Another Fast Break (230) . . .
County Fair (230) . . . Summary (234)

Objective (236) . . . General Plan (236) . . . Procedure for
Option Offense Review (237) . . . Purpose of Pre-Game
Warm-Ups (242) . . . Warm-Up Drill for Rebounders and
Passers (243) . . . Warm-Up for the Back Door (243) . . .
Warm-Up for Dribblers, Talkers, and Switchers (244) . . .
Warm-Up for Passers and Movers (244) . . . Warm-Up for
Passers and Shooters (245) . . . Summary (246)

Chapter One

Installing the Option Offense

IMPORTANCE OF ORIENTATION

The title for this chapter could well have been "Gaining the Confidence of the Reader," because that is what it seems to set out to do. Not too much of the Option Offense, as such, is installed in this chapter. That is left up to following chapters, where it is explained in detail. Here, we stress the importance of indoctrination and teaching, label and characterize the players in the Option Offense, suggest some methodology in its installation, and present the basic and salient features of the offense. This material will promote confidence and enthusiasm, transferable from coach to player as the Option Offense is being installed and perfected, day-by-day and step-by-step.

Confidence, optimism, and enthusiasm are of signal importance when you are beginning to install an organized, rules-oriented style of offense.

Another element that must be inserted right away is the need to establish definite goals as related to the Option Offense and how these objectives are to be achieved through practice and hard work. I suggest that you be very definite about the demands to be placed on the players. Understandings and concepts, particularly those related to the requirements and rules for practice sessions, are of the utmost importance. There must be no doubt about what is to be demanded, and you have to convince the players that the system will work if they devote wholehearted effort to it. Coach Bob Boyd, University of Southern

California, stated at a coaches' clinic that the installation of an offense and the first days of practice make up the "formative time," the time to define what is expected of the players and to "lay it on the line."

The installation of the offense must be gradual. The total offense cannot be understood or perfected from charting its entirety on a chalkboard. The orientation must be more subtle than that. The offense is to be broken down into components and taught by way of drills. At the end of a snappy drill, with the players executing well, you may announce, "That's part of your offense." Drills and basic fundamentals are not a chore to the players when they understand and appreciate that the hard work has a purpose and a place in the offense that is going to be used.

Installation of this offense is marked with repetition of pertinent component drills until skills and habits are polished and movements instinctive. Then it is assembled for utilization by the team, and the work goes on from there in preparation for the opening game. Teaching methods throughout the season, including the "formative time," feature the steps of *Purpose* (the coach states the objective), *Explanation* (the coach, his clipboard, and chalkboard), *Demonstration* (the coach and the models), and *Application* (the players do it).

You operate from a prepared practice plan, organized to meet certain objectives. You are on the floor before the players. When you blow your whistle, all basketballs are rolled to the managers quickly and quietly, and the players run to you, usually at the chalkboard.

Purpose and *Explanation* must be brief, and the players must become acquainted with basketball symbols that are drawn on the chalkboard. As a review, here they are; they also serve as symbolization for the diagrams in this book:

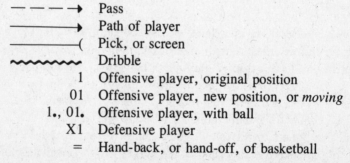

– – – →	Pass
———→	Path of player
———⟨	Pick, or screen
∿∿∿	Dribble
1	Offensive player, original position
01	Offensive player, new position, or *moving*
1., 01.	Offensive player, with ball
X1	Defensive player
=	Hand-back, or hand-off, of basketball

You "talk" your model or models through the *Demonstration* in a professional, business-like manner. Some drills for *Demonstration* could be rehearsed beforehand. The demonstration must be technically and fundamentally sound. In the *Application* phase, it is necessary to have the players charted by name beforehand. Much time will be wasted otherwise.

Figure 1-1 illustrates the original set of the Option Offense. It must be understood at the very first drill and orientation that the players *arrive* at these set areas full speed from the back court into the operational front court, that no sauntering is permitted except where timing or back court help against pressure is involved, and that the initiating pass for any of the three series of the offense may be made while the players are getting into position. This rule particularly applies to 3. He is to appear at the side high post by the most direct means, and he is to receive his pass in the proper area. Here he can expect a battle. Never will an aggressive defense permit him to amble around and stand, waiting for a pass at the place indicated in Figure 1-2. He will be

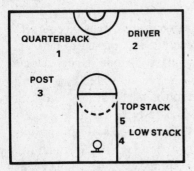

Figure 1-1. Designations.

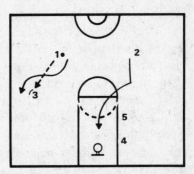

Figure 1-2. Opening moves, Red.

over-played, and there will be constant attempts to force him out. So, the mandatory rule is: the offense gets into high gear in a hurry, the ball is brought down court expeditiously, and the defense is not permitted to *deny* positioning. This may be a patterned, disciplined, rules-oriented offense, but nobody ever strolls going into it.

CHARACTERISTICS OF PLAYERS

Since we have mentioned 3, we may as well go ahead and define his characteristics at this time. He is the traditional big forward who is capable of playing high post at the wing and top-of-the-key. 3 shoots well from the top of the key and from medium-range side areas. He is one of the rebounding triumvirate and is big and strong enough to withstand intimidation as he turns to face the basket and pass to weak-side cutters and the low post. Although the Option Offense guarantees that no one monopolizes the basketball, that everyone does get the "feel of the ball," and that there are options for every player as the movement unfolds, we must expect, at all levels, that 3 will be the high scorer on the team. This is the tendency, for whatever reason.

1 operates in a position of leadership in a customary guard position. He is quick, alert, a good dribbler and passer, confident, and poised. He is the "coach's man" on the floor since he gives signals for the offense.

2 is a prototype of 1. He is an adept dribbler and passer with similar qualities of leadership. He helps 1 bring the ball up court, as necessary, in all situations and works out certain signals and keys with 1. 2 is an aggressive weak-side cutter and likes to penetrate in free-lance style when there is opportunity. As the Option Offense commits itself, he operates generally on his own side of the offensive court (the left), while 1 operates on the right. 2 could be expected to takes 1's place in a substitute role, as necessary, just as 1 would be expected to change over to his position.

4 and 5 are the big men, trained in low post play, rebounding, and setting picks and screens down low. Both are proficient in close-in work with hook shots and turn-around short jumpers. The 4 position calls for more mobility and movement and seems to produce more field goal attempts. 4 is expected to be knowledgeable about the responsibilities of 5, just as 5 could, in a pinch, take 4's place in a substitute situation.

Positions in the offense are referred to by number, not by the traditional position designations of guard, forward, and center. Players have designations as well as numbers. 1, the play-maker, may be called the quarterback; 2 would respond to driver; 3 is a side post, or high post; and 5 and 4 are top stack and low stack respectively. These labels are indicated in Figure 1-1.

GENERAL ASPECTS OF THE OPTION OFFENSE

We will now deal with basic formations of the Option Offense;

the initial movements and keys that initiate and commit it into a Red, White or Blue Series; and the development of routes for all three series up to the Mixmaster phase. Few, if any, specific scoring options will be analyzed, as such, in this section.

The Mixmaster will be referred to separately in a section following this one. Its movements, routes, and objectives are common to all three series. Therefore, to avoid repetitious diagramming and description, a one-time general orientation in a separate section seems feasible. Included in the section will be allusion and reference to the minor positioning adjustment that is made against zone defenses, and a diagram which points out excellent rebounding traits.

The pass from 1 to 3 at the wing, which triggers the Red Series and clears out the side, is shown in Figure 1-2. It always takes place on the right side and is always initiated by 1. In following his pass to 3 to receive the hand-back as shown, 01 presses toward the inside, driving his defensive man back toward the key area; then, he accelerates to his right, swerving to the outside of 3. This coincides with the weak-side cut down the key by 02, as shown in the diagram. This is the first potential scoring option in the Red Series, as 02 uses all his quickness and guile to shake loose from his defensive man. The effort is usually quite productive because the defensive man is uncertain about the intent of 02, and the defensive action is affected by thoughts of a likely collision with the stack barrier of 5 and 4.

Continuing the routes of the Red Series, Figure 1-3 shows the hand-back of the ball to 01 and the clear-out by 03 to the top-of-the-key. 03 looks back at 01 as he moves, gives a head-shoulder fake and feint toward the basket, and then steps back for the possible return pass and jump shot. 02 continues his route, emerging from behind the stack to finish at the foul line extended in the wing area on his side of the court. He faces the basket and is ready to continue his role in the offense.

In Figure 1-4, the stack goes into action in the Red Series. 01 has the ball, 03 has released to the top of the key, and 02 is veering around behind the stack, finally reappearing in the wing area. Using the screening effect, 04 comes around 5, swings across the key, and looks for a pass from 01. If refused, he terminates his route just outside the key, with his back to the basket, ready to continue in a new role as a player at the low post.

After acting as a screen in Figure 1-4, 05 immediately follows 04

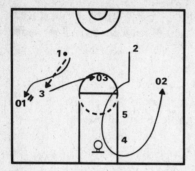

Figure 1-3. Routes of 01, 02, and 03, Red.

Figure 1-4. 04's route out of the stack, Red.

in Figure 1-5 as *second man through*, also looking for a pass in the key from 01. If refused, he swings back to play a low post near his original position with his back to the basket. *Second man through* is a prominent offensive principle in the Option Offense, designed to counter and respond to defensive switching.

Figure 1-6 shows the new set called Mixmaster, which has evolved from the primary routes of the Red Series. No shooting options have been presented so far, and the developing formation consists of 04 and 05 in double low post, 01 and 02 at the wings, and 03 as point man at the top of the key. 01 has the ball.

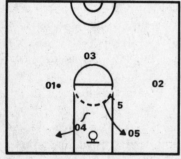

Figure 1-5. 05 as second man through, Red.

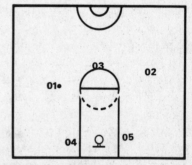

Figure 1-6. Mixmaster set has developed, Red.

The Red Series is ready to go into the Mixmaster phase. We will suspend it there, and go on to discuss the general routes of the White Series.

In Figure 1-7, the ball has reached the front court and the players are reaching their Option Offense areas. 1 has signaled or indicated the White Series. 2 initiates it with his pass to 03 at the top of the key. 03 flashes out to receive the pass, opening up the entire side for the back door cut of 01. The White Series has begun; timing is very important to the success of this first option.

With 01 being refused by 3 in Figure 1-8, 02 is cutting down the

 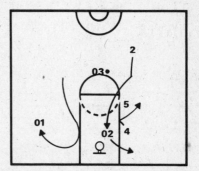

Figure 1-7. White Series begins. Back door by 01.

Figure 1-8. 01 is refused. 02 and 04 cut. White.

key hoping for a short pass from 03. If refused, he continues his route as 04 starts to come around the screen of 5. In Figure 1-9, 04 is hoping for a "high-low" pass from 03. High-low pass action is exciting to watch, since there are all types of passes used by the player at the top-of-the-key high post in getting the ball down to the moving 04 in the low part of the key. If unable to pass to 04, or if 04 is not open, 03 would look down for 05, who is shown in Figure 1-9 as second man through. 02 has reached his wing area, 01 has appeared at his wing area, 04 is at his low post position, and 05 is arriving at his low post position in Figure 1-10. 03 has the ball. The offense has had no shooting options, and the White Series has evolved into the Mixmaster positioning of double low post, two wing men, and a point. The Mixmaster phase would go on without hesitation. It will be suspended now, however, while we go on to a discussion of the Blue Series.

The Blue Series is initiated in Figure 1-11 as 04 pops out from behind 5 to receive the pass from 2. Before going on, we should state that 1 makes "no big thing" out of his signals and keys. With experience and practice, as as a matter of fact, he may do away with voice notification and elaborate hand signals. A simple directional wave of the hand as he passes over to 2 for the Blue Series may be sufficient communication. 04 can be coached and prepared to break out from behind 5 automatically when the pass is made from 1 to 2 or when 02 is dribbling down court on his own and crosses center court on the left side. 03, as well, can start to flash out to the high post, thinking in terms of White. He can always stop short, turn quickly, and go back. There are innumerable ways for the team to work out intercommunication procedures. 02 follows his pass to the outside of 04 and hooks back (Figure 1-12) if the ball isn't returned to him as he goes by. For our purposes of showing primary routes, 04 refuses him, turns, looks down at 5, refuses him, and reverses the ball to 01 (Figure 1-12) at the top of the key. We now have shuffle movement with the reverse pass

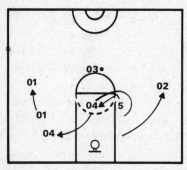

Figure 1-9. 02 and 04 are refused. 05 is second man through. White.

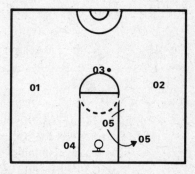

Figure 1-10. 05 is not open. Mixmaster set. White.

Figure 1-11. Start of Blue.

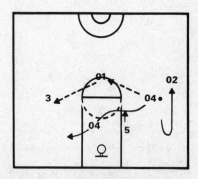

Figure 1-12. 04 reverses the ball and cuts. Blue.

as 04 cuts over the top of 05's screen (05 comes out when the ball is reversed). 01 may return the pass to 04 immediately (give-and-go principle), or he may continue the reversal of the ball with his pass over to 3 (Figure 1-12) as 04 is cutting across the key. If refused all the way, 04 continues to his new low post position, as shown. In Figure 1-13, 05 tried his move as second man through, was refused, and moved back to his low post position. The team has arrived at the Mixmaster set in the Blue Series, having had no scoring options so far.

MIXMASTER PHASE, GENERAL

A few examples of the Mixmaster phase will serve the purpose for this chapter, and then it will be dealt with in more depth in other appropriate places in the book. The players will be enthusiastic about this part of the offense. There is a feeling of freedom of movement, there will be no problems with the simple, but interesting, routes, and the players know the philosophy allows them to deviate and take advantage of an opening that presents itself during the structured movement.

Since Figure 1-13 carried the Blue Series up to Mixmaster, we will continue from that point in Figure 1-14. Although he has other choices, 01 passes over to 3 (Pass A) for the sake of our example, as he activates Mixmaster. He cuts down the key, looking for a return, give-and-go pass. If refused, he continues down the key to come out "opposite," around the screen of 05. 02 replaces 01 at the point and,

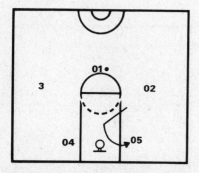

Figure 1-13. 05 as second man through. Mixmaster develops Blue.

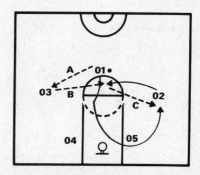

Figure 1-14. Mixmaster, Blue. Point passes to wing.

in our example, receives a reverse type pass from 03 (Pass B). 02 chooses to continue the reverse action with a pass over to 01, who is coming out open at the wing (Pass C). Four rules apply to movement in the Mixmaster, three of which are established in this diagram: (1) the point man cuts down the key after his pass to a wing, (2) the wing man *away from the ball* replaces the point man, (3) the cutter must come down and around the low post screen that is "opposite" the passes, and (4) not shown in this diagram, the point man also cuts down the key when a pass from a wing is going down to the low post. These rules ensure uncomplicated filler and replacement continuity at the wings and point.

Although not a rule, 04 and 05 may exchange at the low posts as the ball moves around outside to counteract fronting and defensive over-play.

Figure 1-15 signifies a new start of Mixmaster, possibly out of the Red or White Series. 03 is located at the point and chooses to start the action with a pass to 02 at that wing. He then cuts down the key looking for a return pass, as 01 re-fills the point. 03 goes around the low post screen opposite and comes out to replace 01.

Figures 1-16, 1-17, and 1-18 carry on from 1-15 as examples of a possible sequence of passes and movement when we would expect scoring options to occur. The sequence ends at Figure 1-18.

In Figure 1-16, 02 passes down to low post 05, so 01 breaks down the key. 03 replaces him. If refused by 05 (he will be open much of the time for a tricky little bounce-pass or short pass from 05), 01 continues around 04 to replace the vacated wing.

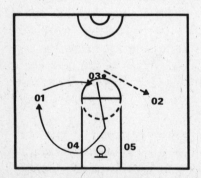

Figure 1-15. Mixmaster, any series. Point passes to wing.

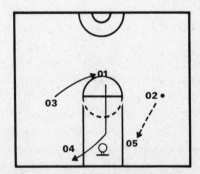

Figure 1-16. 02 passes to low post. 01 cuts. 03 becomes point.

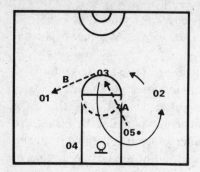

Figure 1-17. Fan-pass out to point. On to wing.

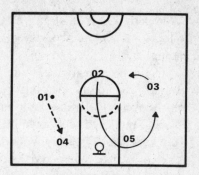

Figure 1-18. Sequence example concludes. Wing to low post.

Although movement is not shown, 02 does not stand idle after his pass to the low post. He moves around in his general wing area to get open for a possible return pass and jump shot.

In Figure 1-17, 05 finds 03 open out at the top of the key, and he would jump high at the low post to deliver a fan-type pass out to the point. For purposes of illustration, 03 passes on over to 01, cuts down the key, and 02 replaces.

The sequence concludes, for our purposes here, when 01 delivers the ball down to his low post man in Figure 1-18, 02 cuts as shown, and 03 replaces.

In Figure 1-19, we show how Mixmaster furnishes a simple way to adjust, if necessary, when the opponent uses a zone defense. The point man, in this case 03, makes a minor positioning adjustment as he arrives at the point by dribbling (or moving, if he doesn't have the ball) to the curving top-side area of the key, as shown. This forms a workable over-load triangle consisting of 03, 02, and 05. Establishment of a side triangle for passing, with concomitant attention to teammates on the weak side and to the sensitive, vulnerable down-the-key lane area, is a classic way of attacking an opponent's zone defense. The principles of Mixmaster, which require continual movement along with the passing, meet all these prerequisites.

Adjustment occurs at the start of Mixmaster, but it must be pointed out that Red, White, or Blue may very well have produced a scoring option long before developing up to Mixmaster. Our confidence in the success of this offense, as it stands, is such that we make no alterations in its original set (Figure 1-1), nor in its philosophy.

"Run your routes of Red, White, or Blue. Move without the ball. Pass to the open man. If scoring options do not accrue, Mixmaster is coming up!"

Only one diagram (Figure 1-19) will be offered to show the ease of transition to the passing triangle; the formation of the triangle, which overloads and overtaxes the defense on that side; the usual (slightly modified) cut down the key by the point man after his pass to the wing (Pass A); his continuance around a screen at the low post; and the added weak-side activity of 01 flashing out to become a replacement at the point.

You may infer that the passing triangle and the weak-side movement swing to the other side and back-and-forth as necessary.

The intent of Figure 1-20 is to advertise the good qualities of offensive rebounding positioning that naturally exist in the Option Offense, particularly when it is in the Mixmaster phase. The triangular concept, as drawn, is fundamentally sound. On a missed shot, two low post men and a point man are on hand for rebounding repossession. Two wing men are in naturally favorable positions for quick transfer to defense if the opponent pulls down the rebound and goes to a fast break.

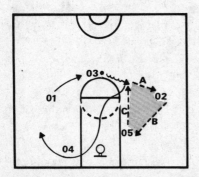

Figure 1-19. Adjustment against a zone.

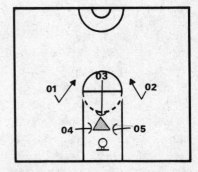

Figure 1-20. Offensive rebounding triangle.

FLOOR BALANCE

Although no specific reference has been made to it as a term, consideration for *floor balance* has been reflected throughout the discussions and illustrations in this opening chapter of orientation. An important integrant of a successful basketball system, *floor balance* is present in a team's offensive schema if (1) the team is able to maintain its distribution and dispersal of players in the operating zone during all phases of the attack, and (2) the team is always distributed and dispersed during offensive attack for prompt and natural transition to defense, if and when the ball is turned over to the opposing team.

The following elements, characteristics, and movements, as they develop, provide *floor balance* in the Option Offense to an outstanding degree:

1. weak side cuts
2. strong side cuts
3. swing passes from strong side to weak side
4. cuts across to the top of the key
5. cuts down the key
6. one man, sometimes two, always at the top of the key
7. triangular concept in offensive rebounding
8. continuity of movement which keeps the defense spread
9. uncluttered driving and approach lanes
10. ease and simplicity of adjustment to changing defenses

Each of these ten items is implicit within the diagrams of the Option Offense presented in this chapter.

Chapter Two

Planning the Option Offense

Against Man-Man Defenses:

The Red Series

GENERAL CHARACTERISTICS

The Red Series is one of the three that makes up the total Option Offense. It is generated by a key or signal given by the quarterback, 1. Before the signal is given, however, the team has looked for the fast break possibility. The team must be coached to always consider the fast break likelihood, with the quarterback assuming the necessary leadership in putting it into effect or calling it off.

Fast break or not, we always come back to the thesis that the hub of this offense system is the pattern, out of which come our options. So, in this chapter we deal, in depth, with the pattern of the Red Series. Many of the option possibilities will be described. It would be impossible to attempt to anticipate and describe all of them.

The diagrammed options, with descriptions, demand the mastery of basketball fundamentals to be attained in practice; so, you may use the diagrams here when you plan your daily practices in fundamentals.

The positioning, or set, of the Red Series has been drawn and described in previous material, so it will not be repeated in this chapter. I must, however, reiterate the importance of players arriving at their set positions as quickly as possible. We must keep in mind that the longer it takes for the Option Offense to get moving into patterns and routes, the more time the defense has to get set, increasing its chances to diagnose the oncoming offensive movement.

INSTRUCTING SELECTED TECHNIQUES

In Figure 2-1, 1 passes to 3. It is critical that: (1) this wing man not be intimidated out of his area; (2) passes of about 15 to 18 feet are maximum; (3) the receiver meets the pass and reaches out for it; and (4) the pass is directed away from the receiver's defensive man.

As this pass is made, things start to happen. 02, with a burst of speed, cuts as shown, over the top of 5, and looks for a swing pass from 3 while flashing down the key. 3 has pivoted to his right, to face 02 as he cuts. 01, after passing to 3, follows his pass, as shown. If 3 finds 02 open, he passes to him, and the Red Series is over because we have scored. If 02 is not open, there is no break in the action. In Figure 2-2 the ball is handed back to 01 as 02 continues down the key and around the stack without the ball. 03 clears out to the top of the key, looking back for a return pass. We have weak-side action as 04 cuts around and over the top of 5 to, hopefully, receive the angle pass from 01.

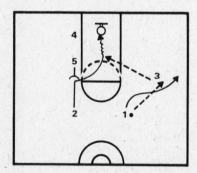

Figure 2-1. First option of Red.

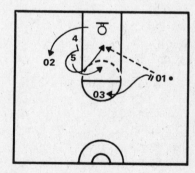

Figure 2-2. Second option of Red.

A word about the fundamentals of the hand-back is necessary at this time. There is nothing careless or perfunctory about the mechanics of this action by 3 and 01, and they must perfect the procedure in practice. First of all, as 3 meets the ball, he maintains *body balance*. He pulls the ball in, pivots, and looks at the cutting 02. If he refuses him, 3 pivots back, still holding the ball. Now, he crouches comfortably, his weight evenly distributed on both feet, which are spread at least to the width of the shoulders. The ball is held firmly, the chin is up, and the head position is directly above the midpoint between the spread feet. 01, after his pass, has acted as if his intention was to go straight down the key, but he changes direction with a hard push off his left leg, quick-steps to his right oblique, and comes over for the hand-back. There may be a tendency here for 3 to get careless or to stuff the ball into 01's stomach, much like the action of a football quarterback as he hands off to one of his backs. We want a well-executed flip pass of about two feet, a firm flip aimed at the waist of 01, right into his hands; and as 3 gets rid of the ball in this manner, he may take a partial step forward with his right foot to act as a kind of buffer against any attempt by 01's guard to reach in and steal the ball. Then 03 gets out of the way, goes quickly to the top of the key area, and looks back for a return pass.

If 04 is not open in his thrust across the key in Figure 2-2, or if refused by 01, he continues through the key to set in a new position as a low post, shown as part of the action in Figure 2-3. 05 follows 04 as second man through, and Figure 2-3 shows him receiving the pass from 01 as a scoring option. If refused, however, he swings back to a low post position close to his original set on the same side. Second man through is a hard-and-fast policy in the offense; the weak-side screener always follows the man he screens for, trying to exploit a potential defensive error in the intricacies of switching, releasing, or sagging off.

The technique of 01's swing pass to either 04 or 05 must be mentioned at this time. 01 is facing the basket after the hand-back from 03, but he does not want to divulge or "telegraph" his intended pass to a potential receiver. The two-handed over-head pass is recommended. Sometimes it is called a fan pass. The ball is held firmly with the hands on the sides of the ball. The ball is brought straight up to a position just above the forehead (don't go behind the head with it), with the thumbs on the back of the ball pointing in toward each other. There is a snap of the wrists as the ball is released, and many passers like to jump with the release of this particular pass, although that depends on the situation.

In Figure 2-4, 01 retained the ball after refusing both 04 and 05 as

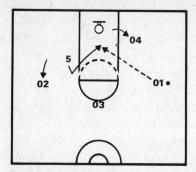

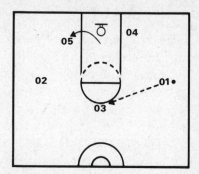

Figure 2-3. Option of second man through.

Figure 2-4. Reverse pass. Jump shot by 03 option.

they cut from the weak side. Then he looked down at the new low post, 04, refused him, and suddenly espied an open 03 at the top of the key. This reverse-type pass usually pays off with a jump shot for 03. His defensive man has never been sure of 03's intent as he moves with a feint toward the basket and then steps back as the pass arrives.

After 03's jump shot, it is appropriate to interrupt the options again, in the interest of fundamentals. We need to mention offensive rebounding, with its triangular concept. It is both a team and an individual requisite. Offensive triangular rebounding is one of the important items of *floor balance*. Notice in Figure 2-5 that 04, 05, and 03 form the triangle after 03's shot. There will be a tendency for the shooter, in our case 03, to stand and admire his shooting effort, but this inclination must be overcome in practice. He, like 04 and 05, anticipates the rebound with proper timing, body slightly crouched, feet well spread (to maintain body balance), level, fingers pointing up, elbows out, palms forward—all the time trying to jostle and jockey for optimum position against the defender without committing a foul. One big reason for keeping the hands up in this situation is to minimize the pushing and shoving with *hands*, which referees will notice very quickly. You should stress in the practicing of offensive rebounding fundamentals, that the player never gives up in his effort to regain the basketball off the boards. Here is one of the most important of all basketball techniques, important to the Option Offense: offensive rebounding from the triangle, which pays off many times through simple, plain aggressiveness, hard work, and effort.

It should also be observed in Figure 2-5 that 01 and 02 are aware of the need for *floor balance* when they get back out, away from the basket, thinking of future defense against the potentiality of the opponent's fast break. If three of our men are working the boards offensively, we want the other two going for *floor balance*, as shown. The Option Offense will never expect 01 and 02 to be offensive rebounders. As a matter of fact, if either is under the boards (except in the case of a dribble-drive or reception of a pass for a lay-up), he is out of position.

PENETRATION AS A WEAPON

In Figure 2-6, the Red Series furnishes the team with one of the most exciting and devastating individual features of offensive basketball. All that is additionally required is an enterprising, imaginative,

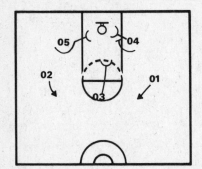

Figure 2-5. Triangular rebounding, offensive.

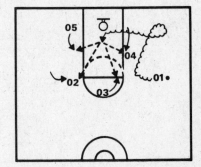

Figure 2-6. 01 penetrates, passes back out.

driving dribbler to make it work. It is called *penetration*. Although Figure 2-6 has to show a dribbling route from the start of the dribble-drive to its conclusion, for the sake of an example, nobody, including the driver himself, knows the ultimate destination or result of the dribble. That is an *advantage*, which makes *penetration* an important element in the offense, to be encouraged as much as possible. We want worthwhile improvisation and free-lance. One-on-one is not discouraged in our Option Offense if the improvisor has gained that important half-step on his guard and is driving toward the basket, close-in. In Figure 2-6, 01 has the ball after the hand-back and has refused all previous options. Surmising that he has his guard out of position (one way of accomplishing this is to apply the rocker step), he starts his dribble-drive toward the basket. A route is shown, but it could be an entirely different one, and the four passing options are shown in Figure 2-6 only to serve as examples of "what could happen." The other four players must move to get open while the drive is taking place, so that at least one will be a target for a pass. The coach must include all kinds of penetration drills of his own in practice sessions. The pass by the penetrator (out to an open man) must be practiced, too. The term "how to" applies. How to suspend dribbling and make a drop-back pass; how to bounce-pass off the dribble without having to stop; how to dribble with the head up; how to be aware of the periphery; and how to jump high, turn, and pass off to an open man while hanging in the air.

LOW POST PLAY IN THE MIXMASTER

In Figure 2-7, we return to the options of the Red Series. 01 has the ball, has refused 03, and has decided against trying one-on-one penetration. So, he passes down to low post 04, follows his pass, makes a head-and-shoulder fake to try to get a half-step on his guard, suddenly pushes hard off his left leg while moving, and flashes to his right a bit, hoping for a return pass and jump shot.

In Figure 2-8, his hope is realized, but to remain with Figure 2-7, we have 03 observing a most important rule. When the ball goes down to low post (either side), or when the ball is passed from the point (top of the key) to a wing man, the point man always cuts down the key and comes back out "opposite."

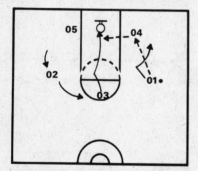

Figure 2-7. Lay-up by 03.

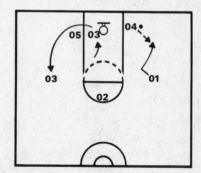

Figure 2-8. Pass back to 01 for jump shot.

In this one part of the Option Offense you must be absolutely unbending. There must be no other interpretation, no better ideas, no improvisation. In order to activate the rotating, mixing movement of the Mixmaster, the point man must follow the instructions of his coach to the letter. He cuts down the key when the ball is passed to the wing or low post!

We are in the Mixmaster phase from Figure 2-4 on. (Point man, two wing men, double low post.)

In Figure 2-9, Mixmaster continues as 04 refuses 03, refuses 01, decides against going one-on-one at the low post, and passes out to 02 (new point man) for a jump shot. 03, 04, and 05 have excellent offensive rebounding positioning (Figure 2-9) as the ball is on its way to the basket.

PLAY FROM THE WINGS IN THE MIXMASTER

In Figure 2-10, 02 is not open for a shot as he receives the pass, but he finds 03 coming out on the left side. In our option example here, 03 receives the pass, stops, turns quickly with his pivot, passes down to 05, and follows his pass hoping for a return pass and a jump shot. In

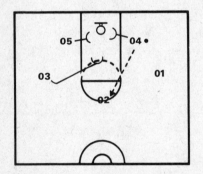

Figure 2-9. Fan pass out to 02 for jump shot.

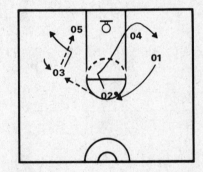

Figure 2-10. To 05 at the low post.

Figure 2-11, we show the return pass and jump shot option by 03 and, again, the attention to offensive rebounding. In Figure 2-12, it is assumed that 03 had no jump shot, so he puts the ball on the floor, starts his dribble, gets 05 to step out for screening purposes, and dribbles around the screen while 05 releases and rolls for the basket. 03 would have a lay-up, or he would hit 05 with a little pass at the end of the roll.

In Figure 2-13, 03 decides to give up the ball entirely by reversing it to 01 at the top of the key. It was stated before that the point man must look for the return pass (give-and-go) from the wing man as he starts down the key. In Figure 2-14, 01 has passed over to wing man 02, and his cut down the key is rewarded with a return pass, a give-and-go which should result in a lay-up for 01. Following a rule paid off for him!

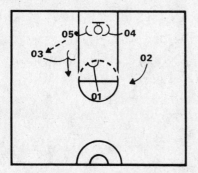

Figure 2-11. Back to 03 for jump shot.

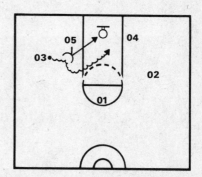

Figure 2-12. Pick and roll.

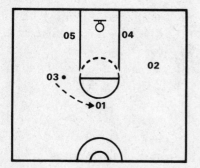

Figure 2-13. 03 decides to reverse ball.

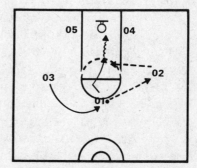

Figure 2-14. Give-and-go.

In Figure 2-15, 01 was not open on the give-and-go, so 02 relayed the ball down to low post 04. 03 was replacing 01 at the point, and as the ball went to 04, we see 03 cutting down the key and continuing Mixmaster, as he is supposed to do. The diagram shows him open for a quick, bounce pass from 04.

Having received the ball from 02 back in Figure 2-15, 04 did not find 03 open, so in Figure 2-16 he returned it to 02 and then stepped out to set a screen as 02 started his dribble. 04 then rolled for the hoop

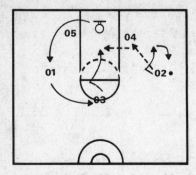
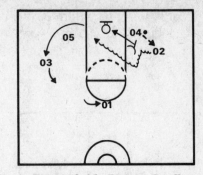

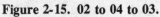

Figure 2-15. 02 to 04 to 03.   **Figure 2-16. Pick-and-roll.**

as 02 dribbled by (Figure 2-16). 01 comes to the point. 03 replaces him on the wing.

MORE LOW POST ACTION

So far, the individual low post play of 04 and 05 has been rather ignored, but only because we have been concerned with other options. Besides their rebounding and screening responsibilities, 04 and 05 are expected to contribute as scorers when the ball is passed down to them. Drills for proficiency in close-in offensive work for them are in Chapters 5, 7, and 12. The hook shot (right or left hand) and the turn-around jumper are the two main scoring tools that must be practiced. This action will not be diagrammed, but we can refer to Figure 2-15, where the ball was passed down to 04, and to Figure 2-10, where 05 received the pass from 03. In either case, 04 and 05 can retain the ball and work one-on-one against the defensive man. They can expect, in many cases, that the defensive man will deny the use of the baseline by means of overplay near the base line as the ball is received. In such a case, low post man 04 must prepare to go to his right with a dribble and put the ball in the basket with the left hand; low post man 05 must prepare to go to his left with a dribble and get his basket with the right hand. The turn-around jumper is also pertinent to both 04 and 05.

ADDITIONAL PENETRATION NOTES

Figures 2-17 and 2-18 serve to point out, again, the important phase of penetration in the Option Offense. The pass from 04 out to 03

Figure 2-17. Pass out to point.
Penetration.

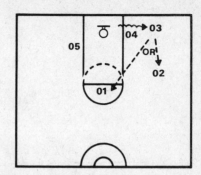

Figure 2-18. Possible passes by
03.

will probably be the two-handed overhead (fan) type, with 04 jumping
to gain velocity and accuracy, and 03 moving to meet the pass. As he
meets the pass, 03 may try to power his way into the penetration
dribble with the lead step, rocker step, or cross-over step. The route
shown in Figures 2-17 and 2-18 is only an example, but it is a good one
which will definitely occur in a game. When he passes back out at the
end of his penetration in Figure 2-18, 03 must know that his pass to 01
is a dangerous one because of the danger of interception. Figure 2-18
also shows 03 with an option of passing out to 02. Not shown is his
own possibility of keeping the ball and continuing his dribble around
the screen of 04 for his own little jump shot. The point to stress here is
directed at the other three players while 03 is dribbling and 04 is
screening: "Don't stand around and watch 03. Get moving, get open!"

Figures 2-19, 2-20, and 2-21 are included to give the reader

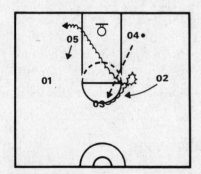

Figure 2-19. Same pass, 04 to 03.
Penetration by 03.

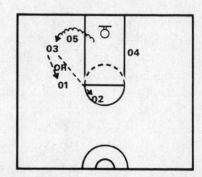

Figure 2-20. Possible passes by
penetrator 03.

Figure 2-21. Still another pene-trating route and passes.

additional ideas as to penetration routes. Figure 2-21 would be especially effective because the pass-offs by 03 are much shorter and the resulting jump shots would be attempted from high-percentage areas. Again, the moves of 03 to gain a half-step on his guard at the top of the key as he starts his penetration dribble cannot be drawn, but they must be practiced. For example, he may take one dribble toward his guard and then spin off the guard with his dribble; or he may rocker step or cross-over.

PRECISION PASSING AND SUMMARY

The programmed options of the Red Series in this chapter end with Figures 2-22 and 2-23. These are options which feature passing.

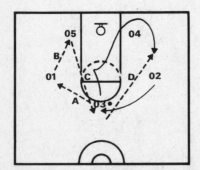

Figure 2-22. Precision passing. Shot by 03.

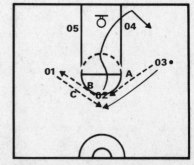

Figure 2-23. Three passes. Shot by 03.

The ball is reversed and shuffled by way of at least four passes in Figure 2-22 and by three in Figure 2-23. The passes work around the perimeter, or periphery, and then inside and back ouside, keeping the offense busy; and there is movement of our offensive people which adds to the mix.

03 has the ball in Figure 2-22, having received it by way of a pass from 04 back in Figure 2-17. Unable to shoot, he starts the Mixmaster by passing to 01 (Pass A); then he cuts down the key as the ball is passed down to low post 05 (Pass B). 02, following the Mixmaster pattern, has replaced 03 at the point, and 05 finds him open with a pass (Pass C). Using 04 as a screen as he "comes around opposite," 03 is open, so 02 passes to him for the close-in shot (Pass D). If not totally satisfied with his opening, 03 might work the pick-and-roll with 04, which has been discussed previously. Or, as shown in Figure 2-23, he may reverse the ball back to 02 at the point (Pass A in Figure 2-23). 02 passes to the opposite wing (Pass B) and cuts down the key as 03 replaces him. This time, 03 comes out open at the top of the key to receive a reverse pass from 01 for a jump shot (Pass C).

Diagramming and discussion of options continue in Chapters 3 and 4 as we go to the other two series. The point should be made that it is impossible to cover every possibility in the three chapters. Too many basketball variables are involved. It should also be pointed out that most, if not all, options of the Red Series apply in one way or another to the White and Blue. In a word, options in all three series are interchangeable, and universal to all three.

In presenting one series of the Option Offense, with probable options described and diagrammed, I hope the following offensive principles (against the man-man defense) are evident: (1) all the items of *floor balance* are present, both when the series sets and during the continuity and flow of the action; (2) the double low post, evolving from the original stack, encourages the inside game and also ensures that there will be excellent positioning for rebounding; and (3) the continuous movement of players is varied, especially in Mixmaster, and features penetration, shuffle, reverse, cut, clear-out, and other solid elements. The result should be balanced scoring, as developed from an easy-to-understand pattern that requires little adjustment whether it is being used for attacking man-man or zone defenses.

Chapter Three

Utilizing the White Series

Against Man-Man Defenses

FIRST OPTION

Just like the Red Series, the White is signaled by the quarterback, 1. As in the case of the Red Series, our offense has considered the fast break before going on to the White. Now, we are committed to the signal by 1, so the initial point of attack will be in the center at the top of the key. The back door is the very first option. It has been discussed to some extent in previous chapters. In this chapter the discussion is especially significant because we are dealing with such an important part of a particular series.

The offensive execution of the back door furnishes one of the most exciting maneuvers in basketball. The basketball purist is excited, as a spectator, when he sees the movement, because good qualities and skills of passing, cutting, and deception stand out so clearly in the execution. Figure 3-1 depicts this, as 03 flashes to the top of the key, receives a pass from 2, and with superb timing completes the back door with his relay pass to the driving 01. The deception comes mainly from 01, who must contrive to get at least a half-step advantage on his defensive man or get inside position on him as he starts the drive.

Used by others in a similar manner, the back door may be posed as a threat and countermeasure against a defense that is overplaying, and they may use it as a called play, to be signaled in special situations.

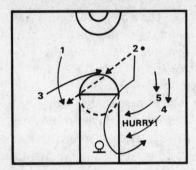

Figure 3-1. Back door on the move.

In the Option Offense, White Series, the use of the back door is unique in that it goes into motion every time the White Series begins, and it may be tried over again by the play-maker if it doesn't work as an option in the first place. To rerun, all he has to do is call out a simple signal which resets the team into the White formation with its initiating back door feature.

I believe that having the back door as an integral part of an offense and drilling it into the team makes it more effective than just having it as a play. Expecting it and trying to react to it every time, the defense is going to make a mistake, get careless, or will pay so much attention to it that it will fail to cope with a following option in the series.

In practicing the back door as a part of this series, you must guard against carelessness and negativism on the part of your players. It is easy for them, in this particular option requiring such excellent timing, deception, and surprise, to rationalize poor effort and execution in practice sessions with statements such as, "It won't work in practice because we all know it's coming," "O1 can't get open as he cuts back door because his guard will sag back on him when he starts to drive," and so on. The rebuttal is to to remind the quarterback that he must *work* for more deception in his effort to gain that half-step advantage against his defensive man. Call the team's attention to the fact that this is just one of many options, and if it doesn't work, we merely go on with the series pattern. Renew the concept that it is entirely possible for the same option to present itself again as the series develops, maybe with greater surprise next time!

The development of 1 as the back door cutter will be an interesting challenge for you. The competence of 1 and the success of the maneuver depends as much, or more, on his own personal application and effort as on the coaching and teaching he has received. As the ball goes from 2 to 03 at the top of the key in a game, we must expect to see individuality and personal effort over and beyond the fundamental teaching. You have taught head-and-shoulder fakes, the push-off one leg when there is a change of direction involved, the spin-off, the hesitation-and-go, the jab step, and so on; now, it really comes to the matter of individual adroitness, deception, and finesse. A sudden un-expected burst of speed, a sudden change of direction, something a little extra—all are actions by 01 that will be successful in proportion to his individual effort and desire. And you must have a hand in the installation of this desire, along with your teaching!

It will be noted in Figure 3-1 that 04 and 05 are moving into their stack positions just as the back door is going into motion. This is most realistic, and it will happen. The White Series may go into gear before 04 and 05 are completely set in the stack, although we do insist that they get down the floor as quickly as possible. The diagram also shows 02's usual move and cut for the key area after his pass to 03. It is timed slightly behind 01's back door as an additional option. 03 can hand off to him as he goes by or return the ball for a jump shot.

SUBSEQUENT OPTIONS

In the sequence of White, if both 01 and 02 are shut off, they continue their routes as shown in Figure 3-2, and the series continues. Neither tarries under the basket, because they must get back on their respective sides of the court for floor balance and continuity. 01 comes around and back to the wing position on his orignal side of the court; 02 cuts around and behind 04, using him as a screen, to emerge on his original side. High-low action follows in Figure 3-2, with 03 turning to face the basket in a pivoting move. 04 comes around and over the top of 5 to receive the high-low pass. If 04 is not open, and we have already raised the possibility that he might not always be, then 05 is the second man through, receiving the high-low pass in Figure 3-3.

Figures 3-4, 3-5, and 3-6 sketch individual efforts by 03 as he decides to keep the ball and go one-on-one from the top of the key in the White Series. In Figure 3-4, he faces the basket; uses a jab step, rocker step, or cross-over; gains a half-step on his guard as he starts his

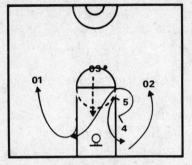

Figure 3-2. High-low pass to 04.

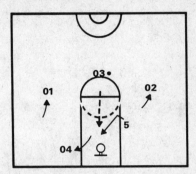

Figure 3-3. Second man through. Pass to 05.

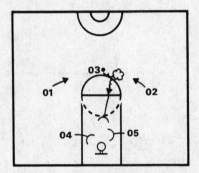

Figure 3-4. 03 goes one-on-one.

Figure 3-5. Penetration by 03.

dribble to the left; reverses, shifts to right-hand dribble, and goes up for his jump shot in a high-percentage area. The White Series has evolved to Mixmaster, and triangular rebounding considerations are also shown in Figure 3-4.

Your belief in the importance of penetration is again illustrated in Figure 3-5. Penetration, and passing out to an open man, is stressed so much in practice that it becomes a natural part of the repertoire of the point man. In Figure 3-5, 03 has moved to gain a half-step on his guard, so he starts a dribble-drive down the key, keeping in mind the 3-second rule and being aware that some of the defense may try to compress and clog the key area. His teammates are moving to get open in their general areas, especially if their guards are releasing from them a bit. Figure 3-6 suggests that the key becomes cluttered, with X5 particularly releasing from our 05 to pick up 03 coming down the key with the ball. A little deceptive bounce-pass to 05 under the basket may teach X5 a lesson about "cheating" or releasing. This kind of penetration must be practiced over and over, with the point man spending a great deal of time and effort in learning how to gain that half-step advantage at the point.

If the key is clogged and no pass option is presented at all, 03 must dribble back out in a hurry, as Figure 3-7 indicates.

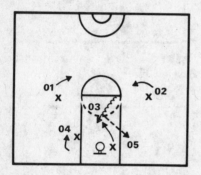 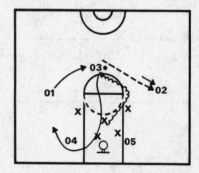

Figure 3-6. 03 to 05 under the basket.   Figure 3-7. Retreat, dribble. Pass to wing.

It has been stated that a feature of the back door tactic is the probability that it could be re-applied during a sequence. The opportunity is afforded, growing out of 03's retreat to the top of the key in Figure 3-7. Looking for the open man, he finds 02 at the wing with a pass (Figure 3-7) and cuts down the key as 01 replaces him at the point. Suddenly, 01 shows his floor leadership by calling "set!" or "White!" Although 02 could respond by passing the ball to his quarterback, he knows that here, in White, the ball would just be returned to him anyway, so he retains possession with a retreating dribble out to his normal set positon while the other team members are re-forming, as shown in Figure 3-8. In Figure 3-9, 02 hits 03 with the pass, and 01 goes back door. The White Series is re-activated.

The options in Figures 3-10 through 3-14 will quicken the interest of 01, 02, and, 03 as they demonstrate the alternatives in the Option Offense that furnish secondary routes and the aspect of free-lance.

In Figure 3-10, 02 continues to dribble and refuses 03 as he flashes out to start the White Series. 01 makes a move for back door and then turns back as he sees 02 dribbling over the top of 03's screen (pick) at the top of the key to go on in for a close-in jump shot. 03

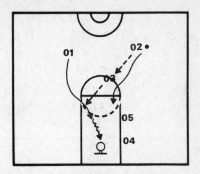

Figure 3-8. 01 calls "White!" or "Set!"

Figure 3-9. Back door, White, all over again.

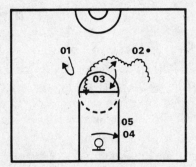

Figure 3-10. 02 goes on his own instead.

releases from the screen as 02 dribbles by and rolls for the basket down the lane. 02 could pass to him as an option. The terminology for this, of course, is pick-and-roll, and this particular action at the high post will be significantly effective against a sagging defense.

It should be understood that the high post pick-and-roll, although not presented as a primary route of the White Series, is definitely considered an integral part of the offense and is not restricted to situations such as the one in Figure 3-10. It can be put into play, for whatever tactical reason, when the ball is brought down court in the usual commitment of the White Series.

03 is given his chance to challenge his defensive man and to take advantage of any defensive lapse in a new White Series in Figures 3-11 and 3-12. There is great potential for 03's one-on-one efforts at the high post area. The coach must encourage 03's exploitation of an

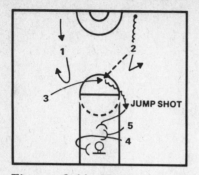

Figure 3-11. New sequence, White. Action by 03.

Figure 3-12. Another new sequence. Action by 03.

opponent who is over-playing or "cheating." If he isn't advised and taught to respond positively and imaginatively (within the scope of the Option Offense), 03 may become discouraged and inefficient in un-usual game situations around the high post. In Figure 3-11, the ball has been brought down court, 02 is keeping it with his dribble, and he passes to 03 to start the White Series. The Series is terminated when 03 realizes that he has a half-step on his guard as he receives the pass, and continues to his right with a one-on-one dribble and drive. We would expect a jump shot from a high-percentage area or a driving lay-up. In Figure 3-12, another instance, 03's guard has been overplaying, in-timidating, and trying to shut off the pass from 02 to 03. 03 did get the pass, however, stops short, spins left with a dribble, and leaves his guard behind at the reception area. Again, the good jump shot or dribble-drive. 01 and 02 stop short and go back.

Both diagrams show the inherent excellence of offensive rebound-ing characteristics.

HIGH POST SCISSORS

Remaining in the White Series and continuing to profit by its diversity at the top of the key, 01 and 02 work out a simple signal as they bring the ball down court in another new situation (Figure 3-13) and execute the scissors, or split, movement off the high post. They are aware that there are defensive antidotes for this movement, but 01 and 02 are depending on surprise, deception, and excellent execution for success. 02 passes to high post 03 as he flashes out from the wing. Instead of following the primary, usual route of White, 01 and 02 work off the high post as shown, with the passer, 02, cutting first. This is a rather standard rule. 03 is turning with the ball, ready to pass to either as they go by in their scissors action. The turning movement culminates in high-low options if 03 chooses not to pass to either 01 or 02 as they go by.

Figures 3-14 and 3-15 carry on with the individual routes which, obviously, mesh and blend with the total White Series pattern, show no interruption in the flow of movement, and reflect excellent floor balance. In Figure 3-14, 03 has turned to face the basket, 04 starts around and over the top of 5 looking for a pass, and the paths of 01 and 02 are crossing as they are starting to turn out to their normal wing positions. There are under-basket options here, created by the natural screen of 01 and 02. 03's pass may find either of them open. 05 goes as second man through in Figure 3-15. With 03 refusing all options so far, the progression has brought us from a scissors beginning to the set of Mixmaster in Figure 3-16. This ends the diagramming. The options of this new Mixmaster phase are a part of other chapters.

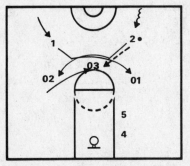

Figure 3-13. White surprise. Scissors.

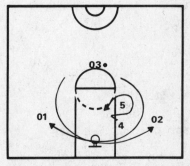

Figure 3-14. Routes of White scissors.

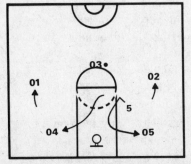

Figure 3-15. Routes near completion. Options.

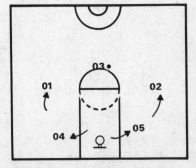

Figure 3-16. Mixmaster Set.

SUMMARY AND NOTES ABOUT SHOOTING

The White Series initially concentrates its attack down the center and then, like both the Red and Blue, progresses into Mixmaster if an attempt at a field goal has not resulted. In its entirety, the White Series produces the back door, give-and-go, high-low passing, penetration, second man through, pick-and-roll, high post scissors, double low post play, and unusual opportunities for the individual to go one-on-one with the wholehearted approval of the coach. The end result will be an unusual amount of lay-up opportunities and close-in offensive work.

Since such excellent close-in jump-shooting opportunities are provided in this series, some reference must be made here to this individual basic skill. No space or attention is given elsewhere in this book to the techniques of shooting, mainly because there is little of innovative interest or worth that I can add to already published material. I am particularly impressed by the book of Coach Bob Fuller (*Basketball's Wishbone Offense*, Parker Publishing Company, West Nyack, New York, 1973) in the chapters on improving field goal percentages and individual shooting skills.

I would add only two general points of my own. First, when you have devised and installed an offense that will give the team good shooting options, you must expect and demand that your offense be given a fair deal and that there be no surprises during a game. For one thing, you should make sure that each player knows his optimum shooting range and stays within it.

We're all acquainted with the hapless coach (and he should be viewed commiseratively) who jumps up screaming, "Don't shoot, don't shoot!" and then applauds wildly and shouts, "Nice shot!" as the ball settles down in the net from far out. This is the "happy" side of "bad" basketball, but some very negative things accrue from a *missed* shot taken by the same player outside his shooting range of capability. Almost always, there is no offensive rebounding because teammates are out of rebounding positions, and the opponents end up with a fast break possibility off the uncontested outlet pass; and probably most negative, the gunnery becomes contagious as the others join in.

This problem of shot selection is a problem for every coach, to be dealt with in practice sessions by you in your own way.

The second point alludes to the teaching of two elements that are particularly important to the total process of jump shooting. I consider these two as most significant because they pertain to both *beginning* and *ending* of the jump shot, and if any effort is begun and ended properly it should be successful! The *beginning* refers to *stance*; the *ending* is the combination of *launch* (jump straight up) and *land* (come straight down to about the same starting point).

As the player consolidates and prepares his base (stance) for the jump shot, his head should be centered in relation to the rest of his body, and level (not tilted back, not too far forward). His body should be in balance and rather erect (not leaning backward, not leaning forward). With the ball in cocked position, the shooter's legs and feet (properly positioned) provide the impetus and energy for the power push, taking him as straight upward as possible. In the end, he lands *in balance* at about the same place as he was in the *beginning* of the shot.

To give the player a point of reference to think about, tell him to imagine that he is jump shooting out of a *phone booth*. This seems to help instill the concept of jumping straight up. Don't forget, however, to rationalize that the phone booth is open at the top!

I will leave all the remaining specific mechanics and principles of the total jump shot to other teachers and authors, particularly the Hoosier coach, Mr. Fuller, cited before. The two points presented here are only a reflection of my personal concern for their importance as they relate to the success of the jump shot in my own Option Offense.

Chapter Four

Employing the Blue Series
Against the Man-Man Defense

GENERAL CHARACTERISTICS

The Blue Series provides the team with an attack aimed initially at the left side of the defense. The Red Series, as it begins, probes at the right side. The White Series causes the defense to worry about its center. In the Blue Series, the 04 man suddenly comes out from behind 5 on the left side of the court to receive the initiating pass from 2. Thus, the Blue Series adds versatility, breadth, motion, and balance to the offensive attack. But it is also important in another way. It is easily signaled and activated and can be used at the spur of the moment as a kind of safety-valve if the offense is having trouble getting 3 open for a pass at the right side or at the top of the key. There is really no defensive way to prevent the pass from 2 to 04 as shown in Figure 4-1, whether against a man-man or a zone defense; and 2 or 1 can make just a simple directional hand signal to get 04 moving out from his place in the stack. He is always eager to get out from behind the shadow of 5 anyway!

EXAMPLES OF MAIN OPTIONS

Upon signal (2 with the ball *can* be the key), the stack goes into action in Figure 4-1 as 04 feints to his left and then pops out to the right, as shown, to receive the pass from 2. 02 follows his pass, which gives 04 a hand-back option. But in Figure 4-1, 04 turns and takes a jump shot. This is the time for you to work with the basic techniques of receiving a pass, stopping, turning, and quick-release shooting.

Attention to offensive rebounding by 05 and 03 is shown in Figure 4-1. 04 must also be coached to go for his own missed shot. This jump shot by 04 will present itself as a simple offensive option more often than any other in the Blue Series because 04 will usually gain no less than a half-step on his guard, X4, as he moves out from the rear of the stack. In the first place, the feint by 04 toward the center of the key will be deceptive; secondly, when 04 swings to his right around the screen by 05, he will hang his opponent on the back or hip of 05, at least temporarily. 01 moves to the top of the key as point man and safety-valve. Refused the hand-back from 04, 02 hooks back for floor balance.

In Figure 4-2, 04 hands back to 02, who dribbles down the side, along the base line, and on in toward the basket, looking all the while for an open teammate. 01, 03, and 05 are likely prospects, but 04 is most likely to be open if 05 will set a screen for him as shown. This will require communication between the two.

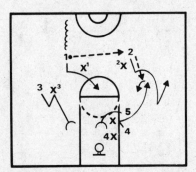

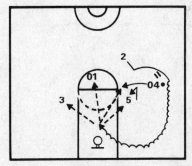

Figure 4-1. Jump shot by 04. Quick release.

Figure 4-2. Penetrate. Pass-out by 02.

Reverse passing and the shuffle principle are features of the option shown in Figure 4-3. Properly executed, this is one of the most exciting and productive options of the Option Offense. 04 receives the pass from 2, refuses him as he comes by, and passes (reverses) to 01 at the point. 05 steps out to set a pick for 04 as he breaks for the key area, while the ball is moving from 01 to 3. 04 receives the pass from 3 for a lay-up. Interesting alternatives present themselves, which are explainable here without diagramming. For example, 01 might want to return-pass to 04, as in give-and-go, just as he comes around 05's screen. Then again, 01 might completely refuse 04 and take a jump shot at the top of the key, especially if his defensive man has stepped back to impede 04. Or, 01 may find 3 completely open on the wing (if X3 has sagged into the lane to help obstruct and check movement in there). Figure 4-3 also includes the second man through part of the offense. 3 passes to 04 in the diagram, but the alternative pass to 05 is not shown. If 04 is not open, he goes on to his low post position, as does 05 if he is refused.

The reverse-shuffle principle is productive against the man-man defense because it keeps the defense spread, opens up driving and cutting lanes, and produces screening possibilities. It is workable against zone defenses because good perimeter-type passing is involved from strong side to weak side and there is movement into and through vulnerable areas which creates over-load situations.

Pick-and-roll, always a threat in other parts of the Option Offense, presents itself again as a promising likelihood in Figure 4-4, when 04 receives the pass from 2. He turns, looks down at 5, refuses

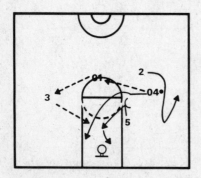

Figure 4-3. Reverse action with a shuffle.

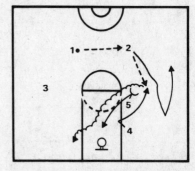

Figure 4-4. Pick-and-roll, Blue.

him, and puts the ball on the floor in a right-handed dribble as 05 steps out for a pick-and-roll. 04 would hope for a driving lay-up. In case he is defensed away from his lay-up, however, he can pass off to 05 as 05 rolls to the basket (Figure 4-4), or, as shown in Figure 4-5, he might suspend his dribble, turn, jump high, and pass back out to either 01 or 03 as they get open for a jump shot. Notice that 05 is completing his roll and going on to his low post position. 04 has already arrived at his low post area. 02 has returned to his former position for floor balance.

LOW POST PLAY IN THE SERIES

We start a new Blue Series sequence in Figures 4-6, 4-7, and 4-8, in illustration of low post play. In Figure 4-6, 04 receives the pass from 2 and refuses to return the ball as he goes by. Instead, 04 pivots with the ball, turns, looks down, and passes to low post 05. This triggers many movements and options, not nearly all of which will be diagrammed here.

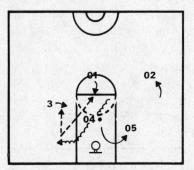

Figure 4-5. Penetrate, Blue. Pass-out by 04.

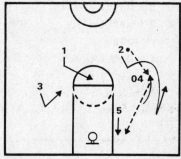

Figure 4-6. To the low post. Blue.

Figure 4-7. Low post to the cutter, Blue.

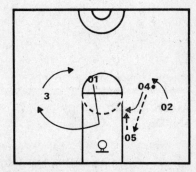

Figure 4-8. Back to 04 for jump shot. Blue.

One option in Figure 4-7 shows 05 passing to the point man as he cuts straight down the center of the key. Another, in Figure 4-8, shows the return pass to 04, who is working for a jump shot after his pass to 05. 03 replaces 01 at the point. 01 comes around and out to the wing. Other options, not drawn, would have 05 going one-on-one at the low post or passing out to 03 at the top of the key for a jump shot, and so on. The philosophy remains the same: Pass to the open man; move without the ball in the pattern; get open!

If 04 doesn't receive the pass back from 05, he moves through the key as usual to his low post position.

A word is in order at this time about the value of low post play in an offense. A successful offense includes the component of an *inside* concept that takes the basketball down low by way of a pass to the under-basket area, and as the coach of that offense you must promote confidence in this passing from *outside* to *inside*. Young basketball players need to be coached and encouraged to look down toward the inside, under-basket area and to pass down, in what could be termed *vertical penetration*. Too often, the young player will pass to a perimeter teammate just for the sake of passing. While it is true that some horizontal passing may be necessary, it is also a fact that too much of it is aimless and invites interception.

With its double low post functioning in the Mixmaster phase, the Option Offense places a great emphasis on low post operation.

We now go back to Figure 4-2, because it is necessary to refer again to the hand-back action between 04 and 02 at the beginning of Blue. It is a point of reference as we go on to Figure 4-9. 04 passes back to 02 as he comes by and then goes through the key to his low post, looking back for a possible return pass. 02 decides to start his own reverse-shuffle by passing out to 01 at the top of the key in Figure 4-10. 01 swings his pass over to 3 at the wing, 02 cuts over the top of 05's screen, and 05 follows as second man through. 3 would pass to the open man for the lay-up.

If refused or not open, 05 goes on to his low post, and 02 continues around and back out to his wing position.

Figure 4-11 considers the possibility that neither 02 nor 05 will be open. Having been taught and coached to never *force* a pass, 3 is able to sustain the precision passing around the perimeter by passing down to 04 at the low post. Options from this will not be detailed, but this is excellent, productive passing and player movement, especially against a zone defense. It will be noted that 01 remembers the rule about breaking down the key when the ball is passed down to the low post. He is replaced by 02.

Figure 4-12 assumes the development to Mixmaster, with 04 in possession of the ball.

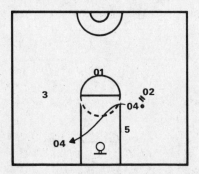

Figure 4-9. 04 hands back to 02.

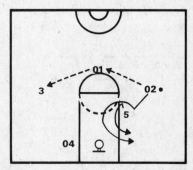

Figure 4-10. Reverse-shuffle by 02.

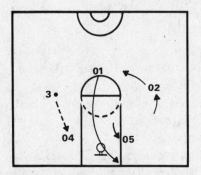

Figure 4-11. 02 and 05 not open. Ball to low post.

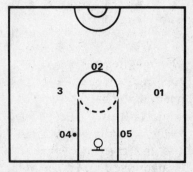

Figure 4-12. Begin Mixmaster.

SOMETHING NEW IN MIXMASTER

To develop the options of Mixmaster from Figure 4-12 would only be repetition of diagramming and description. Instead, we will add something new to it, recommended for use in all three series. The effectiveness of this added option has been proven in many specific instances and situations by my teams over the years.

From low post, 04 dumps the ball out to an open 02 at the top of the key (Figure 4-13). Recognizing an excellent situation for a kind of improvised back door option, 02 keys its development in Figure 4-13 by simply dribbling back out a few steps. By whatever signal (the retreating dribble or a directional signal by a nod of the head could be the key), 04 flashes up the side of the lane to receive a pass from 02, while 03 goes back door in perfect timing and synchronization (Figure 4-14).

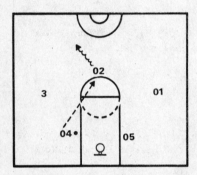

Figure 4-13. 02 decides on Mix-master back door.

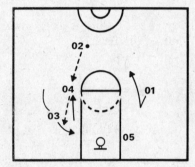

Figure 4-14. Mixmaster back door.

If, for some reason, nothing comes of the movement, 04 is encouraged to turn, face the basket, and go one-on-one, or to pass to an open man. We repeat: Free-lance and improvisation is encouraged, particularly after the planned routes have been committed and the attack is reaching down into the inside areas.

In Figure 4-15, however, 04 sees no openings; so, he passes out to his quarterback at the top of the key. Routes are naturally leading to the Mixmaster set, which is developed in Figure 4-16.

The back door option of Figures 4-13 through 4-16 should be added to Mixmaster options in all three series—Red, White, and Blue.

An opposing army coach remarked after a game, "You know, all those clear-outs with so much back door remind me of a bookie joint when somebody blows a whistle. People seem to scatter everywhere!"

Of course they do. All during a game, 03 flashes out high in the White Series, clearing out the side for 01 to go back door. Now, another back door, seemingly improvised, is added for the Mixmaster phase, to be used in all three series.

Figure 4-15. Back door is closed. Ball to quarterback.

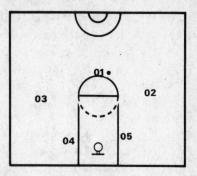

Figure 4-16. Natural return to Mixmaster set.

SUMMARY

As a component of the Option Offense, the Blue Series, with its Mixmaster, is indispensable. A list of the qualities that make it so significant will serve as a summary for this chapter:

1. It will be particularly effective against zone-type defenses.

2. A defense sagging against Red and White can not extend its effectiveness to include Blue. The entry pass from 2 to 04 cannot be prevented. With Red and White restricted for any reason, including that imposed by the sag, the Blue may be initiated as an alternative or safety-valve.

3. The strong-side cut of 02 down the side and hook-back in the beginning worry the defensive man in that area, man-man or zone, because he has to guard a man who has just received the ball (04); at the same time, a second man, 02, is entering the area.

4. Reverse action, so much a part of Blue, continually takes an offensive player *inside*; maintains the offensive capability around the perimeter; and keeps the defense on the move, susceptible to screens, cuts, and drives.

5. The Blue Series encourages and requires penetration.

6. When 04 goes out to receive the pass from 2 in the beginning, he takes a big defensive man with him—and away from the basket (against man-man).

7. Against a zone defense, when 04 goes out of the stack to receive the pass from 2, he is helping to create the overload situation important to offensive success.

8. All five players are unusually involved in the Blue Series.

9. Excellent principles of low post play develop during the Blue Series.

10. Just like the Red and White Series, the Blue Series evolves into Mixmaster, with all the option offerings of that phase added to those of the main series. An option additional to all those of other chapters was presented in this chapter: the Mixmaster back door.

Chapter Five

Anticipating Man-Man Reactions

To the Option Offense

GENERAL EXPECTATIONS TO CONSIDER

To begin this discussion about "anticipation" and "what to expect," it is necessary to comment briefly about certain strengths and advantages usually enjoyed by modern man-man defenses. First of all, because of new coaching approaches in the building of positive individual attitudes and the spirit of confidence and aggressiveness, the man-man defense emerges more and more as a defense of pride and desire. The offense must expect this. In addition, the team on offense can be sure that the man-man opponent is generally strong in all defensive fundamentals and is in good physical condition. The man-man defense will be *physical* largely because of the unusual pride and effort in conditioning preparation. Lastly, you can expect that your offense will have to contend with people who help each other in a relatively new concept that will be discussed later.

By the same token, you should also be aware of certain inherent weaknesses in man-man defenses, with the idea that they may be exploited in the offensive plan. First, and probably most important, there is vulnerability to picks and screens. Second, there is a tendency to commit fouls as the aggressiveness spills over into violations. Third, unlike zone defense, man-man defense can't hide its weakest defensive member. He stands out, ready to be acted upon.

ANTICIPATION OF DEFENSIVE SAG

Of all the specific methods that are a part of modern man-man defenses, the *sag* will be the one that the Option Offense will have to contend with more than any other. Defensive coaches, or coaches who are about to meet up with the Option Offense, will observe the Red, White, and Blue Series—with all the clear-outs, inside cuts, high-low passing action, inside routes of the stack men, and the swing passes from strong side to weak side—and immediately start thinking in terms of *permitting* the outside perimeter and periphery action to a great extent, while making plans to *deny* the inside action.

So, as coach of the Option Offense, you must be ready for a defensive front-court technique which usually establishes an imaginary, semi-circular perimeter called the "critical line" (Figure 5-1), beyond which no defensive member goes unless his individual opponent has the ball. In this diagram, our 1 has the ball in the initial phase of the offensive movement, so X1 goes out to him aggressively. X2 drops back inside the line, clogging the middle. X4 and X5 would ease toward the strong side by moving away from 4 and 5, further clogging up the key where so much of our driving and cutting takes place. And X3 would tighten up on 3 while still remaining within the perimeter. If 1 should pass across to 2 we would see X1 release from 1 and drop back into the perimeter, while X2 would pop out to challenge 2. Any movement of the ball around the perimeter would result in this kind of response: the constant popping out and dropping back by this sagging team. As applied to our own offense, notice in Figure 5-2 (the Red

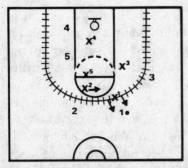

Figure 5-1. Probable sag line against Option Offense.

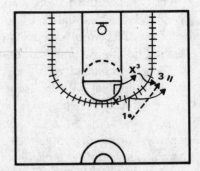

Figure 5-2. X3 pops out. X1 goes back in.

Series is beginning; 1 passes to 3) that X3 pops out to challenge 3, while X1 drops back.

While noting the defensive actions of X3 and X1, one should also infer that our offense presents them with a problem right away: When 3 hands the ball back to 01 (Figure 5-2), how is X1 going to get around his own teammate (X3) and our own 3 in order to get to and challenge 01 outside the perimeter? *We* know that 3, in our offense, is going to cut across to the top of the key after handing the ball back to 01 at the wing, and this will get X1 and X3 out of this particular difficulty, temporarily at least, by way of a switching process. But there *is* an instant when 01 is receiving full screening effect along the side. Look for him to take advantage of it, possibly with a driving dribble around the screen and into the basket area from the side! Figure 5-3 depicts this possible action, which presents X3 and X1 with new defensive problems of adjustment.

It is obvious that the inside driving and passing lanes within the imaginary perimeter will tend to become clogged and cluttered as defensive people sag and sink into the high post man (Figure 5-4), front the low post man (strong side) when the ball is on his side of the

Figure 5-3. X3 and X1 get a new problem.

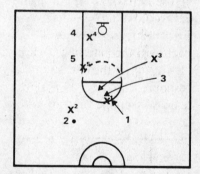

Figure 5-4. Sag into high post by X1.

court in our Option Offense (Figure 5-5), drift away from our offensive men on the weak side (side away from the ball) as in Figure 5-1, and over-play the low post man on the strong side (Figure 5-6).

Another serious nuisance to be anticipated is the man-man half-court pressure tactic with stunting and double-teaming characteristics.

In philosophy, if not in manner of execution, the modern man-

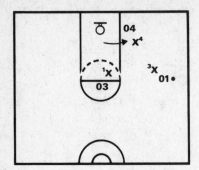

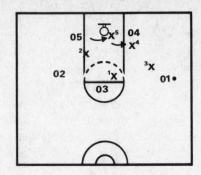

Figure 5-5. Fronting our low post by X4.

Figure 5-6. Overplay by X4, weak-side help from X5.

man sag resembles certain zone defenses, especially if it combines with other techniques and tactics such as switching, releasing, helping from the weak side, sliding, and trapping. A real masquerade is conducted; the defense looks like a zone; and, in modern basketball parlance, a new defensive word is coined: *combination*.

If doubt does exist as to whether a zone or man-man defense is being employed, the normal movement and route of 02 in the Red Series of the Option Offense should serve to dispel the uncertainty. In Figure 5-7, the response of X2 is significant and should be watched. If he goes man-man with 02 down the key and around 4, as shown in Figure 5-7, the defense is surely man-man. In a very sophisticated combination defense, X2 might drop off and release from 02, turn him over to X4, and take on 4 himself. Our Red Series discourages this, however, because our 4 is a big man and there would be physical mismatch between X2 and 4 in such inside switching. Notice that X2 stays within the confines of the sag perimeter even though he never relinquishes the man-man responsibility for 02.

When and if the Option Offense reaches the Mixmaster stage, the sag defense has met its nemesis, especially when the point man has the ball. Just as the Mixmaster will be successful against all types of zones, so will it be successful against a sag. In Figure 5-8, X3 can't sink or sag; that would invite an open jump shot by 03. On the wings, X1 and X2 can't afford to regress or draw back from their offensive opponents, 01 and 02. There is no strong side, and there is no weak side! X4 and X5 must play honest, because 03 could lob a pass to a momentarily free 04 or 05 under the basket. The offensive expectation

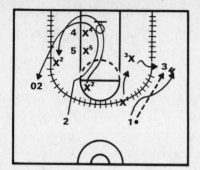

Figure 5-7. X2's response is watched.

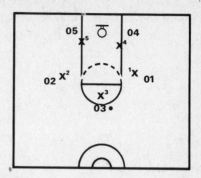

Figure 5-8. Mixmaster against the sag.

should be that Mixmaster can begin its operation without the nuisance of sag. Figure 5-9 stays with the Mixmaster, showing a pass from the point 03 to the wing 01. We can expect defensive sinking and sagging in the key immediately by X2 and X5, as shown, and X4 will be trying to front 04. In this situation, all the work in give-and-go practice comes in handy. 01 return-passes to 03 as he goes down the key (Pass B). Met by a "helping" X5, 03 hardly interrupts the course of the ball as he bounce-passes over to the wide-open 05 for a lay-up (Pass C). In Figure 5-10, 01 refuses the give-and-go and makes X2 pay for his defensive cheating by hitting the open 02 at the top of the key. He has an open jump shot before X2 can get to him. Another example of *hit the open man!*

In Figure 5-11, we have a situation which will occur often enough

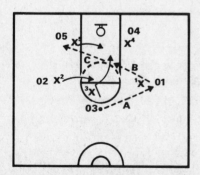

Figure 5-9. Give-and-go, with a pass to 05.

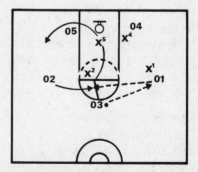

Figure 5-10. X2 is taught a lesson.

for it to be a matter of concern in practice plans. 01 has the ball at the right wing. We are in the Mixmaster. Not wanting to pass to the point man for some reason, 01 decides to dribble down the side in the hope that he can get the ball to 04 from a different angle and position. In reaction to this, X4 has shifted around until he is between 04 and the baseline. This is good defensive basketball as he leans tight while checking on 04's left side, his defensive left arm at full extent projected across the front of 04. The objective is to deny the baseline in this situation and, by so doing, to discourage any pass to 04 that could result in his baseline movement to the basket. This denial of the baseline is a relatively new concept. For years the general opinion and practice was that baseline movement would be tolerated if a choice had to be made. Allowance of 04 to move to his right with the ball, which would result if he was denied the baseline, was unfeasible and almost unthinkable. He would be practically unguarded as he drove under the basket or tried a left-handed hook shot! In recent years, however, this movement is allowed and encouraged more and more by the defense, mainly because of another relatively new concept which reacts to such an offensive move. It is called weak-side help. Figure 5-12 will help to

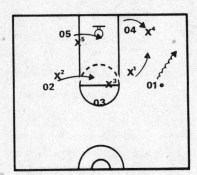

Figure 5-11. Deny the baseline.

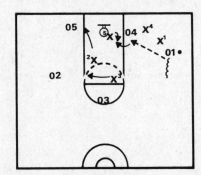

Figure 5-12. Weak-side help at the low post.

clarify this. (Figure 5-6 is also an example.) With X4 over-playing to the baseline, 01 passes to 04's right hand. X4 is willing to allow this pass from 01 and the resulting move by 04, because he knows that his teammate, X5, will release from 05 to help as 04 makes his *rightward* movement toward the key and the basket. Notice that X2 would simultaneously release from 02 in this action to pick up the unguarded 05.

This, by the way, is a classic example of *combination* defense. It is particularly practiced by most professional basketball teams to circumvent the professional rule that only man-man defense is permitted. It's not a zone defense, but zone principles are involved!

The one dependable, infallible strategy for counteracting a sagging, sinking defense is inherent in the Blue Series. With 2 handling the ball (Figure 5-13), his opponent, X2, will be checking him closely, while X1 will sink away from 1 to clog up the key. With the Option Offense set formation being what it is, this sag will be ineffective against the Blue Series; and if X2 anticipates the pass from 2 to 04 and dares sink back into 04 as he comes out of the stack, 02 would teach him a lesson about cheating by holding on to the ball and dribble-driving to his right oblique into the key for a jump shot (Figure 5-14) or by trying some other free-lance technique.

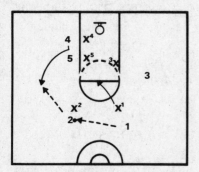

Figure 5-13. Sag by X1 is ineffective.

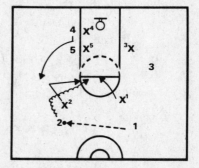

Figure 5-14. X2 sags on 04. Reaction by 02.

A sagging, sinking defense cannot contain the Blue Series. If the other parts of the Option Offense are having trouble, our quarterback can employ the Blue Series as much as necessary, or use it entirely for that matter, until the defense makes a compromise which will leave the door open for the Option Offense to come back into full play with the Red and White.

Realistically, the back door feature of the White Series may encounter some difficulty against the sagging X1 (Figure 5-15). As 2 passes to 03 at the high post, X1 has drifted back, ahead of 01, to shut off the back door option. Among the offensive responses, one stands out: 03, with his back to the basket at the high post, fakes the back-

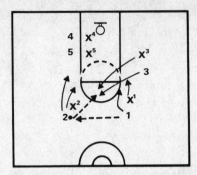

Figure 5-15. X1 neutralizes the back door. Response.

door pass to 01 and then flips the ball back to 02. 02 may free-lance when he gets the ball in view of the fact that X5 always poses a clogging, impeding threat in the key (Figure 5-15). This practice of over-playing, fronting, shifting, sliding, releasing, helping, and denial of the baseline, as depicted and described in Figures 5-1 through 5-15, adds up to the totality of *sag*. It resembles a zone in many ways. With embellishment of switching and other techniques, it has been called *combination*.

ANTICIPATION OF DEFENSIVE SWITCHING

We must expect defensive switching to occur against our Option Offense. A switch usually becomes necessary as a defensive tactic when an offensive screen or pick has taken place. In this situation, there is little choice for the defensive individual but to give up his assigned responsibility and take on another. Many coaches don't like this aspect and teach their players to fight through or fight over screens and picks as much as possible, to switch defensive responsibility only when it is absolutely necessary, and, if it is necessary to switch, to re-assume the original responsibility as quickly as possible.

Three major disadvantages stand out in the defensive switching technique, and our Option Offense must be trained to exploit them: (1) the defensive men must talk to each other (tell each other about intent, give warnings), and too many basketball players are careless about this in spite of all the coach can do; (2) a momentary mismatch usually occurs; and, most important, (3) a natural opening usually occurs at the instant of switching which results in the opportunity for the screener (picker) to release and roll (pick-and-roll) for the basket, with his new defensive opponent a step behind.

Figures 5-16 through 5-25 will help in the discussion of the switching tactic and its implication for the Option Offense. In Figure 5-16, we are in the Blue Series, and 04 has the ball and starts his dribble as 05 sets a rear or side screen on X4. Here, the defensive man *behind* the action, X5, should have called out a warning to X4. If the screen is set properly, X4 will not be able to follow 04 in his dribble, and X5 will have to call, "Switch!" In this example, X5 then picks up the dribbling 04, but a closer look at Figure 5-16 shows the negative aspect of the switch which happens often. X5 finds himself behind 05 in an untenable defensive position, and Figure 5-17 shows the result. 05 turns as 04 dribbles by and finds an open path to the basket as he receives a little pass from 04 (the roll in the pick-and-roll).

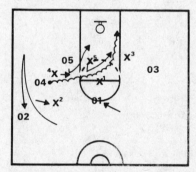

Figure 5-16. Switch by X4 and X5.

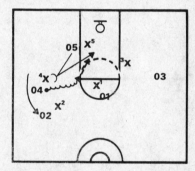

Figure 5-17. Pick and roll by 04 and 05.

Other chapters dealing with the options of the Option Offense will give further examples of the extensive use of pick-and-roll. Figures 5-18, 5-19, and 5-20 demonstrate how defensive switching might affect a part of the Option Offense and what might be expected from the defense when the stack goes into operation. The drawings refer to the high-low options of the White Series. 01 has tried the back door unsuccessfully; he and 02 are at their new side positions. 03 is facing the basket with the ball. 04 fakes toward the center of the lane and then comes around the screen of 5, hoping to receive the high-low pass from 03. In our illustration, X4 calls "Switch!" as he becomes hung up on

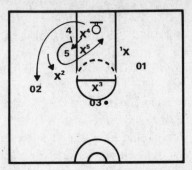

Figure 5-18. X5 and X4 switch.

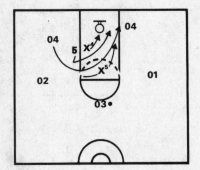

Figure 5-19. X5 has position on 04.

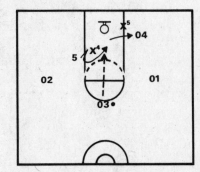

Figure 5-20. 05 is open as second man through.

5. So X5 picks up 04 in the switch and is able, in this case, to discourage the pass from 03 to 04 (Figure 5-19). But we have a response, an automatic one, that just naturally occurs when this option is denied. It is *second man through*. 05 alertly follows 04 through the key area and in Figure 5-20 receives the high-low pass from 03. The second man through is a rule in the Option Offense for all weak side cuts and high-low action.

In this high-low sequence, our expectation should be that if the defense switches, 05 will be open; if it doesn't switch, 04 will be open. We must always assume that defensive switching will, at times, prevent the success of a planned option, just as other defensive measures will cause trouble. It is necessary, therefore, to have planned automatic alternatives, and the players should also be encouraged to take advantage of unexpected openings. There are other expectations. In Figure 5-19, we assume that X5 was able to thwart the pass from 03 down to the cutting 04. This was done for the purposes of illustration, but we must not expect that this will always happen. We must demand of 04 that he *not give up* to aggressive switching; instead, he fights back and does not passively allow X5 to jockey into such good defensive position.

The combat is very interesting when there is no switching tactic. This may take place by design (X4 and X5 may have been instructed to fight through and over picks and screens) or by defensive lapse and "laziness." Figure 5-21 shows the fighting, bristling X4 following instructions, refusing to be pinched out by the screen of 5. He has observed a good rule that he must anticipate and be alert and aggressive *before* his man gets the ball, not just *after* he gets it. When our 04 made his little jab step and a fake inward toward the center of the lane (Figure 5-21), X4 started playing good defense by opening up toward the ball (note that 03 has it) and going into the crouching, boxer stance, with one arm and hand pointing toward 04 and the other hand and arm pointing toward the ball. Then, with 04 pushing off to his right and starting to go around 5, X4 recovers and refuses the pinching process. He jockeys for position, uses his strength legally, fights through, and is responding very well to orders as 04 goes around and over the top of 5. But, right here, he may not be prepared for our response. 04 executes a quick cut-back and goes back door! 04 does that in Figure 5-22 because

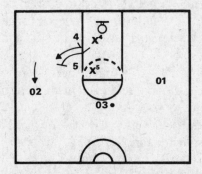

Figure 5-21. X4 fights through. No switch.

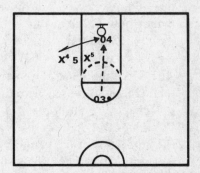

Figure 5-22. A response by 04.

he has been taught to take advantage of an opening or, in the absence of an opening, to make one! 03 passes down to him as he cuts back for this lay-up, back door.

Other alternatives are shown in Figure 5-23. With X4 fighting through, 05 could be open and in front of X5; X4 might get hung up on the back of 5, leaving 04 open for a pass; or 03 could pass off to either wing.

Defensive lapse, or "laziness," is illustrated in Figure 5-24. For whatever reason, X4 and X5 do not switch, do not talk, do not think or

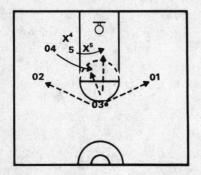 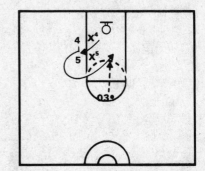

Figure 5-23. Other offensive alternatives.

Figure 5-24. X4, X5 do not switch, do not fight over the top.

play good defense, so 04 will come around the screen of 5 completely open for the pass from 03. In Figure 5-25, X4 and X5 do switch, but this is an example that shows a switch is not always the answer, no matter how efficiently it is executed. 05 follows 04 as second man through. Suddenly, he sees a chance to go back door on X4 and receives the pass from 03 as he does so.

Since the stack plays such an important role in the success of the total Option Offense, there must be additional reference made to it in this chapter in the form of a warning to you. All kinds of defensive "gimmicks" will be devised to neutralize the effectiveness of 4 and 5. Figure 5-26 shows one that has been met before, and it aggravates, as well as inhibits, the offensive operation of the stack unless there is a countermeasure. It can be quite effective.

X5 *fronts* our 4 in Figure 5-26. The plan is, obviously, to completely shut off 04 when he comes around and over the top of 5 in the Red or White Series. X4 is then defensively accountable for 5 without going through the rather chaotic, sometimes ineffective, defensive switching process down in the basket area. Since X5 is also fronting 5

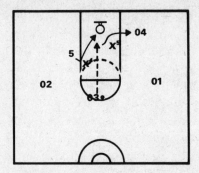

Figure 5-25. 05 goes back door on X4.   **Figure 5-26. X5 fronts 5.**

in this set, he tends to deny and discourage outside passing to 5. His positioning can also be a bother in the Blue Series when 04 pops out from the rear of the stack to receive the initial pass, because X5 would be in a favorable position to defend against 04's turn-around and jump shot or even to "beat him" to the pass.

As I stated, this method has been used against the stack, and it is both realistic and workable. The Option Offense should look for its use by teams that have been met before.

There is always a reaction for every action. A list of just a few offensive reactions (options) follows and could be added to many times over:

1. The play-maker, 1, calls out "Four!" or gives the hand signal for Play #4 as explained in Chapter 8, Figure 8-4. To anticipate later reading, this play calls for 04 to flash out to the free throw line from behind the stack, receive the pass from 1, turn, and take a jump shot. This will cause X5 to ponder a bit, because 04 usually comes around and over the top or pops out to the side.

2. In the Blue Series, 2 refuses to pass to 04 when he pops out to receive the initiating pass. Faking to him and drawing X5 out, he passes, instead, to 5 in an open high post position.

3. In Red and White, 03, from the top of the key, *concentrates* his passes down to 05 as the second man through. This will create a lot of work for X4 and X5. Figure 5-20 is only one of many examples.

EXPECTED RESPONSE TO SCISSORS OFF THE HIGH POST

Figures 5-27 and 5-28 deal with the scissors off the high post, which has been a traditional part of basketball and is a part of the Option Offense. In Figure 5-27 we show the conventional three-man play. 01 and 02 travel the typical routes of the scissors, with 01 cutting behind and after the passer, 02. 03 looks at both as possible receivers of a short pass or hand-off as they come by.

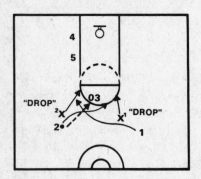

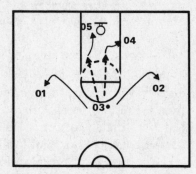

Figure 5-27. Scissors, with *drop* response.

Figure 5-28. Our natural sequential response to *drop*.

There is a defensive answer to the scissors, and the Option Offense must expect it. At his coaches' clinic at the University of Washington in the early '70's, Coach Tex Winter reviewed the *drop* idea, which is included as a part of Figure 5-27. Coach Winter's defensive answer to the scissors was for either X1 or X2 to yell "drop!" Both would then back pedal quickly, drop back to their respective sides on either flank of 03, and merely pick up whoever came by. If they do this properly, there is no screening effect connected with the scissors. This is an excellent defensive idea, and it neutralizes the scissors to some degree.

The Option Offense has a built-in response to the defensive drop. No adjustment need be made. If 03 can't pass to either 01 or 02, he turns with the ball and looks down. From this perspective, he can make a delay pass to either 01 or 02 (they are taught to look back as they go by and also to button-hook back along the sides at about the free throw line extended), or, from the rocker step or cross-over, 03 is encouraged to go one-on-one for the basket from his high post position.

A third built-in response happens naturally and automatically in Figure 5-28. With 03 turned and facing him, 04 makes his usual, basic move around and over the top of 5. 05 follows him as second man through. Figure 5-28 concedes that neither 01 nor 02 are open as they scissors but illustrates the alternative high-low possibilities from 03 to 04 or 05.

SUMMARY

Against all man-man defenses, especially those which combine sagging, switching, and other techniques with the individual effort, three major attack principles must be emphasized: (1) maintain poise and confidence in the Option Offense, (2) move without the ball, and (3) pass to the open man. The first of the three seems most important. Do not make hasty adjustments; instead, continue using the Red, White, and Blue Series. Somewhere along the line, no matter how much sagging or switching is going on, an offensive option will occur. This is the true test of confidence. You must not allow any excuses, rationalizations, or incomplete, half-hearted execution of this offense just because some part of it doesn't produce. The slogan is "Run the offense!"

Chapter Six

Launching the Option Offense
Against Zone Defenses

PRINCIPLES OF ZONE AND MAN-MAN

When a team meets an opponent using a zone defense, the offensive principles as applied against a man-man defense should change very little. This is my opinion, based on the philosophy of the Option Offense. And the general concept of *team* and *movement* should not change at all. The team should continue to move into and out of planned avenues and routes of offensive approach, taking advantage of options and choices just as it does against the man-man defense. Movement with a purpose in mind, spontaneity, and individual improvisation are appropriate particulars, just as before. Since the Option Offense is just as applicable against a zone defense as it is against a man-man, only minor changes are necessary. Simplicity is important in the strategies of basketball; the Option Offense is designed to attack the zone and the man-man in an almost identical fashion; and the philosophy, or the assumption, is that this offense, as it stands, will break down any defense.

The statement of confidence in the Option Offense is made in the face of evidence that zone defenses are becoming more diversified. Although this chapter attempts to do so, it is increasingly difficult to label, define, and evaluate specific zone defenses. They may line up initially in one formation and then shift to another, combine with man-man principles, alternate from zone to man-man during a game, utilize interzonal slides which change individual responsibilities, and continually make other unusual adjustments.

BACKGROUND OF ZONE DEFENSES

It is necessary to furnish some background and make a few general points before dealing with the specifics involved in a discussion of the Option Offense versus zone defenses.

Just as the tactics and techniques of zone defenses have been changing over the years, so have the offensive methods of attacking them. One successful school of thought about beating the zone was led by the late Branch McCracken, coach at Indiana University for 30 years, and it was exciting: "Fast break; get down the floor fast before the defense has a chance to set up." Hence, "Hurryin' Hoosiers."

Another major accepted method was more deliberate. In attacking a defense suspected of being zone, the standard operating offensive procedure was to *send a man through*, with the expectation that the secret of defense would be revealed. If this man's defensive opponent released him as he came through (down the key) or failed to follow him (as he came back out) man-for-man in the front court, the offense was up against a zone. Simple as that!

Upon the guarantee that a zone defense was being met, the common thing was for the offense to move the ball around the perimeter or outside limit of defense, with the prime objective of getting the ball to the team's best outside shooter. The strategy was really very simple: Move the ball around faster than the individual defensive men could move and react within their zones on the outside, and if the "gunner" was hitting a high percentage of his shots, sooner or later the defense would have to abandon its zone strategy and go to a man-man defense. "Move it, move it!" the coach and the fans would scream. And the passes would speed up around the outside—pass, move a step, fake a pass, send a man through the middle and swerve him out to a corner —and most of all, get the ball to an open man, preferably the "gunner," around the outside. Now, if the outside shooting was below par, we had a game that was dreadfully boring and a coach whose team didn't get to shoot many, if any, free throws and whose theory for losing was that his team "couldn't hit a thing."

Surprisingly enough, a great deal of this dogged, uninspiring plan of attack remains with us today, and there are boring games. Luckily, however, there are always coaches who question established procedures and concepts. So, add their inventiveness and theories to the information and ideas coming out of coaches' clinics, professional publications, and books, and we have a modern game of basketball undergoing continual change that is, generally, most exciting and imaginative in its offensive execution, no matter what the defensive strategies are. For the most part, there is *player movement* and offensive penetration as well as ball movement, as coaches send cutters and drivers into the zonal areas, set up picks and screens just as they do against man-man defenses, create mis-matches in relatively weak defensive areas, and overload certain areas with player movement that results in out-numbering situations

In the last few sentences, I find that I have been, inadvertently, describing the Option Offense as it responds to a zone defense.

Now, a word for the coach of zone defense. He has, himself, been forced to innovate, experiment, and develop arrangements, movements, and formations that supplement the traditional zone methods of defense. In short, he has devised modern zone defenses that blend and combine the old and the new. The old continues with the traditional idea that a zone defense must be *compact* as a *unit*, with the *mass* moving as a unit and directing its strength *toward* the ball. The new adds the dynamics of *sliding*, *shifting*, *inter-zone help,* and *trapping*.

In the following material, some facts about the traits, qualities, and peculiarities of the traditional zone defenses that are of interest to you, the Option Offense coach, will be presented. Some of the newer trends and the terminology will be included.

Although there has been modification, as mentioned before, there remain five traditional zone defenses for our concern. They are the 2-3, the 2-1-2, the 1-2-2, the 3-2, and the 1-3-1. In appearance, the 3-2 and the 1-2-2 (sometimes called the jug or bottle zone) are so much alike that we could say there are only four instead of five zones that have been handed down through basketball history and are still in use today.

IMPORTANT GENERAL INFORMATION, 2-3 ZONE

We start with the 2-3, sometimes referred to as the lay-back zone. The coach of this defensive formation breaks down the total area into sections, and each section is assigned to players for individual responsibility (Figure 6-1). This is traditional. Now we go to the modification or the "new."

Figure 6-2 shows the relationship of the original set of the 2-3 to the Option Offense and the moves normally expected of X1, X2, X3, X4, and X5 as our 1 receives the ball. None of them have moved outside their assigned area. But in Figure 6-3, X3 does move forward, ouside his original area of responsibility, in response to the initiating Red Series pass from 1 to 3. This interzonal movement by X3 would be termed a slide. The concurring adjustments by X1, X2, X4, and X5 (Figure 6-3) would, in totality, be termed a shift. To continue this exercise in modern adjustment, in Figure 6-4, 01 passes down to 04 at the low post (Red Series action), and we see a flagrant example of *slide* as X3 releases from his side position and quickly moves down to

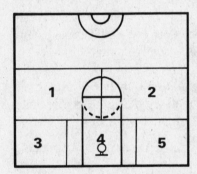

Figure 6-1. 2-3 zone. Traditional assignment of zone sections.

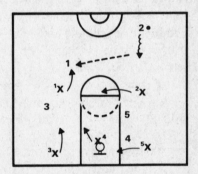

Figure 6-2. X1 replies to a pass.

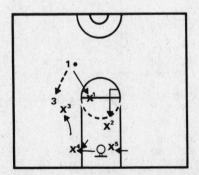

Figure 6-3. X3 *slides*, the zone shifts.

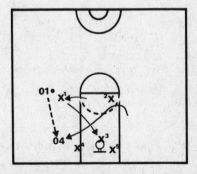

Figure 6-4. X4 goes out. X3 slides down.

replace X4, who has gone out to defend the low post area. The formation has *shifted* again.

Obviously, the 2-3 zone will have to make a dramatic adjustment, either in the way it sets up initially or in its adaptation once our offensive movement begins. X5 is completely outside the realm of defensive action, on the "wrong" side of the stack; and the position of X3 adds nothing to the integrity of the defensive formation—at least, not in the beginning (Figure 6-2).

We must note X1 and X2, the front men. Usually, they will be fast and aggressive as "chasers," with a liking for hard work as they try for pass interceptions. One or the other usually picks up his ball-handling opponent at about 20 to 25 feet. Occasionally, depending upon a signal or policy, X1 and X2 will team up to set an early trap on a dribbler entering the front court. The double-teaming may even extend to the side areas. You will seldom see trapping and double-teaming in the middle area. The 2-3 zone does not lend itself to extensive or sustained double-teaming. It is, usually, more conservative; hence, lay-back zone.

Figure 6-5 shows the general limitations. In the diagram, the shaded areas in the front court represent all the defensive coach could probably designate as trapping places. Figure 6-6 shows an action

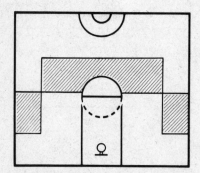

Figure 6-5. Usual limits of trapping, 2-3 zone.

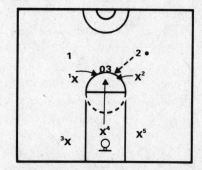

Figure 6-6. Pinch and trap at the top of the key.

which can be expected quite often as a surprise trap. It is sprung by X1 and X2 as they pinch on our 03 at the high post just as he receives the pass from 2 in the White Series.

While it is a gambling maneuver on the part of the defense, the

Option Offense must expect to be subjected to it, because the top of the key is the very center of the White Series operation. In very rare situations, X4 would come forward quickly to make it a three-man trap (Figure 6-6).

I have given brief examples, so far, of the terms *sliding*, *shifting*, and *trapping* as they may apply to the 2-3 zone. As the discussion of other zone defenses and their relationships to the Option Offense continues in this chapter, I will need to make further reference to all three terms. As stated before, trapping is not usually an outstanding feature of the 2-3 zone; however, since the term has been presented, I will continue the discussion of some of its more salient points here, before going on to other zones and the Option Offense. As the Option Offense coach, you had better know a great deal about it. *Trapping* will be used against you!

As stated elsewhere in this book, there is an instructional tendency to go from method to method and strategy to strategy, while failing to consider that concepts and understandings are being overlooked. In other words, the person conducting the orientation must not always assume that everybody is up to date on the terminology and basics. You must heed this warning when you conduct practice sessions, just as writers and lecturers must when they present their views. Right here, then, we must stop short, in the interest of concepts and understandings, to present a definition of the objectives of trap and double-team and to review certain standout fundamentals that pertain to its execution.

The usual objectives of front-court trapping and double-teaming as supplements to a zone defense are (1) to induce panicky, "telegraphed" passes which can be intercepted for fast-break purposes; (2) to force the offense out of its patterns and plans; (3) to cause jump balls, which gives the defense a chance to regain possession and also brings the offensive movement to a halt; (4) to cause foot-work errors that enable the defense to get possession of the ball out-of-bounds; and (5) to cause offensive fouling violations.

To achieve these objectives, the trapping defense relies on increased tempo and aggressiveness, and is willing to gamble quite a bit. Sometimes two players, not one, will go to the receiver just at the instant of the pass reception; other times, one player will go to the receiver and aggressively fix him in place, to be joined immediately by his teammate, who has released from his normal defensive assignment.

If the opponent is dribbling, he is not permitted to penetrate the key and foul lane area. The first member of the trapper-team will go to challenge the dribbler and possibly over-play him in such a way as to force him towards the sideline and away from the key area. (True, some coaches advocate the funneling method of coercing the dribbler towards the *middle*, where the main strength of the defense is concentrated and where there is more congestion.) While over-playing the dribbler and forcing him to enter a desired defensive area, the single trapper is also herding the dribbler into a blind turning action, right into the path of the second trapper coming to help.

In either case, that of the stationary receiver of a pass or that of the moving dribbler, the ultimate double-teaming trap is formed by the positioning of the trappers' bodies as they advance and press themselves closely to the ball-handler, shuffling and slide-stepping in a rather erect stance, with arms extended straight *up*. Pressing as closely as possible in the direction of the movement of the ball without fouling, the trappers restrict maneuverability and obstruct and deny so many options in passing and shooting that the dribbler is forced to suspend his dribble; ultimately, with the trappers jumping, flailing their arms, and pressing closely, the man with the ball has no options remaining. He goes to a jump ball or makes a desperation pass.

Modified, altered, and supplemented, then, by sliding, shifting, and trapping, the discussion of the 2-3 concludes with the following notes, all of significance and consequence to the planning that goes into the Option Offense.

The probable trapping actions of X1and X2 have been briefly discussed. Figures 6-7, 6-8, and 6-9 are now added to show the

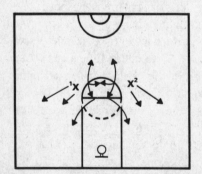

Figure 6-7. Slides of X1 and X2.

Figure 6-8. Slides of X4.

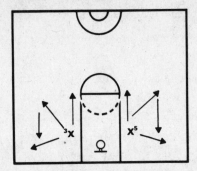

Figure 6-9. Slides of X3 and X5.

customary responsibilities of X1 and X2 in the 2-3 zone, as well as those of X3, X4, and X5. Figure 6-7 outlines the sliding and interzonal responsibilities of X1 and X2. In Figure 6-8, X4 would replace either X3 or X5 as necessary, go to either corner, and flash out to check the area in the middle of the key. He must be alert and highly mobile. In Figure 6-9, X3 and X5 have to be mobile even though they would be the big men. They are expected to (1) clog up the deep key area, (2) go to the corners, (3) go out to the wings, (4) go from wing to corner, and (5) come out to defend against a high post set along the side of the lane.

Here are some strong points of the 2-3 zone:

1. Viewing the formation in Figure 6-1, one can easily see that the 2-3 would have great rebounding capability because of the density of its coverage and alignment around the basket. Rebounding by an offensive team would be curtailed because of the natural protective triangle that would be formed.

2. There is good coverage against low post play.

3. The 2-3 converts very well to the fast break, with two get-away men out front.

4. The 2-3 would be effective against a team that concentrated its power in its big men around the basket; thus, it is very restrictive in regards to under-basket offensive play.

5. If it doesn't try to trap outside and plays more or less traditionally, the 2-3 would be effective against a team that has weak outside shooters. (Because it lays-back, by reputation, and seems willing to give up outside shots.)

Disadvantages and weaknesses are:

1. It is notoriously weak against 12 to 15 foot jump shots on either side of the free throw line.

2. The seam area between the two front men and the three back men can be exploited by good passing and cutting.

3. The seam and sections around the top of the key can be overloaded rather easily.

4. Mismatching is a danger if an offense can cause the 2-3 to move, slide, and switch vertically a great deal.

5. Trapping and double-teaming areas are comparatively limited.

SPECIFIC RELATIONSHIPS, OPTION OFFENSE AND 2-3 ZONE

You, the coach of Option Offense, are advised to stick to the patterns, with minor adjustment, against the 2-3 zone. Certain parts and specific options within the offense will prove effective. They will be recommended and illustrated at this juncture. At the same time, for your benefit every possible effort will be made to avoid redundancy and superfluity in diagramming. Drawings in other chapters will be applicable in some cases.

An important tenet to be followed in attacking a 2-3 zone (or any zone for that matter) is to always attempt to *outnumber* the defense in its weak areas. Another offensive axiom (in broad strategy) in attacking a zone that, traditionally, sinks back into the basket area is to concentrate the power of the offense into the high-percentage shooting areas. In the face of a good shooting percentage, the two front men, X1 and X2, will tend to come out, exposing a horizontal seam between them and the three deep defensive men. This, in turn, opens up the inside aspect of the offense.

At the very beginning of the Red Series, when 3 receives the pass from 1 at the wing and looks for the cutting, driving 02, he will find him open more often than not right at the foul line. Upon receiving the pass from 3 in this seam, 02 can pull up and take his high-percentage jump shot. His chances for a driving lay-up, favorable against man-man, are lessened against the 2-3.

When 3 hands back to 01 at the wing (Red Series) and cuts for the top of the key, he will find the identical seam. The return pass from 01, reverse-style, will produce another high-percentage jump shot.

Still in the Red Series (Figure 6-10), 01's swing pass will be delivered a bit earlier than against man-man, because 04 will also find the seam for an open jump shot just as he comes around and over the top of 5. It must be noted, in the drawing, that X1 is busy with 01, X2 must give attention to 03's move to the top of the key, and these concerns leave only the forward-sliding X4 as a late defender against the jump shot of 04.

Outnumbering will be dealt with in subsequent discussion about other zone defenses in this chapter, but early passing reference should be made since it was mentioned here as an anti-zone offensive principle. In Figure 6-11, note the outnumbering characteristic of the Mixmaster as it begins the mixing process. The two outside men, X1 and

Figure 6-10. 04 comes to an open seam.

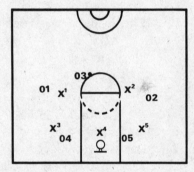

Figure 6-11. Mixmaster outnumbers the 2-3 zone.

X2, are outmanned initially; immediate defensive adjustment will be required by way of sliding, shifting, and inter-zone movement. 01 and 02 really present a problem. They are in their Mixmaster positions about half-way between the sidelines and the sides of the free throw lane and about even with the free throw line. Neither X1 nor X2 can ignore point man 03, although X1 will be the more concerned in Figure 6-11. 03 has made a minor positioning adjustment in order to set an overload triangle on X1's side. If X1 makes a move toward him, 03 quickly passes off to 01, who is open for a quick-release jump shot. Neither X5 nor X4 will feel free to rush forward to defend, because our 04 or 05 would be uncovered in the low post area. It is also well to remember that 03 is flashing straight down the key area after his pass to either wing, looking for a give-and-go pass or a pass from the low post. This is drilled as a standard rule in the Option Offense, and it further burdens the zone's adjustment.

The back door, which bears the earmark of the White Series and initiates it, will be successful against the 2-3 zone defense. When wing man 03 flashes to the top of the key to receive the pass from 2, clearing out the side for 01's back-door move as already described and illustrated in Chapters 1 and 3, the 2-3 zone is in trouble. Earlier in this chapter, the "pinch" capability of X1 and X2 at the high post, combined occasionally with a rear-trap foray by the sliding X4 (Figure 6-6), was presented as a possible nuisance, and this action by the 2-3 zone must be considered in White Series practice sessions. The fact remains, however, that our 03 will be trained in his execution and timing at the high post to the extent that the ball will be relayed to 01 on the cleared side without problem. Meeting the pass, body balance, protecting the ball, footwork, pivoting, turning, going one-on-one—all of these fundamentals are involved for 03 and must be perfected through practice drills.

MINOR ADJUSTMENT BY THE OPTION OFFENSE

The only initial concession made by the Option Offense (whether Red, White, or Blue Series) when it meets any type of zone defense concerns only a slight adjustment in positioning by the point man when the Mixmaster comes into play. This is done in order to establish an overloading triangle on a *strong side* (side where the ball is located) of the court, made up of a low post, wing man, and point man. Triangular passing against an outnumbered defense on that side of the court is generated within this group, with a main purpose of gaining an open, close-in jump shot. The *weak side* (side away from the ball) would consist of the other low post and wing man.

We will refer to Figure 6-12 to illustrate this. Notice that this is Mixmaster except for the minor adjustment made in the top-of-the-key area. The point man generally moves over into the curving area instead of being approximately centered at the top.

Nothing new is claimed in regard to a triangular idea, or grouping, against a zone defense. Its philosophy and objective of creating an overload or outnumbering situation is well-known and established. But at least two important things stand out here that stamp the Mixmaster phase of the Option Offense against the zone in an unusual, revolutionary manner: (1) our players do not have to change their offensive basketball thinking, and (2) the triangle doesn't stand around, as most triangles do, while the passing goes on. No change is made in the Mixmaster philosophy of passing, moving, and hitting the open man as described and drawn in other chapters. I have, therefore, a constantly rotating strong side and weak side and a constant stream of replacement into the wings and point while the ball is moving. Only the double low-post men are relatively stationary. The ball is passed to the wing from the point (Figure 6-13); the point man cuts down the key; the ball goes to the low post. This is strong-side, overloading basket-

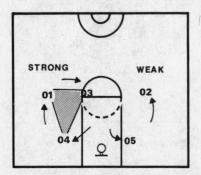

Figure 6-12. Evolvement into Mixmaster triangle.

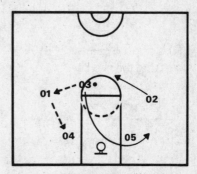

Figure 6-13. Triangular passing, but the same Mixmaster.

ball done the Mixmaster way in the shape of a triangle, which keeps the defense moving, leaning, spread out, and vulnerable to sudden reversal of the ball to the weak side via the new, replacing point man. The reversal of the ball, by the way, acts to rotate the roles of strong side and weak side. Figure 6-14 should aid in clarification.

One highly recommended strategy against zone defenses is the use of double low-post players, with concentrated effort in getting the ball down to them. The Mixmaster *features* the double low post. All of the action there, combined with cuts and drives by players *without the ball* and the swinging of the ball "around the horn" (perimeter) via a point man, adds up to total activity which exerts the greatest possible pressure against any zone defense.

All descriptions and diagrams of Mixmaster movement presented elsewhere in this book pertain and apply here and, except for a few instances, will not be repeated here.

PERTINENT 2-1-2 CHARACTERISTICS

The 2-1-2 is becoming an increasingly popular zone defense. Viewed in a diagram, it sets as two adjoining triangles, with X3 being the common part of both. The broken lines in Figure 6-15 illustrate the configuration. The one deep triangle formed by X3, X4, and X5 gives

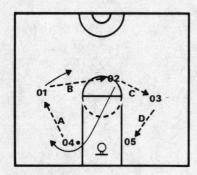

Figure 6-14. Weak side becomes strong side.

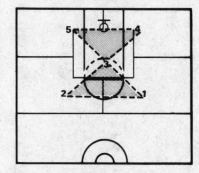

Figure 6-15. The triangles of the 2-1-2.

the 2-1-2 its defensive rebounding strength and also presents a formidable barrier to under-basket and close-in offense. It is a very competitive, combative, and aggressive zone defense. Positive features, in general, are:

1. It defends the foul line area very well against high post play.
2. It is comparatively easy to teach; although sliding is necessary, it is not a complicated process.
3. The 2-1-2 can go to the fast break very well.

Primary areas of responsibility for all players are shown within the heavy, unbroken lines in Figure 6-16. Interzonal movements of sliding are also illustrated. For example, X1 and X2 could be expected to slide toward the middle, toward the wings, and back into the free throw line area. They are quick and aggressive and like to be called *chasers* because they do go out head hunting, trying to intercept passes and steal the ball. They will usually pick up the offense at 25 to 30 feet out, farther out than the two front men in the 2-3 zone. X3 will be assigned the areas in the key, to include the slides down the key to replace X4 or X5 when they are forced to go out to the corners. Occasionally, X3 is expected to slide out to the wing areas, out of his usual zonal responsibility. He is a relatively big, mobile player who must have good basketball instinct and intelligence, because he has a sensitive area to cover and some of the coverage decisions may be left up to him in a free-lancing sense. X4 and X5 have to be unusually mobile big men, in addition to their primary rebounding requisites. Figure 6-16 shows their possible slides out to the corners, out to the wings, and into the deep lane area.

The 2-1-2 has a couple of recognized weaknesses. With X3 on the move with his slides, there is vulnerability to weak side cutters as they flash into the key. An opposing team that shoots well from outside will cause trouble, especially along the sides (where the wing men of the Option Offense operate). The 2-1-2 requires above-average speed.

THE OPTION OFFENSE AND THE 2-1-2

In Figure 6-17, the ball is passed to the wing in the Red Series. Three different coaches might have their teams respond in three different ways, as shown in Figures 6-17, 6-20, and 6-21. In Figure 6-17, one coach would have X4 slide out to cover the wing. X3 replaces him quickly, with the added effort of trying to front the momentarily uncovered low post man. X1 replaces X3 at the free throw line area, and X5 shades over toward the strong side. The usual routes of our 01 and

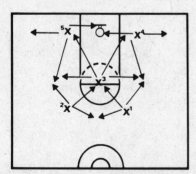

Figure 6-16. Interzonal slides of the 2-1-2.

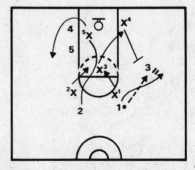

Figure 6-17. One technique of sliding against the Option Offense.

02 are now superimposed, in Figure 6-17, to verify the premise that just the *initial* part of the Red Series will uncover weaknesses.

First, upon receiving the pass from 1, our 3 will find 02 open right at the beginning of his cut down the key *unless* X2 applies some man-man technique and goes with 02. If he sticks unbendingly to traditional zone principles, our 02 is going to have a wide-open jump shot right at the free throw line. The question arises: "Can't X3 prevent this action by 02? The answer is *no*. One can see X3 moving to defend the low post in Figure 6-17 as the initiating pass is made. There is a temporary vacuum at the top of the key and the free throw line. With no need for adjustment on the part of the Option Offense, the vacuum will be used to our advantage.

Secondly, when and if 01 receives the hand-back from 3, X4 is temporarily outnumbered in Figure 6-17, and the possibilities for 01 and 03 for free-lancing are considerable. For one, 01 can reverse the ball right back to 03 at the top of the key, Red Series, almost immediately. X1 cannot react quickly enough, because he is involved in his slide to replace X3. For another, 01 can keep right on going with a dribble down the side after the hand-back as 03 cuts for the top of the key. X4 cannot go to both!

Without the aid of diagramming, which would be repetitious, the reader is asked to visualize the implications of the sequential cuts of 04, and 05 while 01 has the ball at the wing in the Red Series. X1 and X5 are going to be very busy people, and 02 is coming out on the weak side, too. I will agree that X3 is going to have excellent positioning against 04, when he arrives at his low post area (not having received the ball during his cut).

Our Mixmaster, waiting to go into action, will be very "appreciative" as all the individual defensive interzonal *sliding* has been going on, along with the team *shifting*, because the defense has been forced to move around. The defense is being spread out and is being, generally, acted upon by player movement. Now, activated by the reverse pass from 01 to 03 in Figure 6-18, the Mixmaster goes into effect. For specificity, the exploitation of just two *weak spots* will be shown in Figure 6-19 by the letters "WS." There would be others in the course of the movement of players and ball. In Figure 6-19, 03 returns the ball to 01, goes down the key, comes out at the opposite wing, while being replaced at the point by 02. Both places marked "WS" are vulnerable to jump shots.

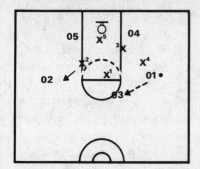

Figure 6-18. Mixmaster starts against the 2-1-2.

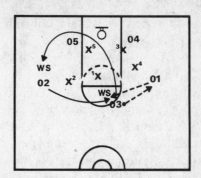

Figure 6-19. Weak spots in the 2-1-2.

Figure 6-20 illustrates the response of a *second* coach to the same initiating pass from 1 to 3 in the Red Series. Here X3 goes out to cover the wing as the pass is made, while X1 slides back to replace him. X2 slides down on the weak side.

In Figure 6-21, the third coach expects X1 to cover his portion of the outside front plus the wing on his side of the court; so X1 releases from 1 and races to challenge 3 at the wing as the pass is made. X3 holds fast at the free throw line, and X2 slides down the side of the lane on the weak side. If X1 is quick and aggressive, this would be the simplest response of all three to the important first pass of the Red Series.

The second coach's response (X3 slides over to defend against 3) will leave the free throw line uncovered just long enough for 02 to be

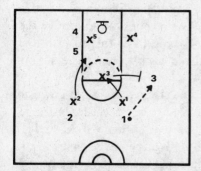

Figure 6-20. X3 reacts to the pass. X1 replaces.

Figure 6-21. X1 reacts to the pass. X3 stands fast.

open as he cuts into and down the key in his route at the beginning of
the Red Series.

The third coach's response (X1 releases and goes to the wing,
while X3 holds fast) leaves our 3 uncovered just enough for free-
lancing.

It should be noted, in all cases, that X5 is outnumbered against the
stack until X2 slides down to help, if the defense sets initially in the
traditional 2-1-2. Since the the policy of the Option Offense is always
primarily to pass to the open man, we should expect some deviation
from our Red Series patterns as open men appear—a result of outnumbering.

Against the 2-1-2, the Option Offense (White Series) must anticipate that X3 will try to get in front of and intimidate our 03 as he flashes
out to the high post. The back door lay-up by 01 in the same series will
also be restricted more than usual, because X4 would be in relatively
good defensive position against it. 01 could, however, take a jump shot
during the action instead of trying to dribble in for the lay-up.

The "high-low" pass from 03 to 04 or 05 in the White Series will
be operative in spite of X2's slide down the side of the lane on the stack
side. He may temporarily impede 04 as he comes around and over the
top of 5, but he cannot go through the key with him. This would take
him completely out of his areas of responsibility.

The reverse-shuffle part of the Blue Series will be repeated here in
diagrams and discussion in order to bear out and clarify an earlier
statement that Blue, with Mixmaster, will be most effective against the
2-1-2. In Figure 6-22, 1 passes to 2, and the signal is on for Blue. 04
pops out from the stack to receive 2's pass. When 02 follows his pass
as shown, an overload has been created right away, comprised of 02,
04, and 05. Who is to defend against 04 as he pops out to receive the
pass? X2? If X2 slides down to check 04, our 02 is free to roam the
side with his dribble, *if* the ball is handed back to him. The side is
open!

If, instead, X3 slides out to take on 04, does X1 slide down to
replace him at the free throw line area? I hope so, because 04 would
rather *reverse the ball* to 01 anyway, as he does in Figure 6-23, and go
through the key. His refusal of 02 fixes X2 in place; his reverse pass to
01 finds 01 completely open for a jump shot. If, for some reason, 01
doesn't take the shot, he can dump the ball over to 3, who is open
there, completing the reversal. Notice, in Figure 6-23, that we have

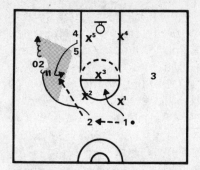

Figure 6-22. Overload by 02, 04, and 05.

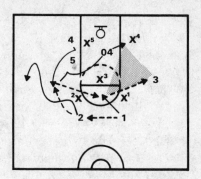

Figure 6-23. Overload by 3, 01, and 04.

now overloaded *that* side of the court (3, 01, and 04 against X4 and X5).

Reverse passing and shuffle movement by Blue will be very effective against the 2-1-2.

THE 1-2-2 AND THE OPTION OFFENSE

Many coaches claim that the 1-2-2, in basic form, is the least complicated of all the formations as far as teaching is concerned. Players are generally drilled to always present the appearance of a jug or bottle (hence *jug zone* or *bottle zone*), with the neck, the two shoulders, and the two points at the base (Figure 6-24). The neck is always aimed toward the point of the ball by way of the point man.

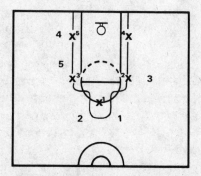

Figure 6-24. The 1-2-2 and the Option Offense.

Sliding is always necessary, but the original symmetry and shape is never lost or changed. The 1-2-2 is a very connective, compressed unit, and is the classic example of the *mass* feature of traditional zone philosophy. Gaining the ball by way of an opponent's missed shot or turnover, it adjusts and converts to the fast break quicker than any other zone, with a point man always thinking in terms of being the get-away man. A coach with generally big, tall, and relatively slow personnel (except for some quickness out at the point) will give serious consideration to installation of the 1-2-2. It is not nearly as physically demanding as other zone defenses because of its compactness. Figure 6-24 shows the shape of the 1-2-2. X1 is the quickest and most agile of all the players, although, because of interzonal sliding and team shifting, he is not always the get-away man on the fast break. Some coaches assign him to trapping and double-teaming activity with X2 and X3 at the wings, and he should be expected to exhibit his quickness in interception of passes that may come back to the area of the point *from* the wings. The Option Offense must be warned about this because of its heavy employment of reverse passes from wing to point (Mixmaster, and so on). And there must be practice in passing and pass reception, in faking and pumping a pass at a receiver, and then finally passing to him as he goes back door against the defensive over-play, the receiver's V-cut, and so on.

X4 and X5 are the big men, and the coach will plan his defensive tactics so that neither will have to go very deeply into the corners on defense. He will want them primarily concerned with under-basket defense and rebounding. As a matter of fact, the coach must be very aware of the built-in, natural weakness of his 1-2-2 defense. It exists in the under-basket areas, where the big men operating there must be physically able to continually shore up these areas and at the same time be responsive to outnumbering attempts. X2 and X3 are very mobile and will usually be responsible for the wing areas and corner areas.

In Figures 6-25 and 6-26, the ball has been passed to the left side to 04 to start the Blue Series. Although there are other responses, in my example the defensive reply to this initiating pass is to send X3 out as the "neck" of the jug. X1 steps back to become one shoulder of the jug as X5 slides up to become the other. X2 slides back and X4 slides over to become the base. Thus, the jug tilts in Figure 6-25, but the integrity of shape is retained, which is unusual. Most zones shift and reshift into different forms with the movement of the ball.

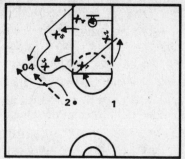

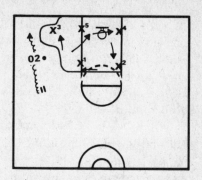

Figure 6-25. Blue Series. The jug tilts.   **Figure 6-26. The jug on its side.**

Figure 6-26 illustrates what the Option Offense can further expect from the sliding 1-2-2 and shows the simplicity of its technique as X5 retains his positioning assignment in the under-basket area with a simple slide. The ball is handed back to 02 in the Blue Series, and he starts down the side with his dribble in the penetration concept. X3 hustles and slides down with him (man-man principle). X5 slides back to form the shoulder with X1. X4 slides over almost to his normal set position, X2 slides out, and they become the base. The motion is easily taught and explained and is readily executed. Simply put, *everybody* moves either clockwise or counterclockwise. There is never any movement by an individual against the grain. The unit moves as a compact unit.

In the Red Series against the 1-2-2, the pass from 1 to 3 may be hampered, so it should not be forced. The hand-back to 01 and subsequent cut by 03 to the top of the key will remain effective, but the team must be trained to anticipate the aggressiveness of X1, or any other point man in the 1-2-2, in "shooting the gap" and intercepting and stealing horizontal-type passes. Figure 6-27 illustrates how inventive coaches have presented a constantly changing and different defensive arrangement during a game by simply sliding one man, X1, from the top of the key down the lane. When X1 is set at (A), the team is in a 1-2-2 zone; when X1 slides down to Point (B), the team has shifted to a 3-2 alignment; if he slides down to (C), the team is deployed in a 2-1-2; and finally, by sliding all the way down to (D), X1 has caused the team to be set in a 2-3 zone.

We cannot underestimate the problems of the Option Offense against the 1-2-2. Outside (around the top of the key) and in the side (wing) areas we will find the 1-2-2 at its strongest. Down low, at the post areas, and in the three-second areas of the lane, the Option Offense should find some weaknesses in the 1-2-2, especially as the offense evolves into its inside game from weak-side cuts, movement down the center of the lane, reverse passing, and other actions of Red, White and Blue.

The 1-2-2 also has some weakness in defending the corner areas, but the Option Offense doesn't particularly try to exploit this deficiency because its movement and effort are not normally directed there. Field goal attempts from the corner areas generally result in poor percentage anyway and the rebound from a missed field goal attempt too often bounces out high and far off the rim, giving the opponent an opportunity for conversion to a fast break.

The high-low pass from 03 down to 04 or 05 in the White Series should go through with effectiveness, because there is an open seam down the center of the lane within the box-like structure of the 1-2-2 where 04 or 05 can receive the ball and within three seconds "put it up" for a shot or pass off to a teammate. 03 should expect some problem and resistance at the top of the key as he pivots and turns to look down for his pass to 04 or 05, because he is in an area of probable defensive strength. The point man of the 1-2-2 would be defending there and sometimes he is joined quickly by X2 and X3 in a double-teaming, trapping attempt.

THE 3-2

The 3-2 is diagrammed in Figure 6-28. Through the years, it has

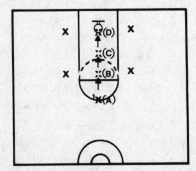

Figure 6-27. Slides which change the formations.

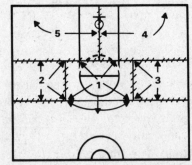

Figure 6-28. Areas of responsibility.

probably been the most popular of all in usage. It does not depend on outstanding speed and quickness in its outside technique. At least two of the three outside men (those two on the wings) can be tall and rangy, the taller the better. With hands up on defense, they discourage passing from outside to inside. If they are outstandingly mobile in addition to their size, the coach has only a bonus. The middle man, X1, is the most agile, and this agility is a requirement. If the coach is trying to use more than one relatively small man out in the front line of three, he may be using the wrong system of zone defense. The 3-2 lays back; that is, it is designed to encourage the offense to commit itself *first*. Then there is response, and it is not as aggressive as that of some defenses unless it has been modified. The original philosophy of the 3-2 was to keep the offense operating around the outside, shut off the driving lanes, force the outside shots, work hard in individually assigned zones, and not go out to trap and steal the ball. As we will see later in our diagramming and discussion, there can be alteration of this philosophy. Another feature in the alteration of the 3-2 is that the outside men are in good position to form for a fast break. As a matter of fact, this zone defense is noted for its adaptability to the fast break system. The 3-2 is not as demanding physically as some of the other zone defenses, and the coach would do well to consider using it if his team is big and lacks some speed.

There are weaknesses. There is vulnerability to sharp passing and quick-release jump shooting around the foul line area. There is a seam between the three men in the front line and the two back men. The Option Offense will concentrate on this weakness, which is compounded if and when the front line is penetrated by cutters on their way to the basket or if all or any of the front men go farther out to meet the offense. Offensive overloading is relatively easy. The corner areas are vulnerable to jump shooting if field goal attempts from the corner is a part of the offensive plan.

Rebounding coverage leaves something to be desired. The rebounding triangle does not develop naturally. X4 and X5 would be a natural part, but the third rebounder for the triangle would have to be improvised because X1, X2, and X3 are constantly sliding in interzonal adjustments as they engage the offense. Figure 6-28 shows the individual responsibility areas of the 3-2 as it sets, but it is subject to alteration by over-lapping inter-zone movement as it modifies itself to go to the ball. The quickest and most active player will be X1. The two best rebounders, X4 and X5, are the back men. The wing men are the tall forwards.

Because they are part of a lay-back zone, the three front men will usually not set up more than 22 to 25 feet from the basket in defensive line. If they do, or if any one does move farther out for any reason, it is at the risk of creating an added weakness in the zonal structure that will be exploited by the Option Offense. For whatever reason, if they do come out, the horizontal seam between them and the two back men is widened and unguarded. The reverse-shuffle movement of 04 in the Blue Series (Figure 4-3), 02 in the Blue Series (Figure 4-9), and the pick-and-roll options in Mixmaster (Figure 4-4) are just three offensive reactions that you may turn to. The high-low pass in the White Series will be effective. Passes from the wing areas down to the double low posts and passes returned to the wings for short-range jump shots will exploit some vulnerability. The Mixmaster will produce high-percentage jump shots from the wing areas against the 3-2.

MODIFICATION OF THE 3-2

Like all the others, the 3-2 modifies its traditional set formation according to situations. An increasingly familiar modification that would apply is diagrammed in Figure 6-29 and described as follows.

Although the Option Offense does not feature perimeter passing and movement (we only pass and move on the perimeter as a means of getting *inside* as quickly as possible), you should know what to expect when your team is initiating the offense on the perimeters of the 3-2. We are starting the Blue Series as 04 comes out of the stack to meet the pass from 2. He hands the ball back to 02 as he comes by, and 02 starts a dribble-drive down the side. The current trend in the method of defending this would call for the modification of original zonal responsibilities. Feinting defensively at 2 just before he passes to 04, X1 slides over to replace X2 just at the time of the hand-back. X2 releases to go down the side with the dribbling 02.

This is modification. Refer back to Figure 6-28, and we see that X2 is sliding into X5's area on the outside. The defensive coach probably wants to maintain X5 in the under-basket defensive area as much as possible, doesn't want him expending energy in fluctuating, back-and-forth movement, and wants no unnecessary distraction in his defensive rebounding job.

ANOTHER MODIFICATION CALLED SPOT-UP

It was stated earlier that the Mixmaster should be able to produce short-range jump shots at the wings. This is easier said than done if the 3-2 modifies itself into what is called spot-up or match-up. In Figure

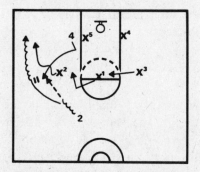

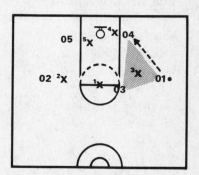

Figure 6-29. X1 and X2 slide in-terzonally.

Figure 6-30. Match-up.

6-30, the 3-2 reacts to the formation of the Mixmaster by having its players match with players within their zone at the time, and each player will be responsible for his opponent as long as he is in that zone. There is definitely a resemblance to a man-man defense as X3 goes to the ball and the others pick up offensive men as shown. There are at least two excellent by-products of this match-up for the defense if a shot is taken from the wings or perimeter. There is excellent defensive rebounding position and very good get-away positioning of the players in the front line for the fast break.

The offensive triangle of 03, 01, and 04 is shown in Figure 6-30, and a pass from 01 down to low 04 is also included. The Mixmaster is in trouble and has no easy chore if it concentrates only on perimeter and low post passing and depends only on the passing to get an open shot, because it is matched. But Figure 6-31 reviews, again, the player movement which, when combined with passing, is one answer to the 3-2 spot-up tactic. Here, we have at least three specific players moving (02, 03 and 01) in normal routes, which affords optional passing by low post 04. In the defensive process, X1 would have to stay with 03, as he moved down the key until he could turn him over to X5. In this, he would have his problems in communication and reaction. X2 would move to the top of the key with our point-replacement, 02. X3 would stay with 01. But a real weakness ensues when 03 comes out to the wing in his normal-route replacement of 02. Who can react quickly enough to get there to defend against him? That side of the floor is wide open. Only one thing is necessary now—to get the ball over to 03 from the point!

Additional reference to spot-up and other techniques will be made when we deal with the 1-3-1 in this chapter.

TIME-OUT ADJUSTMENT TO SPOT-UP

In an important Army game, I was forced to call a time-out and make a change in my Mixmaster of that time because it had been matched-up in similar fashion to Figure 6-30, and it was sputtering. With no previous orientation or preparation, the team, made up entirely of college-level players, was able to work out an adjustment with me which got us out of trouble, and we went on to win the game for an area championship.

Sketched hurriedly then (it is shown in Figure 6-32), it was accompanied by the following instructions: "Point man, when you pass to the wing, follow your pass like you do in the Red Series. Let's open up the seam. *Don't cut down the key.* Go to the outside, get the hand-back, and then hit the weak-side wing as *he* cuts directly into the seam. That's it. If the cutter's not open, he swings back to his same wing. Pass the ball back to the new point man and try it again or pass down to the low post and get something from that."

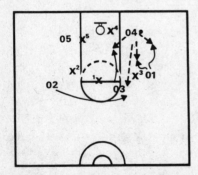

Figure 6-31. Player movement.

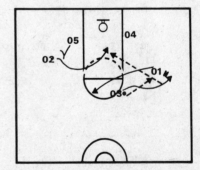

Figure 6-32. Adjustment.

The point being made here, by way of the example, is that certain parts of the Option Offense, including Mixmaster, can and should be altered to meet certain specific situations.

OPTION OFFENSE VERSUS 3-2, CONTINUED

No alteration should have to be made, however, in the initial sets of Red, White, and Blue. There is no way that the 3-2 can match up without losing some of its own integrity of formation. To avoid repetitious diagramming, the reader may link Figure 6-28 (3-2 areas of responsibility) to Figures 1-1, 1-2, 1-3 and 1-4. As Red develops from its original set into the first stages of its pattern, the 3-2 defensive set is in trouble, as can be inferred from Figures 2-2 and 2-3. In White, X1 will be in a dilemma over the high-low action between 03 and 04 or 05 in Figures 3-2 and 3-3, and X3 and X4 will have their problems with the back door of Figure 3-1. In Blue, an immediate overload is created against X2 and X5 (relate the original set of the 3-2 zone to Figures 4-1 and 4-6); and when there is reverse-shuffle of ball and player (Figures 4-3 and 4-10), there is a real problem with sliding adjustment for X1, X3, and X4.

THE 3-2 AND DOUBLE-TEAMING

It has been stated that the 3-2 is not normally an aggressive zone defense. However, Figures 6-33 and 6-34 are based on a few experiences of the Option Offense against the 3-2 double-team in the front

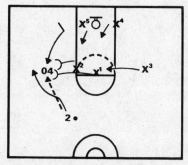

Figure 6-33. Trap by X1, X2.

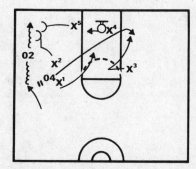

Figure 6-34. Trap by X2, X5.

court. Used as an element of surprise, it caused trouble. When 04 came
out to receive the pass from 2 in the Blue Series (Figure 6-33), X2 and
X1 formed the trap as shown, X3 moved over to protect the foul line
area, and X4 moved over into the lane. In Figure 6-34, 04 handed back
to 02 as he came by (probably in reaction to the trap) and then cut down
the key in his normal route to a low post. 02 dribbled down the side, to
be completely surprised by the trap of X2 (sliding down) and X5
(sliding over). X4 moved over to cover the very sensitive baseline area
vacated by X5, X3 moved from the foul line down to guard the weak-
side baseline and to furnish under-basket rebounding strength, and X1
moved to protect the areas along the key, strong-side.

There are other situations and examples, mostly confined to the
side areas. One specific example should be anticipated. In the back
door action of Mixmaster we might expect pinching, trapping, and
converging action by X1 and X3 on our 04 and 05 as they flash out to
receive the pass at the high post; for example, Figures 4-13, 4-14, and
7-40.

THE 1-3-1 AND THE OPTION OFFENSE

One of the more interesting zone defenses today is the 1-3-1
because it lends itself to the improvisation and formation of many
accessory patterns. For example, besides the conventional 1-3-1 with
its normal slides and shifts, there is the 1-3-1 match-up, spot-up,
combination; the 1-3-1 with chaser; the 1-3-1 front-court trap; and the
1-3-1 press, both half- and full-court.

Because of its success and innovation with the 1-3-1, the University of Kentucky has, for years, had great impact and influence on its
usage and popularity.

As it sets traditionally (Figure 6-35), this defense has a point man,
X1, who meets the ball handler at about 25 to 30 feet. In order not to
overextend and thereby weaken the defensive zones around the top of
the key, he will not permit himself to go beyond an approximate
10-foot limitation at either sideline. X2, X3, and X4 line up across the
free throw line as shown in Figure 6-35. X5 is in the deep key,
under-basket. Out of this basic set-up, 1-3-1 coaches will plan their
slides, switches, shifts, inter-zone movement, and traps; but these are
considered the primary areas of individual responsibility.

X1 is the quick player in this formation. He would probably be the
smallest, most mobile, and most aggressive guard. X3, a big forward
on offense, would, in this defensive job, initially deny the high post

area and would front any opponent flashing into it. He is a strong defensive rebounder. X2, a bigger guard, would be a wing man. And with X4 on the other wing, he would overplay and intimidate the passing lanes from these areas back out to the front, primarily defend the side zones, assist in defense around the high post, and be very sensitive and quick to react when X5 needs help against passes and cutters in the under-basket and corner zones. X4 is a rebounder, more so than X2. X5 is big, but he is also agile and mobile as he defends and tries to front the low post, defends under the basket, goes out to the corner as necessary, and acts as a main rebounder with X3 and X4.

With attention to its integrity as a unit, the standard 1-3-1 tries to keep three men in line (three men abreast) behind the point man at all times. At the same time, it attempts to maintain three men between the ball and the basket. Although greatly simplified, Figures 6-36, 6-37, and 6-38 illustrate the three-deep, three-abreast concept. With the ball

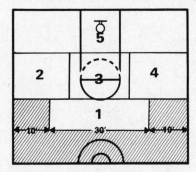

Figure 6-35. 1-3-1 formation.

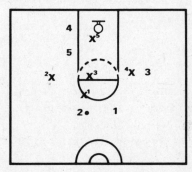

Figure 6-36. Three deep, three abreast.

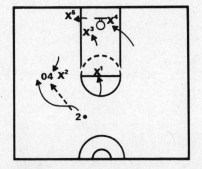

Figure 6-37. Blue Series pass against 1-3-1.

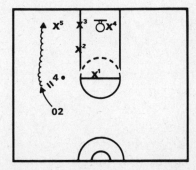

Figure 6-38. Ball goes in corner.

at the point in Figure 6-36, X1, X3, and X5 form the three-man tandem in depth, and the three-abreast feature is maintained at the same time. Inter-zone sliding is necessary in Figure 6-37 when the ball is passed to the wing (as in our Blue Series). X2, X3, and X5 are within their original zones of responsibility, but X1 has moved down to maintain the three-abreast integrity, while X4 slides down and out of his zone to preserve the three-man tandem (depth) concept.

We would expect the same general response to the initiating pass in the Red Series.

If 02 dribbles down the side after receiving the hand-back (Figure 6-38) in the Blue Series or passes down to a teammate in the corner (not in the Blue Series, but it could happen), the 1-3-1 could be expected to react as shown in Figure 6-38. X5 goes to the ball, the tandem of X5, X3 and X4 is along the baseline, and X3, X2,and X1 are roughly three-abreast.

Some of the advantages and strengths of the 1-3-1 zone defenses are as follows:

1. Can alter and adjust itself very well.
2. Is relatively strong against diagonal cutting and dribble-play of a pivot man there.
3. Is relatively strong against diagonal cutting and dribble-driving into the free throw lane from the sides and front.
4. Adjusts very well against the overload triangle.
5. Covers the high-percentage jump shot areas very well.
6. Requires but one chaser with special skills.

Disadvantages, weaknesses:

1. Corner areas are vulnerable.
2. Is one of the weakest zones in rebounding.
3. Does not convert as well to the fast break as some other zones.

A MODERN TENDENCY: SCREENING AGAINST A ZONE

For many years in basketball, the idea of using picks ands screens against a zone defense was highly questioned and seldom practiced. Modern offenses, and most certainly my Option Offense, contradict this fallacy that screening is an illogical offensive measure. Now, the offense should go about attacking all defenses, zone or man-man, with all weapons, and in the same general manner, until a weakness is found and exploited.

To set the record straight for the modern coach, screening does have a place, an important place, in the repertoire against any zone defense. We will investigate this statement now as we continue our discussion of the 1-3-1. We will hold our examples to three, keep them simple, and prepare diagrams to clarify.

Inside screens will not be as effective as those on the outside. The screen in Figure 6-39 is an example. It is a part of the White Series and has been shown before to illustrate other points. Against a zone such as the 1-3-1, this outside screen action by 03 should produce a jump shot opportunity for 02. If X4 moves in to contest the jump shot, 01 would be left open for a pass from 02.

The reverse action of the Blue Series is shown in Figure 6-40 to further demonstrate the successful application of outside screening against a zone. There is no departure from the normal Blue Series

Figure 6-39. A simple screen of the Option Offense against zone.

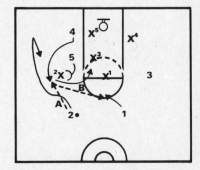

Figure 6-40. Screen against the zone.

pattern. 2 passes to 04, (Pass A), follows his pass, and button-hooks back. 04 reverses the ball to 01 (Pass B), and comes over the top of 05's screen just as in man-man action. Blocked and screened by 05, X2 has no choice; he has to be there, because it is his zone of responsibility. Figure 6-41 is drawn in continuation, and it clarifies the effect of the screen by 05 and the ensuing diagonal cut by 04 through the key. 01 is provided with at least three passing options (labeled C). He might continue the direction of the reversal by passing over to 3; he could return-pass to 04; and, very likely, he would sense that the zone was "leaning" and shifting toward the direction of the reversal, so he could *counter-reverse* the ball over to 02, who will be wide open along the side by way of an overload. The latter option is an effective one. When an offense, in its *normal* procedures, is able to entice a leaning effect by reverse action of ball and players and then suddenly shift the ball opposite, or counter, to the established flow, it is an excellent offense. Especially when there is a player just naturally there to receive the pass!

The third screen combines with an overload to establish its effectiveness. It is illustrated in Figure 6-42. It could have been described as a part of the Blue Series in Chapter 4; instead, it is shown here for specific use against a zone. This screen is part of what has been called *blast*, and it comes out (against a zone) from the normal actions between 02 and 04 in the Blue Series. 02 follows his pass to 04 as usual. Suddenly, he goes on by, "blasting" down the side. 04 turns with him and hits him with a pass down in the corner area. X2 is screened out right away. X5 is the only defensive hope to recover and get over to check 02, but he may be distracted by our 04, who is making his normal diagonal cut through the key. 02 is encouraged to free-lance when he receives the pass. He is in a favorable high-percentage shooting area.

Figure 6-41. Options resulting from the screen.

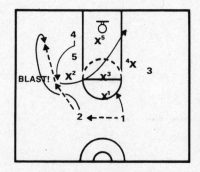

Figure 6-42. The *blast*.

ADDITIONAL REFERENCE TO SPOT-UP (COMBINATION)

I have already stated that the unusual initial set of the Option

Offense (stack, and so on) poses problems for the set of the 1-3-1 (Figure 6-35), just as it does for all zone defenses. Serious as the defensive dilemma seems to be in the beginning (where to go, how to adjust, how to line up), it multiplies as the Option Offense develops its Red, White, and Blue Series unless some defensive improvisation is planned and practiced beforehand. Past experience has shown that many zone defensive coaches, including those of 1-3-1, prepare to meet the Option Offense by using the spot-up, or combination technique. Against top-flight Service teams, the Option Offense received the most trouble from those teams that came back on defense and presented a standard, traditional zone front such as the 1-3-1 (Figure 6-35), created an illusion that they intended to play that way, suddenly shifted and moved just as the offense moved, and went along with it. This was, and is a *combination* tactic which appears to be both man-man and zone. Out front, the defense would let our man go on through (such as our 02 man in the Red Series) to be picked up by defensive players in the back or wings. Figure 6-43 illustrates the reaction of spot-up when Mixmaster begins. X3, middle man in the 1-3-1, slides quickly down to pick up one of our low post men, 05. X5 moves over to check the other, 04. Figure 6-44 continues the sequence. Our 04 and

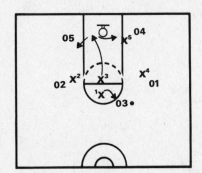

Figure 6-43. Match-up.

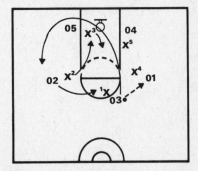

Figure 6-44. Spot-up against Mixmaster.

05 men (double low post) are fronted. All five defensive men face the ball. X2 and X4 try to pinch and converge at the free throw line area and also help X1, as necessary, at the top of the key. In Figure 6-44, our 03 passed to a wing and cut down the key. In the spot-up or combination procedure, X1 would retreat as far as the free throw line, where he would trade 03 off to X3, who moves up into the lane from

the weak side. X2 slides down to take X3's place. X1 moves back to his original area to pick up the next offensive man coming in from the other wing.

It is not at all unusual, then, for a modern team to set in one type of zone, such as the 1-3-1, and then switch into modification, in order to mix up the offense, to present certain strengths of its own personnel, and to take advantage of weaknesses of the opponent. One way of doing this is to use the spot-up, or combination, method, and we have discussed it at some length in conjunction with the 1-3-1. The following additional notes are provided, pertinent to the plans of the Option Offense:

1. There is the deception of going into a defensive set with *hands up* in a formation indicating a zone defense and then shifting into a man-man defense with no zone principles whatever, just as the ball gets to the operational areas.

2. There is the combination of man-man with zone. There will be switching out front and other evidence of man-man principles, but when the opponent cuts or drives into the key, or penetrates into certain other areas he is released by his original defensive man and picked up by another. The defense seems to be playing man-man, but it is also playing some zone.

3. There may be shifting from one standard zone to another upon voice or other signals by the defensive captain.

4. There is the policy of *go as the offense goes*. If it is a 1-3-1 offense, then the defense starts out in a 1-3-1 formation, using the 1-3-1 zone, and so on. Or, upon getting back on defense, the team sets up in a decoy formation (such as the standard 1-3-1) and then goes to a spot-up by shifting into whatever formation the offensive team is using, with particular attention paid to the location of the ball at all times, and using free-lance zone principles, moving as the offense moves.

5. There is the tactic of shutting off the point man by the 1-3-1 and its modification, the combination or spot-up. Every effort will be made to *deny* territorial rights to our player who is rotating there, and to the pass which will be coming to him from the wing. Constantly rotating players going from wing

to point, the feature of Mixmaster, are intimidated, over-played, and forced away from the point by the well-coached team using combination. If they do make it to the point and receive the ball, they are overplayed and sometimes double-teamed. The wing, if unable to swing the ball back to the point, still has the remaining option of passing down to the low post, but some of the effectivenesses of our offense will be restricted unless we counter with poise, good passing, and *retaliating aggressiveness*. We cannot passively accept any-thing that detracts from our offense. There is always coun-teraction.

COMBINATION: AN INTERESTING PAST

For the sake of including some basketball history that is appro-priate to this discussion, it is interesting to note that the philosophy of combination is a product of college basketball in the eastern United States, with coach Joe Mullaney as one of the pioneers. It is no acci-dent, then, that it went West to form the defensive base in Seattle University basketball under Bill O'Connor, who was a player and assistant coach under Mr. Mullaney, and that it became a part of professional basketball as Coach Mullaney moved into the National and American Basketball Association ranks. Rules of professional basketball prohibit the zone defense, but the shadings of zone princi-ples, within the guise of man-man, do not go unnoticed by students of basketball. The popular explanation for the success of an NBA team recently, and its championship status, is that it "really plays as a team." A more scientific one is that it sags, releases, picks-up, switches-off, double-teams, leaves one offensive opponent wide open (even close-in), and obviously operates defensively within zones of differing intensity and maximum-minimum effort. An NBA coach commented recently that to be successful, a professional team is going to have to learn how to play against a combination defense.

THE CHASER OPTION IN THE 1-3-1

A number of coaches claim that the 1-3-1, in order to be success-ful, must utilize a chaser at all times. Some would use the chaser in a fatiguing full-court role (and substitute chasers more frequently) and include chasing work even after the ball is brought across the center line. Others would have him operating only in half-court, after the ball comes across the centerline. Still others would have him chasing in the back court, but suspending the effort when he nears the vicinity of his usual place in the 1-3-1. Figure 6-45 shows X1 in this latter capacity as he goes to the ball-handler to chase and harass while his teammates hurry to their normal set defensive positions after giving up the ball.

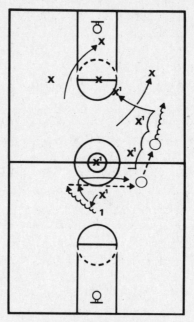

Figure 6-45. Chaser.

This is not full-court press, because only X1 is active in the back court. It is a one-man press of intimidation. Once in a while X1 will cause a turnover. He will pose a constant threat; the dribbler will have to give unusual attention to his dribbling; passers will have to be careful; and play-makers may become disconcerted as they try to set up the offense. The Option Offense has a built-in response which takes away the effectiveness of the harassment. Two men (01 and 02) bring the ball down-court as a twosome.

SUMMARY

The task of the offense against modern zone defenses is becoming

increasingly complicated. It is not at all unusual for a modern defense
to form into a straight or traditional zone and then shift and switch into
any one of many modifications in order to confuse the offense, to
utilize certain strengths of its own, and to exploit weaknesses of the
opponent.

Modification has called for changing terminology. There are sliding, trapping, sagging, and switching tactics, which make the defense
more complex. More and more sophisticated formations are being used
to supplement the traditional zones; namely, the box-and-one, triangle-
and-two, diamond-and-one, and combination (spot-up, match-up, and
so on). Only the latter was dealt with to any extent in this chapter
because of its complicity with the traditional five that were discussed
and diagrammed in detail.

The unusual, unorthodox set of the Option Offense will cause any
zone defense to think about modification right away.

The *principle of replacement* is a significant procedure of the
Option Offense against a zone defense. Featured in Mixmaster, this
method creates situations, by constant movement and rotation, in
which one defensive man must attempt to guard one offensive man
leaving a specific area and a second offensive man *entering* the same
area at the same time.

By minor adjustment in placement of the point man, the Option
Offense overloads against a zone. Overload is defined as the situation
in which more offensive players are located in an area than there are
defensive players to guard them. The Option Offense creates this situation, developing overloads which rotate from one side of the court to
the other.

The weakness of most offenses against zone defenses is the lack
of movement by players. The day of moving the ball faster than the
zone can move is over. Perimeter passing (around the horn) depends
too much on shooting from the outside. The Option Offense takes the
ball inside, sometimes in conjunction with the overload, sometimes as
a separate pattern. A double low post (04 and 05) operates there, and
the ball also moves to the vulnerable wing areas. Figure 6-44 is a prime
example.

All traditional zone defenses, regardless of modification or alteration, have strengths and weaknesses. In attacking a zone defense, the
offense should operate with screens (picks) and player movement with
the same effort that is used against man-man defenses. The only difference is the need for offensive overload. This feature must be a built-in
part of the offense.

Some parts of certain zone defenses will cause more problems for the Option Offense than others, but that is the reason for the philosophy of *option*. A statement of confidence has been made more than once in this book that the Option Offense, and particularly the Mixmaster within it, has been successful against zone defenses. In spite of my respect and concern for the problems presented by a well-drilled zone defensive team, and my references to the troublesome *combination*, I reiterate this positive, optimistic statement.

Chapter Seven

Developing and Conducting Drills:

Breaking Down the Offense

PURPOSE OF DRILLS

This chapter deals only with those small-unit drills that pertain directly to the Option Offense. There are no frills. It would be relatively easy to prepare a potpourri of drills for the improvement of offensive skills that would apply to any basketball player and any system of offense. Instead, the work here is designed to be applicable and specific to our own system, and we keep players busy with basic fundamentals within the scope of the Option Offense. All the effort here is also projected toward using *time* intelligently while getting the players accustomed to each other in a progressive, gradual manner.

A word about *time*. All of you must have a common problem with the implication of this word above all others. In nearly all cases, the coach is, first and foremost, a teacher with students to teach and advise, parents to call and meet, meetings to attend, lessons to plan and prepare, and classrooms to be managed. The additional teaching of basketball to young men and women as a part of the school day only makes *time* more complicated. It is important, therefore, that you take full advantage of every means and method that will help in your preparation. In the interest of budgeting time, your main practice drills should relate to the offensive system.

If the material in this chapter will expedite your planning and alleviate some of your problems with time, an important purpose has been achieved. The drills, as they stand, can be transferred to the preparatory plan for practices quite readily.

PLANNING AND DESIRED OUTCOMES

During early season practices, the Red, White, and Blue Series, complete with patterns and options, must be demobilized, broken down, and dispersed to separate parts on a coach's worksheet or format. This done, and with the drills of the two-man and three-man units (as organized and described in this chapter) predicated on teaching skills in basic fundamentals that are uniquely pertinent to the success of the Option Offense, we will be better able to assemble into five-man units for the operation of the total offense later on. In the end, the whole of the Option Offense, in efficiency and competence, will be greater than the sum of its parts.

Anticipated improvement and acquisition of certain skills should be listed on your worksheet. Simultaneous work at both halves of the court must be planned and described. This method of organization ensures that all players are busy in purposeful, coherent effort within the structure and framework of the system. Also, you should include a Master Chart of recapitulation to provide a means of recording the cumulative practice activity. No matter how well-organized you are, it will be difficult to refer back to your teaching and instructional effort unless you maintain a chart such as this.

To summarize, the following points are important as we go on to the Option Offense breakdown of drills that follow:

1. This chapter is, obviously, designed to help the busy coach. You may use it verbatim as a ready-made plan, use it only as a reference to build on, or utilize it in any way to fit your needs as you go about an early organization of the Option Offense system.

2. Expect the players to demonstrate good spirit, effort, and morale as they operate within the scope of this chapter. The breakdown of the system into two-man and three-man modules creates a closeness that makes each player feel that you are giving more individual attention and that his work is being appreciated and observed.

3. The concept of teamwork and pattern discipline begins here,

and players working together toward an objective gain confidence in themselves, their teammates, you and your system.

4. The work done in the drills of this chapter will pay off in timing and execution when the five-man units are assembled. A popular truism in basketball maintains that any type of offense is successful only in direct proportion to the excellence of timing and execution within it.

5. The coach/assistant coach relationship will be enhanced. Given specific teaching responsibilities, your assistant will respond here with his best effort. He will feel more secure in the belief that you have confidence in his ability and that he is contributing his own expertise to the varsity effort. It is certainly important (and too many times overlooked) that the assistant be given opportunity to gain confidence in himself and in the Option Offense as well. Needing all the help you can get, you should be happy in the professional growth of your assistant and proud that you can delegate some of the varsity work to him.

6. The recapitulation of the skills-yield from the drills of this chapter (Master Chart), will be an excellent reference for you. Based on your inspection of the recapitulation, you can turn to other materials in the book to add to, adjust, and reinforce the general basic skills and fundamentals that are not being stressed to your liking.

7. For purposes of simplicity in a chapter that is specifically for drills, no distinction is made between the original and new positions of players.

OPTION OFFENSE DRILLS FORMAT

DESCRIPTION: RED SERIES DRILL #7-1. (FIGURE 7-1)

Drill is for 1's, 2's, and 3's. Coach, one manager. Short dribble by 1, pass to 3, 1 follows pass as 2 cuts down the key. 3 turns to pass to 2. Lay-up or free-lance by 2.

Skills:

Dribble, 1, and possibly 2. Pass, 1, and 3. Get free, meet pass, turn, 3. Feint, cut, 1 and 2. Lay-up, 2.

Main concerns:

Coordinate with material in Chapters 2 and 12. Passes of 15 to 18 feet. Stress move of 2. Timing.

Programming:

Suggestion for simultaneous drill at other end, see Drill 7-2.

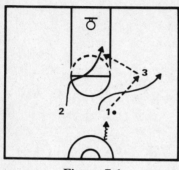

Figure 7-1

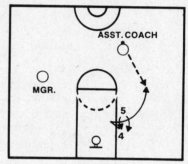

Figure 7-2

DESCRIPTION: BLUE SERIES DRILL #7-2. (FIGURE 7-2)

Drill is for 4's and 5's. Assistant coach and manager in charge. Assistant coach passes to 4 as he pops out for a jump shot. 5 acts initially as screen for 4, then steps back into low post position. 4 turns, jump shoots. 5 goes for offensive rebound, puts ball in basket if the shot is missed; also practices outlet-passing to manager, who passes to assistant coach to keep the drill going.

Skills:

Screen by 5. Pop-out, 4. Meet pass, 4. Stop, turn, look down, jump shot, 4. Low post positioning, 5. Offensive rebound, 5. Outlet pass, 5.

Main concerns:

4 and 5 communicate and work together. Coordinate with material in Chapters 4 and 12.

DESCRIPTION: RED SERIES DRILL #7-3 (FIGURE 7-3)

Drill is for 1's, 2's, and 3's. 1 passes to 3, follows his pass. 2 cuts down the key, but 3 refuses him, and hands the ball back to 1. 3 cuts to top of the key. 1 does rocker step, feints, and then passes over to 3 at top of key for jump shot. 3 may free-lance instead of taking a jump shot.

Skills:

Passes, 1. Meet pass, 3. Feint, cut, 1, 2. Rocker step, 1. Jump shot, 3.

Main concerns:

Hand-back by 3. (See Chapter 2.) 3 must look back as he goes to top of key. Coordinate with material in Chapters 2 and 12.

Programming:

Suggestion for simultaneous drill at other end, see Drill #7-4.

Figure 7-3

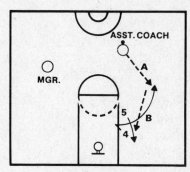

Figure 7-4

DESCRIPTION: BLUE SERIES DRILL #7-4 (FIGURE 7-4)

Drill is for 4's and 5's. Assistant coach passes to 4 as he pops out from the stack. 4 stops, turns, looks down, as 5 sets himself at the low post. 4 passes down to 5. Vary the options. Have 5 work for his shot, and also pass back out to 4, who has been maneuvering to get open after his pass to 5.

Skills:

Screen, 5. Pop out, 4. Meet pass, turn, look down, 4. Low post positioning and maneuvering, 5. Feinting, head-shoulder fake, maneuvering for opening, 4.

Main concerns:

Communication between 4 and 5. Don't allow 4 to stand around after his pass to 5. Coordinate with material in Chapters 2, 3, 4, and 12.

DESCRIPTION: RED SERIES DRILL #7-5 (FIGURE 7-5)

Drill is for 1's, 2's and 3's, with the main objective of training 1's and 2's in controlled dribbling-penetration techniques. 1 passes to 3, and follows his pass as 2 makes his usual cut down the key. 3 hands back and cuts to top of key. 1 fakes a pass, gives a head-and-shoulder fake, executes rocker step, then dribble-drives down the side and into the under-basket area. 1 and 3 maneuver to get open for jump shots, with 1 getting the ball back out to them as shown. 1's and 2's alternate.

Skills:

Passing, 1. Dribbling, 1. Head-shoulder fake and rocker step, 1. Manuever to get open, 2 and 3. Jump shot, 2 and 3. Stop dribble, find open man, pass out, 1.

Main concerns:

Make 1 work to obtain a half-step on his imaginary opponent. *Head-up* during dribble. Coordinate with materials in Chapters 2 and 12.

Programming:

See Drill #7-6 for simultaneous work at other end.

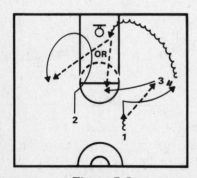

Figure 7-5

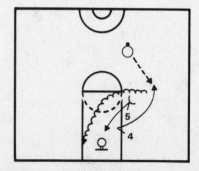

Figure 7-6

DESCRIPTION: BLUE SERIES DRILL #7-6 (FIGURE 7-6)

Drill is for 4's and 5's, with main objective of perfecting the pick-and roll. Assistant coach passes to 4 as he comes out of the stack. 4 has a signal or key with 5 which causes 5 to come out to pick. As 4 dribbles by, 5 rolls for the basket. Vary by having 4 pass to 5 on his roll for the basket.

Skills:

Meet pass, turn, look down, 4. The screen by 5. Dribble, 4. 4's pass to 5 on roll. Lay-up, 4 and 5.

Main concerns:

"Heads up" by 4 on dribble. Communication between 4 and 5. Footwork of 5 as he turns to roll. Coordinate with material in Chapters 1, 2, 4, and 5.

DESCRIPTION: RED SERIES DRILL #7-7 (FIGURE 7-7)

Drill is for 1's, 2's, 3's, and 4's. 1 passes to 3 and follows his pass as 2 makes his customary cut down the key. 3 refuses 2, and hands back to 1. 3 cuts to the top of the key, as 4 runs his route out of the stack around an imaginary 5. 1 fakes to 3, fakes a dribble-drive, and passes to 4 at the first opening. 4 goes one-on-one for his shot, or drives in for lay-up.

Skills:

Passes, 1. Cuts, 1, 2, 3, and 4. Fakes, 1. Shot (any type), 4.

Main concerns:

Timing. Make sure there is no carelessness in options before the ball goes to 4. Make sure 3 looks back when he goes to the top of key. Coordinate with materials in Chapters 2, 5, 6, and 12.

Programming:

See Drill #7-8 for simultaneous work at other end.

DESCRIPTION: BLUE SERIES DRILL #7-8 (FIGURE 7-8)

Drill is for 5's, with the objective of making 5 aggressive in

Figure 7-7   **Figure 7-8**

getting offensive position, and working at the low post. Assistant coach passes to him. Variety of passes: bounce pass, jump pass, lob pass. 5 works for shot, guarded by X5. 5 and X5 fight for rebound. Have 5 and X5 rotate.

Skills:

Work for position, 5. Reception of pass, 5. Work for shot while guarded, 5. Defense, X5. Rebounding, 5 and X5.

Main concerns:

Make 5 rebound after his shot attempt. Make both X5 and 5 be aggressive, but call fouls. X5 may overplay, but not *front*. Coordinate with materials in Chapters 4, 5, 6, and 12.

DESCRIPTION: RED SERIES DRILL #7-9 (FIGURE 7-9)

Drill is for 1's and 3's, with the objective of learning how to counteract the defensive aggressiveness and disruptiveness of overplay. 1 is having trouble passing the ball because 3 is being overplayed and intimidated by an imaginary X3. Unable to pass, 1 continues his dribble, suddenly stops, pumps the ball toward 3, draws it back; then, with no break in the action, he passes (two-handed chest pass) to 3 who has gone back door for a lay-up.

Skills:

Getting open against pressure, 3. Pumping technique, 1. Pass, 1. Back door, lay-up, 3.

Main concerns:

Communications, 1 and 3. Footwork basics, 3. For information on *pumping* and fundamentals of foot work, coordinate with Chapter 12, Figures 12-37, 12-38, and 12-39.

Programming:

See Drill #7-10 for simultaneous work at other end.

Figure 7-9   Figure 7-10

DESCRIPTION: BLUE SERIES DRILL #7-10 (FIGURE 7-10)

Drill is for 2's, 4's, and 5's, with the objective of perfecting the option of penetration. 2 passes to 4. 2 follows pass as usual, receives hand-back option from 4, and continues with power-drive dribble down the side and into the under-basket area. 2 jump shoots, or goes on in for lay-up. 5 rebounds. For variety, have 2 pass back out to 4 for jump shot, or bounce-pass to 5 as he cuts for the basket.

Skills:

Pass, 2. Meet pass, hand-back, 4. Dribble, penetrate, 2. Jump shot, 2 and 4. Lay-up, 2 and 5. Rebound 5.

Main concerns:

Hand-back action between 4 and 2. Dribble technique of 2. Coordinate with material in Chapters 4, 6, and 12.

DESCRIPTION: BLUE SERIES DRILL #7-11 (FIGURE 7-11)

Drill is for 1's, 2's, 4's, and 5's. 2 passes to 4, coming out of the stack. 2 follows his pass, but ball is passed down to low post 5. 1 has moved to top of key. 5 sees 1 open, and fan-passes out to him for a jump shot. Both 4 and 5 rebound offensively. Drill applicable against zone.

Skills:

Passes, 2, 4, and 5. Meet pass, turn, look down, 4. Low post positioning, 5. Get open, 1. Meet pass, jump shot, 1. Rebounding, 4 and 5.

Main concerns:

Jump shooting techniques by 1. Fan-passing by 5 out to 1. Coordinate with materials in Chapters 2, 4, 6, and 12.

Programming:

See Drill #7-12 for simultaneous work at other end.

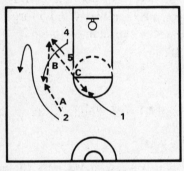

Figure 7-11

Figure 7-12

DESCRIPTION: RED SERIES DRILL #7-12 (FIGURE 7-12)

Drill is for 4's, guarded by an opponent, X4, at the low post. Assistant coach passes to 4 at low post. Bounce pass, jump pass, lob pass. 4 works for shot, guarded closely by X4. Have them change places.

Skills:

Work for low post position, 4. Receiving the pass at low post while being intimidated, 4. Work for shot, 4. Rebounding, 4 and X4.

Main concerns:

Instill aggressive spirit in 4. Do not allow him to be intimidated by overplay of X4. Coordinate with material in Chapters 2, 3, 5, 6, and 12.

DESCRIPTION: RED SERIES DRILL #7-13 (FIGURE 7-13)

Drill is for 4's and 5's, with the objective of instilling confidence in second man through. When 4 comes around 5's screen and makes his cut across the key, have X5 and X4 *switch* on defense. Coach passes to 5, who can free-lance for his shot.

Skills:

Screen, 5. Using a screen, making a cut, 4. Receiving pass, working for shot, 5.

Main concerns:

On his cut, 4 must look for pass, even though he doesn't get it. He must, also, go on through, get out of the way. Don't let 4 and 5 forget about offensive rebounding. Coordinate with material in Chapters 2, 3, 5, 6, and 12.

Programming:

See Drill #14 for simultaneous work at other end.

DESCRIPTION: RED SERIES DRILL #7-14. (FIGURE 7-14)

Drill is for 1's, 2's, and 3's. 1 starts this with his pass to 3,

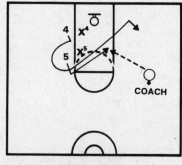

Figure 7-13

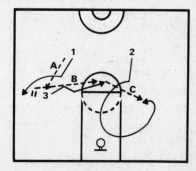

Figure 7-14

follows his pass, gets the hand-back while 2 makes his usual cuts down the key. 1 fakes a pass to an imaginary 4, then to an imaginary 5, before swinging his pass over to 3 at the top of the key. 3 continues the reverse-shuffle with his pass to 2, who takes his jump shot. Drill is applicable to zone defense situations.

Skills:

Passes, 1 and 3. Cuts, 1, 2, and 3. Look back while cutting, 3 and 2. Meeting passes, 3 and 2. Stop, turn, look down, jump shot, 2.

Main concerns:

Timing. Aggressive cutting behind an imaginary 5 by 2. B and C are brisk, chest-type passes. Stress meeting the passes. Stress the pivot, look, hand-back action of 3. Coordinate with material in Chapters 2, 5, 6, and 12.

DESCRIPTION: RED SERIES DRILL #7-15. (FIGURE 7-15)

Drill is for 1's, 3's, and 4's, with the objective of demonstrating our rule that the point man always cuts down the center of the key when the ball is passed down to either low post. 1 starts the Red Series by passing to 3, follows his pass, receives the hand-back, and 3 cuts to the top of the key as 4 comes around the screen of the imaginary 5. 1 fakes his pass over to 3, fakes his own drive, and passes down to 4. 4 finds 3 open as he comes down the key for a lay-up.

Skills:

Passes, 1 and 4. Cutting, 1, 3, and 4. Lay-up, 3. Low post positioning and action, 4.

Main concerns:

4 must get position at low post. 1 must fake moves and passes before passing to 4. 3 must get a half-step on his guard at the top of the key. Timing is important. 4 always looks at the cutter first, as he did here. Coordinate with materials in Chapters 2, 3, 4, 5, 6, and 12.

Programming:

See Drill #7-16 for simultaneous work at other end.

Figure 7-15

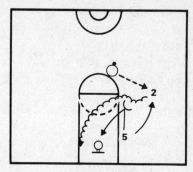

Figure 7-16

DESCRIPTION: RED SERIES AND MIXMASTER DRILL #7-16 (FIGURE 7-16)

Drill is for 2's and 5's, for more work with pick and roll. 2 has run his usual Red Series route, and receives the ball at the wing. Guarded closely, with no jump shot possibility, he puts the ball on the floor as 5 comes out to set the pick. 5 rolls, as 2 dribbles by. 2 may pull up for a jump shot, dribble all the way in, or pass off to 5 on the roll.

Skills:

Communications between 2 and 5. Screen and roll by 5. Dribble by 2. Lay-up by 2. Jump shot by 2. Pass to 5 by 2 as 5 rolls.

Main concerns:

Side screen by 5. Be sure the "body barrier" is at its widest, and that 5 releases and turns properly, facing and going with the dribbling 2. Heads up dribble by 2. Coordinate with materials in Chapters 1, 2, 4, and 5.

DESCRIPTION: RED SERIES AND MIXMASTER DRILL #7-17 (FIGURE 7-17)

Drill is for 1's, 2's, 3's, and 4's. Routes, movement, and passes are of the Red Series, ending with the options of a pass to either 1 or 2 for a jump shot (Pass C). The idea is for 1 to get open for a return pass from 4 (Pass C), or for 2 to be open at the top of the key for a pass from 4 (Pass C). 1 passes to 3 (Pass A). Hand-back to 1, pass down to 4 (Pass B). 3 has cut to the top of the key. 2 has run his route. When the pass goes to 4, 3 cuts down the key. 2 replaces him, coming open at the top of the key. Skills: Passes, 1, 4. Cuts, 1, 2, 3, 4. Low post play, 4. Jumper 4, 1.

Main concerns:

Aggressive cutting down the key by the point man, and flashing movement from the wing to the top of the key as replacement. Meeting passes. Aggressive zig-zag movement by 1 to get open after pass down to 4. Stress *push off* by the leg involved. Coordinate with material in Chapters 1, 2, 5, 6, and 12.

Programming:

See Drill #7-18 for simultaneous work at other end. Send at least one 2 man to work with 5's and the assistant coach at that end.

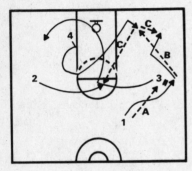

Figure 7-17

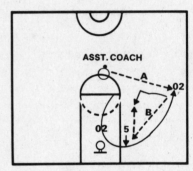

Figure 7-18

DESCRIPTION: RED SERIES DRILL #7-18 (FIGURE 7-18)

Drill is to improve the pattern relationship between 2 and 5. Assistant coach passes over to 2 at the wing, as he runs his route. He stops, turns, looks down, passes to 5, then works for a return pass and an open jump shot. The 2 man here at this end can alternate with a 2 man in the drill at the other end. For purposes of the drill, have 2 start from about the free throw line, make him go full speed around 5's screen and out to the wing.

Skills:

Cut down the key, and around a screen, 2. Meet pass, stop, turn, look down, pass down, 2. Low post play, 5. Work to get open, 2.

Main concerns:

Make 2 use head-shoulder fakes, feints, and other individual moves to get open for the pass back from 5. 15 ft. pass from assistant coach to 2. Coordinate with material in Chapters 4, 5, 6, and 12.

DESCRIPTION: WHITE SERIES DRILL #7-19 (FIGURE 7-19)

The beginning of the White Series (back door) is broken down here. 4's and 5's work in this drill at the high post, alternating with 3, in order to improve general skills, pivoting skills, and in the interest of interchangeability. 1 goes back door as 2 passes to the high post. High post to 1 for the dribble-drive and lay-up.

Skills:

Passes, 2 and 3. Cuts, 1 and 2. Flash-out, 3. Faking, feinting to go back door, 1. Meet the pass, fake the ball to 2, protect the ball, pivot left, pass to back door, 3. Dribble-drive, 1. Lay-up, 1.

Main concerns:

Timing, deception, change of speed, 1. Body balance of 3 at high post. Footwork of 3 at high post. Pivoting of 3 at high post. Coordinate with material in Chapters 1, 3, 5, 6, and 12.

Figure 7-19

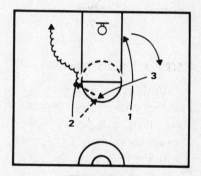
Figure 7-20

DESCRIPTION: WHITE SERIES DRILL #7-20 (FIGURE 7-20)

Same drill as in 7-19, except 1 is refused by 3, and this option is from 3 to 2. 2 passes to 3 at the high post, gains a half-step on his defensive man, and receives a return pass from 3. He may stop quickly, and jump shoot, or work one-on-one with a dribble, using the stack as a screen. Drill is for 1's, 2's and 3's, with 4's and 5's also taking part at the 3 position (high post).

Skills:

Passes, 2 and 3. Cuts, 1 and 2. Flash-out, 3. Faking, feinting, 1 and 2. Dribble, 2. Jump shoot 2.

Main concerns:

Timing, deception, 1, 2, 3. 3 must follow in for offensive rebound each time, as a part of the drill, and for rebounding training. Coordinate with material in Chapters 1, 3, 5, 6 and 12.

DESCRIPTION: WHITE SERIES DRILL #7-21 (FIGURE 7-21)

High-low action. Drill is for 2's, 3's, and 4's, with 1's and 5's at other end in a separate drill (#7-22). X3 is added, to complicate the work of 3. Receiving the ball at the high post, 3 turns and faces the basket as 4 comes around and over an imaginary 5. Pass from 3 to 4, with X3 playing aggressive defense.

Skills:

Passes, 2 and 3, including bounce passes and jump passes. "Look one way, pass another." Defending the high post, X3. Movement, 4. Lay-up, 4.

Main concerns:

Stress importance of not "telegraphing" passes. Stress various passes from 2 to high post. Since the pass from 3 to 4 must be aggres-

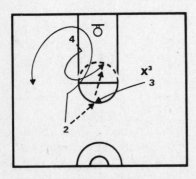

Figure 7-21

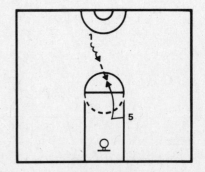

Figure 7-22

sively contested by X3, give 3 the option of going one-on-one against X3. Timing by 4 is important. Make 2 run his usual route, remind him of need to get back for floor balance. Coordinate with material in Chapters 1, 3, 5, 6, and 12.

Programming:

See Drill #7-22 for simultaneous work at other end.

DESCRIPTION: GENERAL OPTION DRILL #7-22 (FIGURE 7-22)

Drill is to encourage the relationship of 1 and 5 as an option in the offense. Sometimes 5's guard will get careless against the stack and not expect action from 5. At such a time, 1 should meet 5 with a bounce pass as he pops out to the free throw line. 5 turns, and takes a jump shot.

Skills:

Pass, 1. Fake, feint to get open, 5. Meet the pass, 5. Pivot, turn, protect the ball, jump shot, 5.

Main concerns:

Communications between 1 and 5. Footwork, feints of 5. Teach him to spin-off in change of direction, to get the half-step he needs. Turn, shoot, without an aimless *one dribble* (a common mistake) by 5. Make 5 go in to rebound his own shot.

DESCRIPTION: GENERAL OPTION DRILL #7-23 (FIGURE 7-23)

Drill is to improve lateral movement of 4 as he plays low post; improve his coordination; improve his aggressiveness in getting position; train him to always expect the pass when he goes strong-side; improve his shooting skills around the basket; and make him appreciate the effect of defense. Coach has ball at point, with managers as wing men. With the movement of ball from point to either wing, 4 moves strong-side. Guarded by X4, he receives the ball when he is open; then, goes one-on-one for his shot. Fight for rebound if shot is unsuccessful. When shot is successful, X4 steps out-of-bounds and practices his fast outlet pass to either manager. If he rebounds an unsuccessful shot, X4 practices his outlet pass to either manager.

Skills:

See above (Description). Have X4 and 4 alternate.

Main concern:

Aggressiveness, both 4 and X4. Shooting skills.

Programming:

Drill #7-24 for simultaneous work at other end.

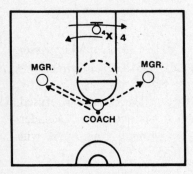

Figure 7-23

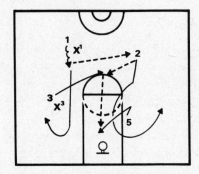

Figure 7-24

DESCRIPTION: WHITE SERIES DRILL #7-24 (FIGURE 7-24)

Drill is for 5's as second man through. To add realism, have X1 guard 1 as he dribbles, have 1 pass over to the moving 2, and have X3 guard 3 as he comes out to high post. 1 and 2 make their cuts, 3 turns, fakes a pass to an imaginary 4, then passes to 5.

Skills:

Passes, 1, 2, and 3. Cuts, 1, 2, 3, and 5. High post play, pivot, turn, 3. Dribble against pressure, 1. Shot, or lay-up, 5.

Main concerns:

Have X1 exert pressure on dribbling 1. Check distance between 1 and 2 at time of pass (15 foot rule). Allow no carelessness in this rule. Don't allow 3 to be intimidated by X3. Don't allow carelessness by 1 and 2 in running routes. Coordinate with material in Chapters 3, 5, 6, and 12.

DESCRIPTION: WHITE SERIES DRILL #7-25 (FIGURE 7-25)

Scissors option in White Series. Drill is for 1's, 2's, and 3's. 2 (or 1), passes to 3 at high post. 1 and 2 "scissors." Options make up the drill, with 3 passing to 1 as he comes by; then, to 2; then refusing both, turning for a jump shot. Jump shots by 1 and 2, also dribble-drive.

Skills:

Passes, 1, 2, and 3. Cuts, 1, 2, and 3. Jump shots, 1, 2, and 3. Dribble-drive, lay-up, 1 and 2. Screen by 3 after hand-off pass.

Main concerns:

The passer cuts first, the non-passer after, and behind the passer. Head-shoulder fakes by both, with leg action (push off) on changes of direction. Make sure that 1 and 2, if refused, look back as they go by. They do not completely turn their backs on 3. They must, if refused, button-hook and get back for floor balance. Keep them out of under-basket area. 3 always goes for offensive rebound. Coordinate with material in Chapters 3, 5, and 12.

Programming:

See Drill #7-26 for simultaneous work at other end.

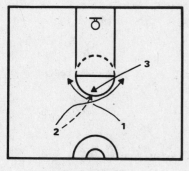

Figure 7-25

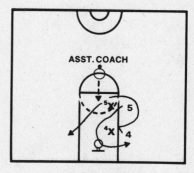

Figure 7-26

DESCRIPTION: WHITE SERIES DRILL #7-26 (FIGURE 7-26)

Drill is to help both defensive and offensive procedures, with X4 and X5 (defense) alternating with 4 and 5, and to train them in the

high-low action. Ball is at point. One time, 4 makes his move around 5
to receive the pass from the top of the key. Then, 5 receives the pass as
second man through. X4 and X5 play good defense. Pass will go to
open man. Lay-ups, short jump shots.

Skills:

Calling and executing switches and slide-throughs by X4, X5.
Fighting over the top, X4, X5. Techniques of 4 and 5 in running routes
and reacting to defensive action. Under-basket area shooting, 4 and 5.

Main concerns:

Jab step by 4 (when behind 5 in the stack) toward the lane, then
the quick move around 5. Head-shoulder fake of 5 as second man
through. Individual reactions of 4 and 5 when, and if, X4 and/or X5
cheat and *anticipate* on defense. Coordinate with material in Chapters
3, 5, 6, and 12.

DESCRIPTION: WHITE SERIES DRILL #7-27 (FIGURE 7-27)

This drill presents 3 with an imaginative option at the high post,
teaches him that he has to take individual, free-lance action at times,
and by having 4 and 5 also taking part (acting as 3 in the drill) adds to
their mobility skills as the big men of the team. 1, bringing the ball
down court, passes over to 2, who passes to 3 coming out to the high
post. Knowing that he is being overguarded and overplayed to his right
as he comes out, 3 suddenly turns to his left when he receives the pass
for a jump shot or dribble drive. Vary the drill by assuming that 3 is
being overplayed on his left, so he goes to his right after receiving the
pass.

Skills:

Passes, 1 and 2. Meet pass, stop, pivot, swing leg over and
around the pivoting leg, protect ball, dribble-drive and/or jump shot, 3.

Main concerns:

Coordinate, specifically, with Figures 3-4, 3-5, 3-11, and 3-12
(Chapter 3) and 12-34 and 12-35, (Chapter 12) for basic skills and
fundamentals to be stressed, and related options.

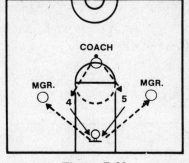

| Figure 7-27 | Figure 7-28 |

DESCRIPTION: GENERAL OPTION DRILL #7-28 (FIGURE 7-28)

Coach has ball at point. Manager at each wing. 4 and 5 on each side of lane area, with their backs to the basket. Coach alternates his passes to them, as they turn for a jump shot. Both go to the board for offensive rebounds, and outlet-pass to their respective side (manager).

Skills:

Jump shooting, moving for rebound, outlet passing, 4 and 5.

Main concern:

Rebounding techniques as described in Chapter 12. Turn, jump shoot.

Programming:

See Drill #7-29 for simultaneous work at other end.

DESCRIPTION: WHITE SERIES DRILL #7-29 (FIGURE 7-29)

1's and 2's work at the 2 position, combining with high post 3 to execute a free-lancing pick-and-roll, as a part of the White Series. 2 decides to put the ball on the floor, which signals 3 to set a screen, as shown.

Skills:

Communications, 2 and 3. Dribble, 2. Pick-and-roll, 3. Jump shot, or driving lay-up, 2. Rebound, 3.

Main concerns:

Much work will be needed with 3, because this is his only requirement for pick-and-roll. Teach him to set a side screen, using the "widest body barrier" concept. As 2 dribbles by, teach him to turn, face the dribbler, trap the defensive man, and roll for the basket, as shown. Coordinate with material in Chapter 3.

Figure 7-29

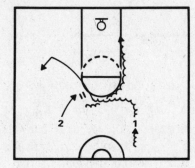

Figure 7-30

DESCRIPTION: WHITE SERIES DRILL #7-30 (FIGURE 7-30)

Drill teaches 1 and 2 to communicate in improvising a reaction to a sagging defensive situation at the high post, White Series. 1 keeps the ball on the floor, heads for imaginary high post teammate 3. A natural screen occurs as he hands off during his dribble to 2, as illustrated. Vary the drill for 2 with jump shots and dribble-drives.

Skills:

This trains 1, a floor leader, to read the defense, while staying within the Option Offense; causes him to communicate while dribbling; and teaches 2 to take advantage of a natural screen.

Main concerns:

Watch for traveling violations at the time of the hand-off. Make 2 execute a change of direction before the hand-off (push off left leg, in this case). Check jump-shooting technique of 2. (Chapter 12 for teaching reminders.)

Programming:

See drill #7-31 for simultaneous work at other end.

DESCRIPTION: WHITE SERIES DRILL #7-31 (FIGURE 7-31)

Each manager has a ball at the wings. 3 is at high post, with 4 and 5 at low post positions. 3 receives passes while going to his right and left. To vary the drill, the passes may be made while 3 is stationary, and he can go one-on-one after he receives the pass. Jump shots by 3.

Skills:

Drill is multipurpose in that 4 and 5 work on rebounding skills, while 3 improves his jump-shooting skills in a White Series situation.

Main concerns:

Coordinate with Chapters 9 and 12 for rebounding fundamentals. Pivoting, footwork of 3 must be stressed. Techniques and basics of shooting, particularly quick release, must be stressed.

DESCRIPTION: BLUE SERIES DRILL #7-32 (FIGURE 7-32)

This is a drill, using 1's, 2's, 4's, and 5's. The simultaneous drill at the other end (Drill #7-33) also requires a 1 and 4, so they can alternate from one drill to the other. Drill is applicable to zone situation, as well as man-man, because of the left-side overload of 4, 5, and 2, with the reverse-shuffle pass to weak-side 1. 2 passes to 4 as he pops out of the stack. 2 follows his pass, as 4 reverses the ball to 1 at the top of the key. 1 return-passes to 4 as the cut is made over the top of 5. To vary the drill, have 1 refuse 4, and take a jump shot.

Skills:

Passes, 2, 4, and 1. Meet pass, stop, turn, 4. Screen, 5. Jump shot or lay-up, 4. Jump shot, 1.

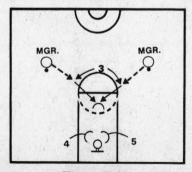

Figure 7-31

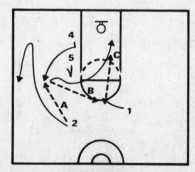

Figure 7-32

Main concerns:

Timing, 4 and 1. Screen by 5. Pass from 1 to 4. Coordinate with material in Chapters 4 and 6.

Programming:

See Drill #7-33 for simultaneous work at other end.

DESCRIPTION: BLUE SERIES DRILL #7-33 (FIGURE 7-33)

This is a prime example of the multiple aspects of the Blue Series, with its screening and cutting characteristics against man-man, and by its principles of overload, reverse-shuffle, and weak-side movement against a zone defense. Same drill as #7-32, except the coach takes the place of 2 (and doesn't follow his pass), and the ball is further reversed to 3. 4 receives the swing pass from 3. To vary the drill, have 3 refuse 4, and take a jump shot.

Skills:

Passes, 4, 1, and 3. Meet pass, stop, turn, 4. Meet pass, 1. Screen, 5. Jump shot or lay-up, 4. Jump shot, 3.

Main concerns:

Timing of 4's cut through the key with Passes B, C, and D. In Drill #7-32, he has been able to move over the screen of 5 without delay; in Drill #7-33, we assume he has been held up momentarily, and that 1 has to re-establish the timing with his pass over to 3. Coordinate with material in Chapters 4, 5, and 6.

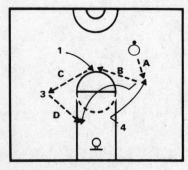

Figure 7-33

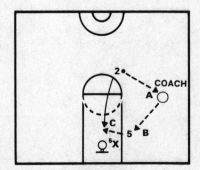

Figure 7-34

DESCRIPTION: MIXMASTER DRILL #7-34 (FIGURE 7-34)

2 has the ball, passes to coach at the wing, who passes down to 5. X5 is guarding 5. 5 to 2, cutting down the key. Applies to inside game against a zone.

Skills:

Positioning at the low post, 5. Cut down the key, 2. *Shovel* pass, 5 to 2. Lay-up, 2.

Main concerns:

Establish the instinctive down-the-key move of 2 (point man) when the ball is passed to the wing, and especially when it goes on down to the low post. Make sure 5 establishes a passing method to the cutter (underhand, shovel pass, bounce pass, look one way, pass another, and so on). Coordinate with Chapters 2, 3, 4, 5, 6, and 12.

Programming:

See Drill #7-35 for simultaneous work at other end.

DESCRIPTION: MIXMASTER DRILL #7-35 (FIGURE 7-35)

This drill emphasizes the role of the Mixmaster against a zone defense, with 3, 1, and 4, during the normal development of the Mixmaster, setting the triangular passing overload on the right side. Notice the slight adjustment of the point man, against a zone. He shades toward the strong (overloading) side. 1 passes to 3, who passes it back to 1. 1 passes down to 4, the triangle is established, and the

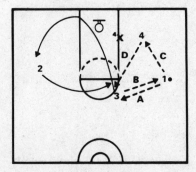

Figure 7-35

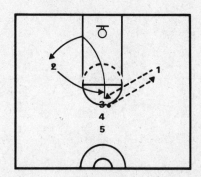

Figure 7-36

zone is outnumbered and leaning, as 3 cuts down the key, looking for an inside pass from low post 4. 4 refuses him, and re-establishes the triangle with his pass to the replacement, 2. Vary the shooting options, with 3 jump-shooting, 2 jump-shooting, 4 working one-on-one at the low post, and 2 getting a pass for a lay-up from 4. Have 5, if not busy at other end, act as X4.

Skills:

Passes, 1, 3, and 4. Cuts, point man. Jump shooting, point man. Low post play, 4. Defense against low post, X4.

Main concerns:

Teach point man to recognize a zone situation, and make his adjustment at the top of the key. Stress passing in the triangle. Don't allow a player to "telegraph" his pass. Emphasize the cut down the key as an effective inside scoring threat against a zone. It also discourages defensive overplay because of the give-and-go characteristic, and it keeps the zone busy. Coordinate with materials in Chapters 2, 3, 4, 5, 6, and 12.

DESCRIPTION: MIXMASTER DRILL #7-36 (FIGURE 7-36)

Bring 4 and 5 out to work with 3 at the point position. 3 has the ball to start the drill, passes to 1, and cuts down the key, looking for the give-and-go. He comes around opposite as 2 replaces him at the point. 1 to 2 for a jump shot.

Skills:

Pass, 3 and 1. Cuts, 3 and 2. Jump shot, 2. Rebound triangle at jump shot, 1, 2, and 3.

Main concerns:

Meeting passes. Timing. Technique of jump shooting. Coordinate with material in Chapters 1, 2, 3, 4, 5, and 6.

DESCRIPTION: MIXMASTER DRILL #7-37 (FIGURE 7-37)

Continuation of drills for Mixmaster proficiency. 2's at the point, 1's on one wing, and 3's, 4's and 5's are combined at the other wing. 2

passes to 3 and cuts down the key to come out opposite, replacing 1 at the wing. 1 has moved to the top of the key to receive the pass from 3. 1 gets a jump shot.

Skills:

Passes, 2 and 3. Cuts, 2 and 1. Jump shot, 1.

Main concerns:

Wing men always look quickly down to low post before passing back out to the point. Check shooting techniques of 1. Coordinate with material in Chapters 1 through 6 and Chapter 12.

Figure 7-37

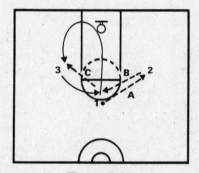
Figure 7-38

DESCRIPTION: MIXMASTER DRILL #7-38 (FIGURE 7-38)

The ball is given to 1 at the point to start the drill. He passes to 2, then cuts down the key to go opposite. 2 passes to 3 as he comes to the point position. 3 completes the reversal with his pass to 1. Jump shot for 1. Have 4's and 5's work at wing positions.

Skills:

Passing, 1, 2, and 3. Cuts, 1 and 3. Jump shot, 1.

Main concerns:

Quick-release jump shot by 1. 3 must create deception at the point as he passes over to 1. Coordinate with material in Chapters 1, 2, and 6.

DESCRIPTION: MIXMASTER DRILL #7-39 (FIGURE 7-39)

Drill sharpens the Mixmaster back door for the players involved. 3 gives signal with back-off dribble. 4 comes out. 1 releases to go back door. 3 to 4 to 1. Take free-lance options if back door pass isn't feasible.

Skills:

Dribble, retain and protect ball, 3. High post positioning, 4. Pass, 3. Pivot as necessary, pass, 4. Pass reception, 4, 1. Deception, cut, 1. Alertness, technique in cutting down key, 3. Lay-up, 1.

Main concerns:

Recognition of signal, 1, 4. Timing by 1 on back door move. Warn 4 not to force pass to 1. Keep ball moving to other open man if no back door is possible. Coordinate with materials in Chapter 4. Work on options: give-and-go, 4 to 3; pass from 4 to 3 at top of key for jumper; turn-around jump shot by 4, and so on.

Programming:

See Drill #7-40 for simultaneous work at other end. 1's, 2's, and 3's will have to be divided, can alternate for Drill #7-39 and Drill #7-40.

DESCRIPTION: MIXMASTER DRILL #7-40 (FIGURE 7-40)

Drill illustrates that the Mixmaster back door applies to both sides

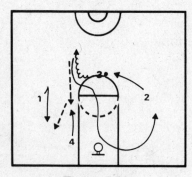

Figure 7-39

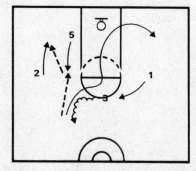

Figure 7-40

of the free throw lane. Same signal as in Figure 7-39, with 2 going back door to receive the relay from 5.

Skills:

Same as Drill #7-39 for players involved.

Main concerns:

Same as Drill #7-39.

DESCRIPTION: BLUE SERIES DRILL #7-41 (FIGURE 7-41)

Drill applies to the "blast" move by 2, usually against a zone defense. It is described as a special part of the offense in Chapter 6, Figure 6-42. 2 passes to 4, who has popped out from the rear of the simulated stack, as in the Blue Series. 2 goes by, as usual; only this time he accelerates suddenly and gets open in the side-corner area. 4 turns, pivots with him, and passes to him (probably an over-head, fan-type). Jump shot or free-lance by 2. The "blast" adds dimension to options of Blue against a zone.

Skills:

Passes, 2, 4. Meet pass, turn, pivot, protect the ball, 4. Cut, head-shoulder fake, change-of-pace move, 2. Jump shot, 2. Offensive rebounding, 4.

Main concerns:

Make sure the players recognize and appreciate the overload characteristics of the "blast." This is a power play on the part of 2. A signal must be worked out between 2 and 4. This is really the first part of the Blue Series, with the ball going to 2 instead of being reversed, or passed down to low post 5.

Programming:

See Drill #7-42 for work at other end.

DESCRIPTION: MIXMASTER DRILL #7-42 (FIGURE 7-42)

Triangular passing drill, appropriate to attacking a zone defense.

Figure 7-41

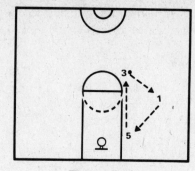

Figure 7-42

Any number of passes, as announced by the coach. Jump shots by 1 or 3, or low post one-on-one by 5.

Skills:

Passing, all types, 3, 1, 5. Jump shots, 1, 3. Low post one-on-one, 5.

Main concerns:

Positioning of 3 must be appropriate to formation of triangle against a zone. Keep the triangle open. There is a tendency to bunch up. Stress quick-release shooting. 5 must rebound.

RECAPITULATION OF CHAPTER SEVEN DRILLS

SKILLS FOR RED, WHITE AND BLUE	1's (names)	2's (names)	3's (names)	4's (names)	5's (names)
High post play			III	II	II
Dribbling	THL	THL	III	I	
Passing, including hand-back	THL THL THL THL	THL THL III	THL THL THL II	THL III	THL
Cutting, moving without the ball	THL THL IIII	THL THL THL I	THL THL THL I	THL II	III
Dribble-driving for hoop	II	II	I		
Meeting and receiving pass	III	II	THL	THL THL	III
Stop, turn, look down	I	II	I	THL II	
Low post play				THL	THL II
Penetration with ball	I	I	I	I	
Footwork	II		III	III	I
Screen and/or pick-roll	I		II		THL II
Offensive rebound	I	I	II	THL	THL I
Feints, fakes	THL I	IIII	I	I	I
Lay-up	III	THL	II	THL	IIII
Jump shot	THL IIII	THL IIII	THL III	THL III	THL
Outlet pass				I	II

Chapter Eight

Integrating Special Plays

Into the Option Offense

FEATURES OF SPECIAL PLAYS

Special plays are especially effective (1) at the start of a game, (2) at the beginning of a period of play, (3) right after a time-out, (4) when the regular offense is bogging down, and (5) when the team really needs a field goal to re-establish momentum.

You can find special plays in professional books, magazines, and coaches' clinics. The best idea probably is to select a very few which seem to fit in with the regular offensive plan without too much upheaval and change.

Special plays need not take away from individual improvisation and initiative. A well-executed special play could produce options of all kinds, during which any member of the team may have the opportunity to score, in line with the open man concept.

It seems that present-day professional teams rely, more and more, on special called or signaled plays. The impact of this trend on teams of a lower level will be interesting to evaluate in the future of basketball. Many of the plays, such as the high post scissors, have stood the test of time and are well-known. Teams have identical plays, the only difference being in the signal, or key; and some of the old standards are in constant limelight, spruced up with variation and modification. Since so many of the professionals' plays are polished and smoothly executed, there is an outward appearance of free-lance, but the observer must not be deceived. The plays have attachments of variation and alternative, they have been honed to a fine edge through practice, and the players have a great awareness of the open man.

Special plays have an important role in basketball—they form the proverbial base in the offense of many great teams at all levels, and are being used to an increasingly high degree.

ILLUSTRATIONS AND DESCRIPTIONS OF SPECIAL PLAYS

Special plays are most effective if they start, or appear to start, in the same manner as the regular pattern. The best example of this is shown in Figure 8-1. As we remember the Red Series, 02 has been running his route as usual (Figure 8-1), going over the top of the stack and down the key as the ball goes from 1 to the wing man. But, in Figure 8-2, we give 02 a special play, where he suddenly changes his route and cuts down the other side of the stack, to receive the swing pass as he comes out under the basket at the bottom of the stack. We call this "number two" because, ideally, 02 gets the shot. This special play for 2 is simple and uncomplicated, but like all special plays, success depends upon perfection of such things as timing, fundamentals, technique, and deception.

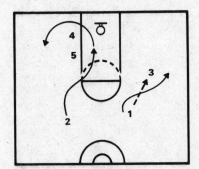
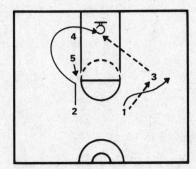

Figure 8-1. Usual route of 02 in Red.   **Figure 8-2. Special play for 2.**

All the diagramming of X's and 0's, all the effort and dedication of a coach, and all the team's sweat in practices goes for naught if 02, in Figure 8-2 for example, fails to feint and deceive his guard as he comes to the top of the stack. His guard must be misled and mis-directed as to the intent. Is 02 going to the right of the stack or to the left? If he goes to his left and down the outside of the stack, will he suddenly stop, spin off, reverse, and come back around and over the top of the stack?

Action and reaction. Proper execution. Technique and use of fundamentals learned in practice. Trickery. Important words in basket-ball, particularly significant in special plays. A sloppy pass from 1 to 3 right at the beginning will doom the play. Or, consider that failure by 3 in performing any one of the following skills can bungle the total play assignment: (1) fails to meet the pass at the proper area, (2) fails to use good catching technique, (3) fails to pivot in conjunction with the catch, resulting in a loss of timing, or (4) fails to get the pay-off pass to 02.

Notice that 02's first move seems to be only repetition of the Red Series. This is deception. Suddenly, he pushes hard off his right leg, gives a head-and-shoulder fake, goes left as he comes to the top of the stack, gets that important half-step on his guard, or even gets him hung up on the pick-screen by 05.

Options? Yes. For one, if X4 or X5 dare release and pick up the cutting 02, our 3 is trained to pass to the man who is momentarily left open during the switching process.

Another special play with great similarity to the regular offense is shown in Figure 8-3. The signal is given as the ball is brought down the floor, and 1 passes to 3 as in the Red Series. 3 reverses the ball back to the top of the key to 02, who meets the pass. This buys time for 05 and 04 to come across the key and reset very quickly on the opposite side. 02 passes 03 as he comes over the top of the stack, or 03 may choose to go around and behind. A sure-fire play! Call it "number three," be-cause 03 gets the shot.

To add variability to the offense, every member of the team (by position) should have a special play. We have already described plays for 2 and 3. The spirit and morale of the team will be enhanced if every position has its own sure-fire potency. We must always keep in mind that basketball is a team game. Every player on the team must feel that he has a right to the scoring action. Workable, simple plays for 1, 4, and 5 can be planned that fit the offense, just like those for 2 and 3.

In Figure 8-4, 04 gets a jump shot as he receives a pass, turns, and faces the basket at the free throw line. The play-maker calls or signals the play (we have used the fist signal for this one) as he brings the ball

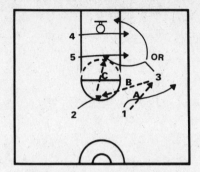

Figure 8-3. Special for 3.

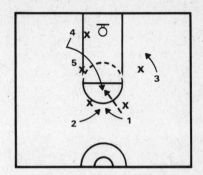

Figure 8-4. Special for 4.

down court. 04 feints to his right (as if he is going to pop out in the Blue Series), but this time he jab-steps to his left, using 5 as a screen, and comes out to the open free throw line for the pass. The rest is up to him.

Offensive rebounding characteristics? In Figure 8-5, notice the classic triangle of 5 (already in place), 03 (coming in from the other side), and 04 (having just taken the shot). This is such a perfect example of a natural offensive rebound situation that it could be used as a drill for just that purpose. By the same token, the play could be used from beginning to end as a rebounding drill.

To illustrate that options must be considered in every facet of the offense, including special plays, we will go back to Figure 8-4. If 5's guard switches to 04 as 04 pops out, 1 should pass to 5 because he will be momentarily open before X4 can pick him up on the switch. Notice also that 03 can go back door as the ball goes to 04; and that 02 and 01 are in ideal scissors position, as the ball goes to 04.

We show partiality in giving 4 another special play, one that could be used in a tight situation after a time-out late in the game. We demonstrate again that the stack offers many exciting possibilities. In Figure 8-6, the defensive man on 04 is caught napping or cheating. 2 passes down to 5 at his normal place in the stack; 04 starts his usual pop-out move as in the Blue Series, then suddenly reverses to go backdoor just as the ball is relayed to him by 5. 5 need not completely turn for this action. He should be so confident through practice and timing, and so sure about the fundamentals of his teammate, that he merely executes a slight turning action to his left as he bounces the ball back door for 04.

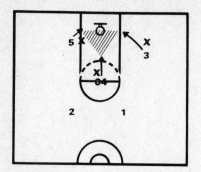

Figure 8-5. Offensive rebound triangle.

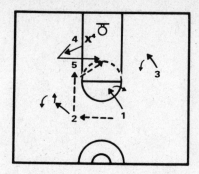

Figure 8-6. 04 goes back door. Special play.

Work this play just once in a close, exciting game; basketball purists in the crowd will be your fans for life!

Again, options. 05 refuses everybody, goes one-on-one; 03 has a half-step on his guard; 01 flashes open at the top of the key for a jumper; or 02 follows his pass, and gets a return pass on that side from 5. Hit the open man on special plays!

05 must be trained to drive to the basket for an offensive tip-in if 04 should happen to miss.

A special play for 1 is drawn in Figure 8-7, and follows the same format as the others in that its initial movement deceives the opponent into expecting the usual offensive movement that has gone before. 01 passes to 3 as in the Red Series, and follows his usual route. But 3 does not hand back; instead, he reverses the ball to 02 at the top of the key, just as 04 and 05 are coming over to set a new stack as shown. 01 moves around the stack, either over the top or behind, to receive the pay-off pass from 02.

Special plays for each member of the team are difficult to perfect and call for much practice. In a given game, not a single one may be used. In another game, they might be exploited to form the bulk of the offense.

I have a special play for 5, shown in Figure 8-8, so now all members of the team have their own to contribute to the total effort. 1 calls the play ("five"), and passes over to 2 as 05 fakes forward, turns, and goes around and behind the screening 4 to receive the pass from 2. 05 can free-lance, but more often than not, he will have a nice jump shot opportunity.

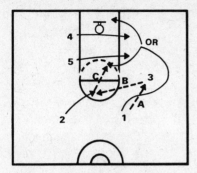
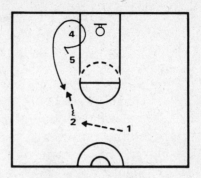

Figure 8-7. Special play for 1.   **Figure 8-8. Special for 5.**

OUT-OF-BOUNDS, UNDER BASKET

Opinion is divided among coaches about the worth and advisability of including planned, practiced, out-of-bounds plays in the offense. Once in a while they work, the detractors admit, but not often. They further suggest that the time spent on learning the plays during practice could be better spent on some other phase of the game, that the results don't justify the effort. In many ways, what they suggest may be valid. It takes just one member of the team, possibly a substitute, to forget his individual part, or it takes just the excitement of the time and a loss of poise to cause an errant pass; or for the other team to unexpectedly line up under their own basket in a zone formation as our offensive team gets ready to in-bounds the ball. Sure enough, any one, or all, of these negative things happen too often, and all the time spent in practice seems to go down the drain.

On the other hand, we see the coaches who don't believe in pre-planned plays *attempt* to outline a play in an environment of chaos and noise when there is little or no chance of success, simply because of those two factors: noise and chaos. From the stands, it looks as if good strategy is being planned because the coach does have a pencil; he has paper on a clipboard; and he is shouting, giving orders and instructions over the confusion, pointing at his work, and seemingly getting his idea across. But if the truth were known, too many times the team in this situation goes back out knowing little of what transpired. Surprisingly, many times this team will leave the time-out and go out to score the winning field goal in their own improvised way in spite of the instructions.

Other coaches suggest that the detailed, confused, hurried planning that takes place in the exigency of the moment should be supplanted by the time-out in which only very general instructions are given. Like the coach in the preceding paragraph, this coach has no use for pre-planned, practiced, signal plays that are a part of an offense; he prefers to call a time-out and give a broad, general plan. Call a time-out? Yes, indeed. He is behind by one point near the end of the game, he is being awarded the basketball under his own basket, and nine seconds remain on the timer's clock. Not much doubt about it, this coach calls a time-out. Listen in: "We've got plenty of time. John, you throw the ball in. Hit an open man on the in-bounds pass! If nobody is open, don't lose your cool. Call another time-out! We've got one left. Now, the rest of you. Move, get in close, move in, move out, get open. Get open for John's pass. If the ball comes to you, you've still got nine seconds. Take a good shot, don't dribble unless you absolutely have to. If you see somebody who has a better shot, dump the ball to him in a hurry. You've got time. Go to it."

The team goes out. Chance of success? Hard to say, but probably better than we think, if for no better reason than the fact that five young basketball heads are uncluttered. They just go out to play basketball and get their winning field goal. It does happen!

Figures 8-9 through 8-14 illustrate a pre-planned, under-basket play that can be practiced and polished by coaches who believe in a *pre-planned* system of in-bounding. I believe that a team should have plays as an integral part of the offense. I believe that every time a team is awarded the ball under its offensive basket, right at that moment, it has an advantage over the defense, and the advantage should be exploited. If the defense makes a mistake, make them pay for it! The position itself is advantageous. This factor of position, combined with planned movement and planned passes, should be expected to produce a field goal at a most opportune time. Possession of the ball under one's own basket is such a rarity. Make the most of it!

In offering just one under-basket play, the following points are taken into consideration:

1. There are hundreds of under-basket plays diagrammed in coaching books by the experts of basketball. It would be presumptuous and a waste of time for me to attempt to fill these pages with repetition. It is best to offer, for purposes of the Option Offense, just one that I have confidence in—that has conformity and symmetry with the total offense.

2. An out-of-bounds play must have options and alternatives which will make it effective against a zone defense under-basket as well as against man-man.

3. It must be as simple as possible.

4. It must have safety-valve features in order to prevent panic or loss of poise if all doesn't go according to plan.

5. Although it has been worked on and polished in practice, this play may be reviewed in certain time-out situations. The coach using pre-planned and practiced plays needs a time-out, and will call it, just as quickly as the coach who believes in ad libbing. He calls his time-out as necessary, and goes over the play with his players, with a lack of confusion.

Figure 8-9 shows the line-up, or set, following the offensive sets of the regular Red, White, and Blue Series (except, of course, for the man passing the ball in-bounds). 1 and 4 are on their usual side of the

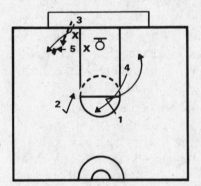

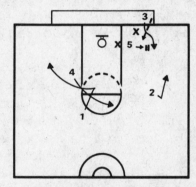

Figure 8-9. Basic under-basket set.

Figure 8-10. Other side.

court; 2 is at about the same position he would be after running his route in the early part of Red and White. So, our people are in familiar territory, and this is important. 3 is designated as the in-bounds passer. What we're saying here is that every 3 on the team, including those sitting on the bench during the game, has been drilled to be the in-bounds passer, just as all the others are specialists by their number. I have already stated in other chapters that if you are using this offense you should give your players a number, substitute by that number, and specialize in skills that tie in with the number in the totality of the team effort. 5 is near his usual low post position. In Figure 8-9, 3 may be looking everywhere in fakery to conceal his passing intention. He has slapped the ball once to set the play in motion. Now, he merely makes a little bounce pass in to 5, who may have to lean over to receive it; steps in to make an attempt to rub off his man on 5; swings out to receive a quick, short pass (almost a hand-back) back from 5; and has a short-range baseline jump shot. On the other side of the court, in the meantime, there has been interchanging movement between 01 and 04 for the primary reason of furnishing a safety-valve, and for the secondary reason of furnishing them an offensive option. 04 could be open at the top of the key after the natural screen; 01 could be open farther down.

Figure 8-10 shows the same action if the referee has handed the ball to 3 on the other side. The ball will never be handed by the referee directly under the basket.

You must explain to 3, 5, and/or 4 that if any cheating takes place by their defensive men, they are to take advantage of the cheating instead of trying to force the play (by cheating, we mean anticipating, or taking a chance). More than anywhere else, this will take place in practice, because all team members know the basics of the play, and they will be anticipating in order to get an advantage in practices and scrimmages. In a way, this action is helpful to the perfection of the play because it forces the team to react with options.

In Figure 8-11, if X3 would dare to cheat and set himself where he thinks 03 will receive the ball for his jump shot, 03 must make him honest and teach him a lesson, as shown. 3 tosses the ball out high to 04 and flashes in-bounds for a return pass and lay-up, while his cheating defensive man, anticipating that the play will go as it did in Figure 8-9, is caught between the baseline and 5. If X5 switches to take 03, then 5 is open for the pass from 04, or a little bounce pass from 03. 03 shouldn't be surprised, by the way, to find 04 wide open at the top of the key at the very beginning, because of the effect of the natural screen (interchange) by 04 and 01.

Figure 8-12 shows an option if 03 is not open for his baseline jumper after receiving the short pass back from 5. Notice the resemblance to the reverse action of the Blue Series. Same idea, same principle. Reverse the ball and cut from the weak side! 03 passes out to 02 (or to 04 at the top of the key), and cuts over the top of the screening 05 for a return pass (Pass C). If 03 isn't open, 02 might be for a jumper, or he can pass over to 04 at the top of the key. This is reverse-shuffle in an out-of-bounds situation which conforms completely to the philosophy of the offense. Pass, hit the open man, reverse the ball at every opportunity, cut from the weak side, and swing the pass from the new strong side. Look for alternatives!

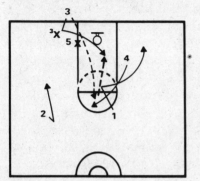

Figure 8-11. X3 is cheating.   **Figure 8-12. Reverse option off in-bounds play.**

Figure 8-13 shows an important option for the under-basket play. It could almost be termed another play. Just as 3 is about to pass in to 5, the latter realizes he is being overguarded and overplayed, so he suddenly flashes to his right and receives the in-bounds pass directly under the basket for his lay-up. This is very effective as a sudden change in the pass-in action between 3 and 05.

Figure 8-14 shows the same thing on the other side, which serves as a reminder that the action in Figures 8-11 and 8-12 applies to either side, even though it is not diagrammed.

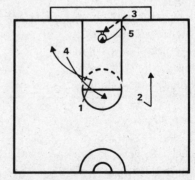

Figure 8-13. X5 gets careless. Pass to 05.   **Figure 8-14. Other side, under-basket.**

POSSESSION OF BALL, OUT-OF-BOUNDS, SIDE

It is recommended that a team using the Option Offense have at least one side-court, out-of-bounds procedure. Many of you may make it a policy to run a planned procedure every time the team receives possession of the ball out-of-bounds, along the side. I go along with this thinking. Planned execution overcomes pressure defense and intimidation, becomes a part of the total offense, and directly contributes points on the scoreboard for the total offense.

Figures 8-15 through 8-27 illustrate one plan which fits in with the Option Offense, with the general form, plan, and movement out of which come the broad option possibilities. Only one end of the court, both sides, is involved in the diagrams. The same line of action would apply, as turned around and transferred to the other end, so there is no need for repetition.

Right away, I want to point out just three of the solid elements of excellent offensive basketball that are naturally present in Figure 8-15, and stand out in the diagram:

1. There is horizontal interchanging movement by outside men, 01 and 02. The natural screening that takes place answers pressure and intimidation.

2. There is a back door feature.

3. There is a scissors movement off a high post.

A fourth element is not immediately evident in Figure 8-15, but it shows up as a sequence in Figures 8-18, 8-22, and 8-26. It is high-low action.

It would be impossible to describe and diagram all the options resulting from this plan. It can be practiced, expanded, and polished as you see fit, the day before the game.

Figure 8-15 initiates our plan, with 3 given the permanent assignment as the in-bounds passer, just as he is for the under-basket special play. The optimum area of effectiveness is between center court and top of the key. As a matter of fact, if the ball is to be in-bounded deeper along the sides (for example, between the top of the key and the baseline), this plan is not to be used. Notice in Figure 8-15 that the referee has handed the ball to 3 about half-way between center court and top-of-the-key. As 3 signals the start of action with a slap of the ball, 4 and 5 are already in a stack on the strong side, 1 is on his side of the offensive front court, and 2 on his. This formation points out again the importance of simplicity. The horizontal interchange between 01 and 02 occurs simultaneously with the move of 04 as he pops out of the stack, generally as shown. We are going to pass the ball in-bounds to 02 as he comes away from 01's screening action. The ensuing action in the same diagram shows 01 releasing from his pick to go back door, and the passes from 3 to 02 and 02 to 04. The ideal option would be the back door, with 04 pivoting to his right to feed the ball to 01. 03 and 02 scissors over the top of 04 as a sequential option.

Figure 8-16 shows the back door option.

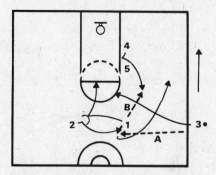

Figure 8-15. The team with a plan.

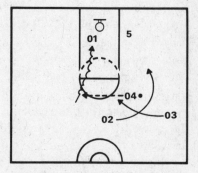

Figure 8-16. The back door.

Figure 8-17 gives 04 the option of refusing 01 and the back door. Instead, he finds 03 open for a short pass or hand-off as he comes by in the scissors movement. 01 is in high gear, getting back for floor balance and the transition to future defense. The diagram suggests that 03 dribbles in for a lay-up, but various other alternatives could be presented. Figure 8-18 illustrates the possibility that 04 has refused everybody, and has turned to pass down low to 5. The two scissors men, 02 and 03, have continued going for the basket, so they are on either side of 5 as he receives the high-low pass. There are options galore if timing and execution have been done properly—for one, 05, with his back to the basket, can refuse them, turn, and go one-on-one from his low post position; for another, he can pass off to either 02 or 03 as they flash by. Again, the maxim applies: Pass to the open man. He could even be 04 or 01!

Figures 8-19 through 8-22 allow 3 to exercise his option of pas-

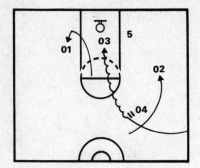

Figure 8-17. Scissors.

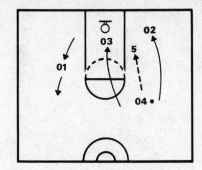

Figure 8-18. High-low.

sing in-bounds directly to 04. This could be considered a safety-valve principle instead of a choice—01 or 02 (depending on the side of the court) may not always come out open for the in-bounds pass. "Look one way, pass another," and "Meet the pass," are admonishments that must be stressed, at any rate.

In Figure 8-19, the pass goes directly to 04. General routes remain the same. 01 and 02 have interchanged, with 01 going back door. 03 and 02 run the scissors over the top of 04. Figures 8-20 and 8-21 re-illustrate these familiar moves, and Figure 8-22 shows the high-low action.

I have diagrammed identical action as it applies to the other side of the court. If you plan on using this procedure, you can not afford to assume that your players can transfer their proficiency from one side to the other without explanation and practice. By the same token, I must be sure that you have been oriented completely to both sides of the court.

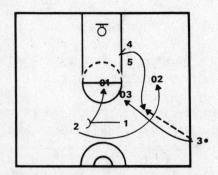

Figure 8-19. Pass-in directly to 04.

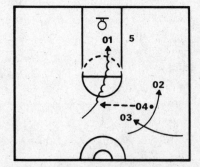

Figure 8-20. Same back door results.

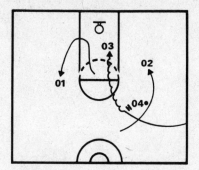

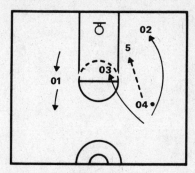

Figure 8-21. Scissors off the direct pass.

Figure 8-22. High-low off the direct pass.

Figures 8-23 through 8-26 pertain to the other side of the court when the ball is passed in to one of the outside men, 01. The back door

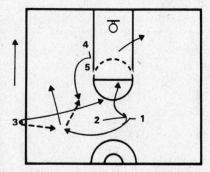

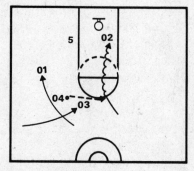

Figure 8-23. Other side, to 01.

Figure 8-24. Other side, back door.

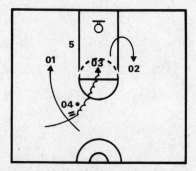

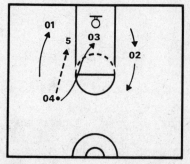

Figure 8-25. Other side, scissors.

Figure 8-26. Other side. High-low.

to 02, the scissors by 03 and 01, and the high-low action between 04 and 5 have already been described.

Figure 8-27 shows the in-bounds pass directly to 04, just as Figure 8-19 did. I will not repeat the diagrams and descriptions. You may refer to Figures 8-24, 8-25, and 8-26.

SUMMARY

In a National Basketball Association championship play-off game, 02 received the pass from 1 (Figure 8-28). 03 faked toward the ball, then cut over the top of 04's screen to receive the pass from 02 for a jump shot or dribble-in. No obvious signal was given, there had been no time-out to set up a play, and there was no particular tactical need for a two-point play at the time. It just seemed to be an automatic method of in-bounding, and it was used more than once, with variations and options, during the game. The professionals do it, too!

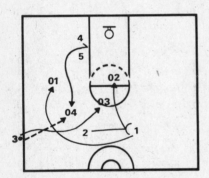

Figure 8-27. Pass-in directly to 04.

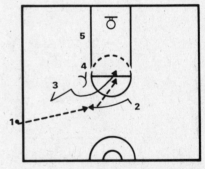

Figure 8-28. In-bounds, NBA professional team.

Special plays are important to the Option Offense. They add dimension to the attack, and those described in this chapter blend into the philosophy and formation of the offense very well. The players have an enthusiastic attitude because of the feeling of contribution that comes from having an individual special play. The under-basket play and side-court in-bounds procedure presented in this chapter are realistic and workable parts of the total Option Offense.

Chapter Nine

Coordinating a Fast Break Plan
Into the Option Offense

NEED FOR A PLAN

During a period of time in the history of basketball, the fast break, however the method of execution, was the principal weapon used by nearly all teams, with the eastern teams and Rhode Island University in particular, serving as examples. Indiana University, in the 1940's and 1950's under Branch McCracken was probably the most famous of all fast break teams. They were called the "Hurryin' Hoosiers" for good reason. This era was followed by a short period during which the vogue leaned toward the deliberate, mechanical, set-up style. Now, most teams at all levels seem to mix the patterned, disciplined style *with* the fast break. Ask almost any modern coach starting a new coaching position about his plans for offense, and a typical answer would be, "We'll *run* every chance we get. If the fast break isn't there, we'll go into an offensive pattern in the front court."

I like the idea, best presented by UCLA during the '60's that players should be trained to apply offensive pressure constantly, through movement of both player and ball, in the hope that the opponent will be *outnumbered* on the way to the basket. Then, if the outnumbering process doesn't work, you go to the pattern immediately, with no break in the action.

You should have a fast break plan. Basketball is too unpredictable for you to assume that you can depend entirely on a patterned, planned, disciplined type of offense. Sometimes the team needs to change to a faster tempo, and you can break the game open with a flurry of baskets. It is a fact that a fast break is the quickest way to score, and the shots derived from it are usually lay-up or close-in attempts. The fast break also tends to worry the other team. It can destroy their offensive rhythm because they start worrying more about getting back on defense, they get careless and hurried in regard to their offensive plan, and they hurry their shots.

There are, of course, as many fast break plans as there are coaches. You should have your own favorite method, one that fits the needs and capabilities of your team.

The traditional fast break consists of the following major components, all of which must work together as an integral whole. Any breakdown in a part will result in the failure of the whole: (1) the defensive rebound off a missed free throw, or off a missed field goal; (2) the outlet pass; (3) the immediate establishment of three lanes of fast, coordinated movement; (4) the decisive penetration by the man in the center lane with the ball; and (5) the approach of the two wing men ahead of the ball who are converging toward the basket at a 45-degree angle.

There are other outnumbering situations besides those derived from defensive rebounding. A fast break can occur when possession of the ball has been gained anywhere on the court by dint of super-fast response to opportunities: a stolen pass, quick handling of the ball after the other team scores, a stolen dribble, a free ball, off a jump ball, and so on.

It must be stated again that there must be intelligent leadership on the floor in the person of the quarterback, 1, and a coaching staff on the bench that preaches restraint, poise, and patience. Be quick, but don't hurry. Even at best, in fast break situations, we are going to have more ball-handling errors and turnovers because of the increased tempo. So, if we have a fast break plan it must be a simple one, with built-in restraint, poise, and patience based in the ability of the team to recognize the existence or non-existence of a fast-break situation; and the team must be drilled to near perfection in the facet of increased tempo.

Two errors that you must look for in practice drills are: (1) tendency of the team to take poor-percentage shots during the fast break and (2) the tendency of a player to take a medium to long-range shot with not a single teammate in offensive rebounding position.

FORMATION FOR FAST BREAK

Figure 9-1 points out the lineup of our team when the opponent has a free throw opportunity. 4 and 5 are lined up outside the lane in close proximity to their accustomed low post positions on offense. 3 is out high along the lane, charged with the rebounding responsibility of flashing in (as the arrow indicates) and blocking out the shooter as the ball makes contact with the basket. Thus, the classic triangle is formed in the case of a missed, rebounding free throw. 1 and 2 are on their usual working sides of the court. Simplicity of adjustment is the concept, again, as we are in our set for the ensuing fast break if the free throw is missed. More often than not, the players would just naturally be in these general areas as the opponent misses a field goal attempt. Figures 9-2 through 9-5 show a method of fast break that applies to both a missed free throw situation and a missed field goal.

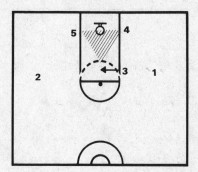

Figure 9-1. Set, and triangle concept.

In Figure 9-2, our 05 rebounds the missed attempt and outlet-passes to 02. In Figure 9-3, 04 rebounds and passes out to 01. The rebounder in each case becomes the important trailer in the fast break, as will be noted in the diagrams. We want either 02 or 01 to always be the center man, so 03 will cross with either of them in order to get to one of the outside lane positions. Notice the crossing movement of 03 in both Figures 9-2 and 9-3. Timing is essential, right at this beginning of the break. The center man is shown in both diagrams as the dribbler down the middle, with the outside lanes occupied by 02, or 01, or 03. This is the ideal situation, but passing may be necessary between the center man and the outside lanes before the three-man convergence at the end.

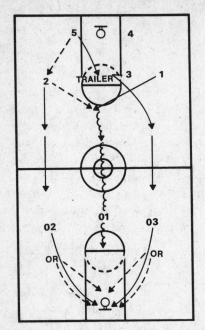

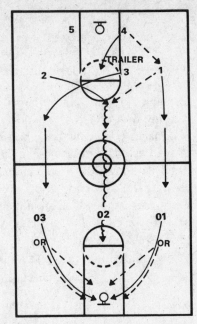

Figure 9-2. Outlet right. Fast break.

Figure 9-3. Outlet left. Fast break.

COACH'S INSTRUCTIONS

The following is presented as if you are verbally engaged with the players in practice and instruction. For the sake of simplicity, no distinction is made between the original and new positions of players.

1. Defensive rebound (4 and 5).

   "If the ball is shot from the left side, most of the time it will come down in rebound on the right side. If the attempt is from the right side, most of the time it will come down on the left side. Now, you have to get yourself set and wait for the ball. Block out, get position, box out with your elbows up, hands up as high as the shoulders, plant yourself firmly, and remember the term *body balance*. Your feet should be spread a little wider than the width of your shoulders. Go up! Grab the ball and pull it straight down with both hands as if you're pulling on the rope of a bell. Straight down. Jack-knife as you come down with the ball, and I want to hear you snorting and stomping the floor. Let everybody know it's your basketball! Don't bring the ball down lower than your chest!"

2. Outlet pass to the side (4 and 5).

     "This is the absolute key to the fast break. Elbows out.
Ball up to eye level. Pivot away from the basket. Don't turn
into your opponent behind you. Pivot away from him. Body
balance! Don't let anyone move you. Establish good passing
position. Turn to the nearest sideline. Look for the outlet man
on your side. Get rid of the ball quickly. Speedily. Accu-
rately. Use the two-handed chest pass, the baseball pass, or
the two-handed overhead pass. If there's no side man, don't
pass! Maybe you should dribble out a step, then look. Or
look to the middle. Maybe the center man is wide open.
Follow your pass, because you are the trailer man."

3. Fill the lanes (1, 2, and 3).

     "Side outlet man, don't drift, don't run away and leave
the pass. If anything, MEET IT! Don't make the rebounder
throw out a pass that is too long. Don't let it get intercepted.
Once you get the ball, look for the man in the center lane, and
get the ball to him. He is the leader of the break. Then, time
your speed and movement down the side with your teammates. Stay in front of the center man, unless there's a *fast
break reason* why you shouldn't. Watch the center man as
you run."

4. Penetrate, center man (1 and 2).

     "You have the ball, and you are nearing the top of the
key with your dribble. This is offensive penetration. Keep
your head up. The wing men are on the periphery. Keep
going in. Is one of them already open for a pass? Bounce
pass? No? Then, make their defensive man at the key commit
himself. Is he coming at you at about the free throw line?
Yes? Then, look one way, pass another. And after you pass,
follow it for a step or two, go toward the man you passed to,
but only as far as the side of the lane out in the key. Don't go
opposite, and don't go in after your pass. You must be available as the point man if your teammate wants to return the
pass to you (check Figure 9-4).

     "But the defensive man is not challenging you as you're
dribbling in? Then go all the way in yourself and score! But
don't force anything. If there's nothing, anywhere, back up,
dribble back out, pass back out, yell 'Set,' and get the ball to

the quarterback, or get it started in a pattern. Then get set in your own place in the pattern.''

5.   Convergence (1, 2, or 3).

''This is where speed and poise come in, and it's the payoff. Use your quickness, but stay under control. You have been running down the side, looking at the center man. Maybe he's even passed to you, and you've passed it back. You've stayed wide, and now as you go past the foul line extended, you must square up, make your strong diagonal cut at about 45 degrees, and go! Look for the pass from the center man. If you get it, dribble on in for your lay-up, if possible. If not possible, don't take a bad shot, don't throw the ball away. Pass back out, quickly, to the center man, who is on your side out at the point. You are not to try to force a pass *across the key* to your other teammate. It will just get intercepted. Let the point man pass to him.''

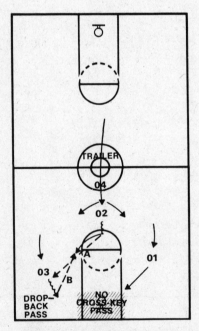

Figure 9-4. Trailer. Dropback pass. Convergence.

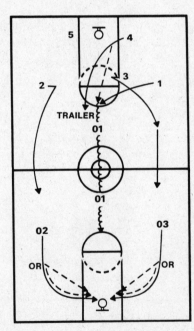

Figure 9-5. Outlet pass to middle.

SPECIAL SITUATIONS

In Figure 9-5 we see the possibility that the outlet pass must go directly to the center man. It is an option to consider. Possibly the opponent is starting to anticipate the pass to the side, and there is danger of interception; or there is *prevent* overplay along the sides. Notice the simplicity. There is no change in the general fast break suggested routes. 01 and 02 are having problems getting free and open for the outlet pass, so 04 looks to the middle for an opening. 03 has faked his move to the middle, then crossed as usual with teammate 01. This creates a natural screen, and helps to assure that 01 will be open at or near the top of the key to receive the outlet pass from 4. 03 continues on to fill a lane, and 02 already is in his lane. 01 is shown dribbling all the way, and the probable routes of 02 and 03 in the fast break are also shown. 04 is the trailer.

Figures 9-2 through 9-5 have dealt with the fast break off a missed free throw or field goal. In Figures 9-6 and 9-7, the opponent has

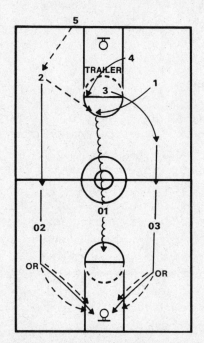

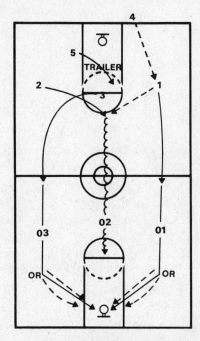

Figure 9-6. Opponent has scored. No full-court press.

Figure 9-7. Other side.

scored in either case, and is not applying any full-court pressure. All instructions and comment pertaining to a missed free throw or field goal will apply to *this* in-bounds situation except, of course, for rebounding. Instead of the rebounding instructions and comment, I would only insist that 04 and 05 grab the ball quickly (as soon out of the net as possible), step out of bounds, and in the same motion, hit 01 or 02 on the sides, or 03 in the middle, with the in-bounds pass.

The in-bounds work of 04 and 05, and the quick, instinctive moves of 01, 02, and 03 in going to their positions must be practiced over and over in the interests of speed, precision, and timing.

The trailer in all diagrams must be noted. No attempt has been made to discuss the place he would have once the ball is committed down the floor. Different coaches would expect different things from him. I have always considered the trailer as a kind of safety-valve as he comes down the floor behind the action. My favorite use of the trailer in the fast break involves the center man stopping near the top of the key, pivoting, turning, and handing off to him as he comes by on either side. If he is really hungry for the ball, the trailer may call ''right,'' or ''left,'' or ''behind you'' to remind the center man that he is a part of the action and wants the ball.

SUMMARY

The fast break is not a harum-scarum operation, but is a well-planned and practiced part of the Option Offense. Its objective is to develop an outnumbering situation en route to a close-in shot or lay-up, starting from the time of possession at the defensive end, and ending with the offense having more players down court than the opposing team can muster for defense. Outnumbering requires, first of all, the most-important outlet pass, which comes from a rebounder, an interceptor, or an out-of-bounds passer. In the movement down court there are two outside flankers in their speed lanes, and a middle man who is a good dribbler, passer and leader. The flankers stay about six to eight feet within their sidelines, and also run slightly ahead of the middle man all the way down. The payoff for the fast break is between the foul line and the endline, within which the flankers converge for the basket while expecting the final pass from the driving middle man. There must always be a trailer. He comes in behind the three attackers, and in many instances will be the decisive man in the outnumbering effort.

Players on a team that has a fast break in its repertoire will appreciate the prerogative to run when the opportunity is there. The fans will enjoy the excitement generated by a fast break.

The fast break is a spectacular part of the Option Offense, outstanding in its simplicity, and requires detailed attention to the basic basketball skills of passing, dribbling, jumping, and running in a speed situation. Good physical conditioning, discipline, and intelligence are additional prerequisites.

Chapter Ten

Organizing an Attack

On Pressure Defenses

THE CHALLENGE

The team that emphasizes pattern-continuity might as well get prepared for the test of pressure. Aware that it is meeting a team of pattern philosophy, the opponent (who has just scored) will test and challenge the ability of this team to (1) get the ball in-bounds in the back court (2) maneuver the ball to, and past, the centerline within ten seconds, and (3) go into its prepared offense in the operational zone.

The complexity and cleverness of pressure defenses is increasing. All of them are enterprising and aggressive as they apply physical and mental pressure on the offense, with harassment and double-team action wherever possible. Sometimes the pressing team will permit the throw-in of the basketball in the back court without challenge; other times there is a *denial* set-up.

Although most pressing teams have the usual objectives of trying to tire the offensive team, forcing turnovers, and making steals, the main goal against our particular offensive team will be to disrupt the offensive plan. The expectation will be that pressure will force the team into distraction and disorganization of its patterns, and that it cannot improvise.

At least two things could cause this anticipation to boomerang: the exhibition of a polished, efficient plan that will overcome pressure, and the maintenance of poise, with the confidence that the offense contains built-in options that will counteract any kind of pressure.

We mentioned in the first paragraph that the first phase of the pressing challenge is to prevent the orderly pass-in of the basketball in the back court. Actually, the technique of *denial* or *prevent* is applied in most erratic fashion—"sometimes they do, sometimes they don't." The man-man press will probably send a deny man to the baseline more often than will the zone press. At any rate, the best reaction to the denial, whether applied by either zone or man-man, is to in-bound the ball as quickly and informally as possible (retrieve it and throw it in to the first open man, and "take off" to get across the centerline). The professionals have this procedure down to such a fine art that few teams are challenged by any sustained pressure in the back court. But at lower levels, "in-bounds fast and take off" is easier said than done. If we're up against a full-court press, we may as well accept the fact that the pressing team is just as quick, or quicker, in getting into pressing position as we are in retrieving the ball and looking for a receiver.

So, we must have a plan involving a basic set positioning, no matter the type of pressure. The plan must be as simple as possible. We will not vary from the basic concepts within it, and we will go into it quickly as the ball is being retrieved by 5.

The triangular concept, so much a part of the Option Offense, is used again, against both man-man and zone. I call it the triangle-and-one, because a weak-side man, 2, operates with the trio of 1, 3, and 4. 5 passes the ball in-bounds, as shown in Figure 10-1. The triangle must think as a unit, move as a unit, and be prepared to rove cross-court, parallel to the baseline, to and fro, if 05 has to run the baseline to escape denial pressure (Figure 10-2).

It will be observed that all five players have been brought up to run the offense against the press. I feel that all hands are needed to overload, to triangulate, and to operate the weak-side feature. It takes all five.

EXAMPLES OF PRESSURE

Figures 10-2 and 10-3 show the concerted movement of the trio, the maintenance of the triangle, and probable passing opportunities within it. In Figure 10-2, X5 is exerting pressure on 05 at the baseline,

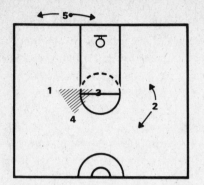

Figure 10-1. Basketball is a game of triangles!

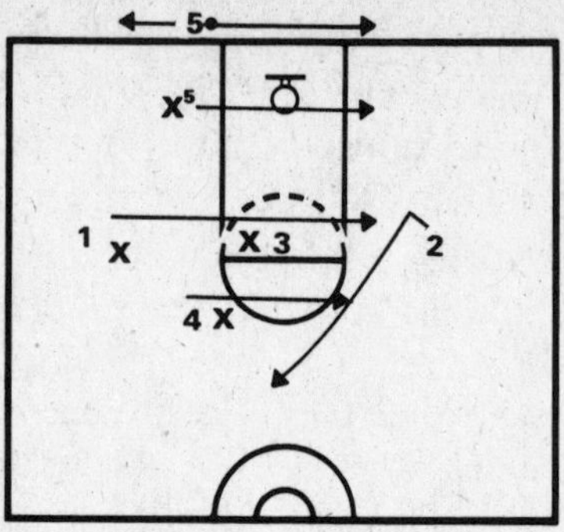

Figure 10-2. Movement as a unit.

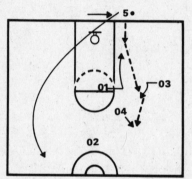

Figure 10-3. 01 comes open during shift. Triangle passing.

so he runs the baseline, with X5 aggressively trying to deny the in-bounds pass all the way. 01, 03, and 04 move as a triangle with 05. 02 would clear out, as shown. Figure 10-3 shows the example of 01 getting open for the in-bounds pass. Remember, 05 has just five seconds! 03 slides down the triangle, as does 04. 01, after receiving the in-bounds pass, is shown passing within the triangle to 03, who turns, and passes on down to 04. 05 goes weak-side and is thinking about possible post duty in the middle farther down.

Figure 10-4 goes back to find 05 again under pressure from X5, but able to pass in. 01 and 03 demonstrate an excellent way to over-come their man-man defensive pressure by moving as if to criss-cross, then suddenly stopping and opening up as 04 flashes in between them to receive the pass from 05. In another example, 01 and 03 may go ahead and complete the criss-cross, thus creating a natural screen as they do so. In such a case, the in-bounds pass could go to either one at either corner of the triangle instead of to 04 at the point. 05 is going to have to be very clever, in all cases, because it is a man-man press and he is being denied the easy pass-in. As 04 receives the pass in Figure 10-4, (with details of the action expanded in Figures 10-5, 10-6, and 10-7), 03 and 01 must slide and move to enlarge the passing triangle.

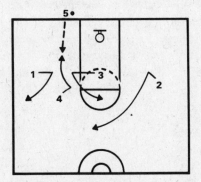

Figure 10-4. 01 and 03, open up. 04 flashes in.

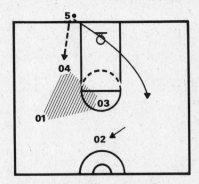

Figure 10-5. The triangle of Figure 10-4, with weak-side action by 05 and 02.

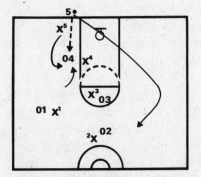

Figure 10-6. Trapping reaction of X4 and X5.

Figure 10-7. Passing options of 04.

02 shifts over, vacating his weak side, to either get in the middle seam, or to overload the side. 05 replaces 02, and if not needed in the immediate action, continues down the side and into the middle, as necessary, to act as low post on either side of the centerline.

As the ball is passed in to 04, we should expect X5 to release from 05 and go to form a quick double-team with X4 on 04, as drawn in

Figure 10-6. We have to anticipate that trapping principle. On the positive side, however, such an act gives our 05 some freedom of action.

04 has been afforded many passing options, drawn in Figure 10-7. We would prefer that he always pass ahead, in this case to 02. He would pass to 05 early, only if he were in trouble and needed a safety-valve. Right here, in Figure 10-7, the press is beaten. No more diagramming in this sequence is necessary. There are options galore for passing, and too many to diagram. Now, there are two major things for the team and the play-maker to think about at the end of Figure 10-7: (1) have we outnumbered the defense, can we go on to the basket? and (2) shall we set up our offense and get it moving without any stoppage or slowdown in the action?

FACTORS TO CONSIDER

A certain salient feature should be pointed out which makes this press-breaker plan effective. Dribbling against man-man, full-court pressure has been kept to a minimum. Dribbling is not completely frowned upon as one of the tools against man-man pressure. Against a full-court zone press, however, dribbling is thoroughly discouraged.

The fact remains that in this plan the dribble would not be the main weapon. The pass, and purposeful movement, would be. For example, 05 has moved down the side, away from the ball, replacing weak-side 02. Then he cuts down into the middle, knowing that he might be needed as a post man. In Figure 10-7, 02 has moved onto the strong side, and also turns back into the middle. This is purposeful movement which adds dimension to the plan. With them setting up, as necessary, in this manner as the ball moves down court, we can have a continual, high-post low-post situation right down the elongated middle seam.

While defeating the press, the fast break possibility must not be ignored. We want 01, 02, and 03 involved in the three fast-break approach lanes as much as possible. Figure 10-8 illustrates the ease of positioning for the fast break, as 02 dribbles down the middle while 01 and 03 go down the sides.

In Figure 10-9, 02 realizes he cannot go to the fast break, so he finds 04 arriving in the middle, and hits him with a pass in the high-low tradition. With 01 and 03 already filling the lanes along the sides, the

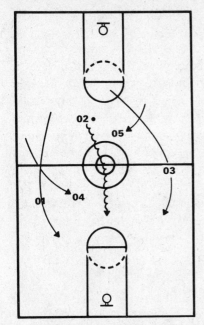

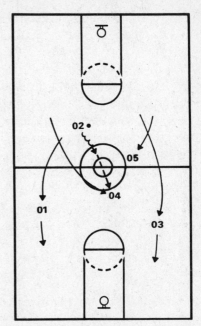

Figure 10-8. Fast break!   **Figure 10-9. No fast break. High-low, 02, 04, and 05.**

defense, in many cases, will be off-balance and poorly positioned to the extent that 04, 01, and 03 can go ahead with a fast-moving, precision-passing, 3-on-3 attack in the front court. In this ideal situation, they can demonstrate that all the 3-on-3 practice sessions will pay off.

Figure 10-10 is another example of the team's perception that there is no outnumbering situation, and of the ensuing leadership action that must be expected of 01. He yells, "Set!" and the team goes to a pattern (series) quickly, with the ball being passed to 01. The natural screens that develop when 02 crosses with 05, (Figure 10-10), and when 03 crosses with 04 and 05, are subtle by-products, and provide impromptu free-lancing possibilities. I will make no attempt to diagram them. If you want to appreciate this classic example of transitional basketball, you should program the situations of Figures 10-9 and 10-10 into your practice planning. The team will instinctively react to the natural screen possibilities, with no diagramming necessary. If no options result, we are still playing under control, because all the players are running normal routes into the Option Offense.

CONTINUING RESPONSE TO MAN-MAN PRESSURE

Another example of beating the press begins in Figure 10-11. The pressure is still man-man as the ball is passed in to 03. 04 has flashed in between 01 and 03, but 05 chooses to pass to 03. 02 heads for the middle, vacating the weak side, and 05 follows his weak-side route. 01 and 04 open up the triangle quickly as 03, turning to look down-court, passes to 02 (Figure 10-12). He could have passed to 01 in the triangle, or to 05 as the safety-valve, although these passes are not included as possibilities in the diagram. The best pass, down the seam to 02, is shown. 02 turns, looks down quickly, and has options to dribble or pass to 03, 01, or 05. In Figure 10-12 he decides to dribble down the middle. Both Figures 10-12 and 10-13 illustrate this decision. This creates the fast break, with 01 and 03 on the wings, and 02, himself, in the middle.

The fast break from the back court did not develop, as Figure 10-14 suggests. Hung up by a defensive check when he turns, 02 finds

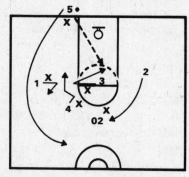

Figure 10-11. A new example. Pass-in to 03.

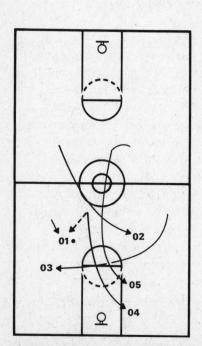

Figure 10-10. No fast break. Run the offense!

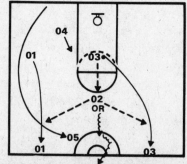

Figure 10-12. 03 passes down the middle. Pass-options of 02.

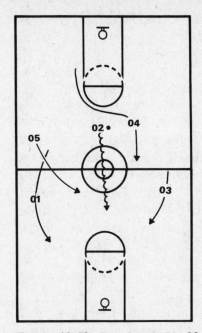

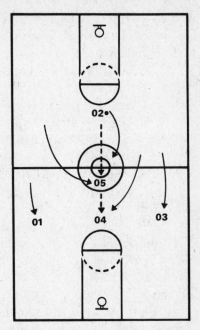

Figure 10-13. Fast break for 02, 01, and 03.

Figure 10-14. No fast break. High-low, 02, 05, 04.

05 barging into the middle, as he's been trained to do, and hits him with a pass. 05, in turn, passes down to 04 at a lower post location. Any press is picked apart by this precise, meticulous passing which aims at intrusion and invasion of the middle. This method, concentrating its passing avenue down the middle, causes the pressure to converge and contract there; this defensive shifting exposes and uncovers the side and wing areas all the way down court, on either side.

Figure 10-14 could be expanded to a following diagram showing three-against-three action and/or movement into the set of the Option Offense, but it would be somewhat repetitious of Figure 10-10.

FULL-COURT ZONE PRESS

So far, the attack plan has focused on the man-man full-court press. Although the general method of attack should change very little, if at all, when a full-court zone press is met, it is advisable to discuss some of its ramifications that are important to the Option Offense.

The modern zone press, with all its trappings, can be devastating to an unprepared, unsuspecting offensive team. It can also be very

effective against a team that is prepared. The full-court zone press
became truly noted as a weapon of terror in its application by Coach
John Wooden's UCLA teams in the 1960's. Particularly effective was
his 2-2-1 formation, demonstrated in Figure 10-15. Most of the time
there was no denial of the in-bounds pass, as there is none in Figure
10-15, although occasionally, either X1 or X2 would suddenly go to
the in-bounds passer to try to prevent the pass-in; or, suddenly, jump in
to intercept the in-bounds pass. Figure 10-15 shows no denial of the
pass-in, but we see the trapping and double-teaming that can be expected as the permissiveness changes to aggressiveness. X1 goes to the
receiver, who has started a dribble. With quick hands and footwork,
X1 forces him to commit the mistake of turning his back while dribbling in the back court. X2 releases from his area and flashes over to
meet the dribbler as he blindly completes his forced turn. X1 and X2
work together now, to force a turnover. The leadership in the 2-2-1
comes from X5, who from his back position calls out directions and
signals.

A lot of revision and addition has taken place in recent years; zone
presses, whatever their formation, have become more sophisticated
and complicated. The main purpose remains, however, to invoke
chaos and disruption among the members of the offense while trying to
regain possession of the basketball.

TRIANGLE-AND-ONE AGAINST THE 2-2-1

In Figure 10-16 we see the initial reaction as our triangle-and-one

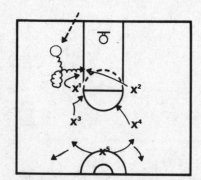

**Figure 10-15. 2-2-1 zone press.
Pass-in permitted.**

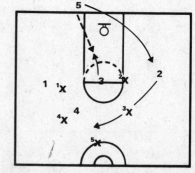

**Figure 10-16. Triangle-and-one
and the 2-2-1.**

comes up against the 2-2-1. It is apparent that the 2-2-1 poses no initial threat to our in-bounds pass. The zone is overloaded, and we have a weak-side man. It has always been my contention that this is the classic way to attack a zone, anywhere on the court. In Figure 10-16, the uncontested pass is made to 03. 02, weak side, clears over toward the middle as 05 replaces him. The reaction of the 2-2-1, in its usual full-court pressure method, is interesting. Would X1 and X2 go to the trapping, double-team technique against 03? Yes, usually. But our 03 is not going to be trapped. He has been trained to turn immediately (no dribble), look down court, protect the ball, and find an open teammate with his pass. He has certainly been taught that the least desirable thing he can do against a zone press is to start a dribble. Figure 10-17 shows at least three passing options for 03, pressure or no pressure.

In Figures 10-18 and 10-19, for the sake of a good example and to

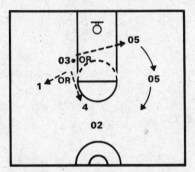

Figure 10-17. Passing options for 03.

Figure 10-18. An unfavorable situation for the Option Offense.

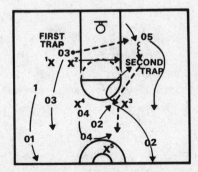

Figure 10-19. Traps against our 03 and 05.

demonstrate the validity of our triangle-and-one plan against pressure, we attack under unfavorable circumstances. We assume that X4 is denying the triangle pass to 4, and that X1 and X2 are teaming up to shut off the pass to 1; so 03 makes the safety-valve pass to 05. This is the man who isn't supposed to handle the ball very much, isn't supposed to dribble very much, and besides, we want him down court as soon as possible, without interruption. In this case, however, 03 had no choice but to pass back to 05. Now, we go to the actions of the 2-2-1. As stated before, X1 and X2 have responded to the in-bounds pass by trying to trap 03 ("First Trap" in Figure 10-19), and 03 has passed back to 05. Right now, X3 is frozen in place because of indecision. What to do? 02 has vacated the weak side, but a man with the ball, 05, has replaced him! X5, farther down court, also has a problem—he must not commit himself too recklessly to the move of 02, because of the sensitive area behind him. Figure 10-19 is a continuation of what appears to be very complicated action, but is easily explained. X2 releases from 03 and goes for 05, who has tentatively put the ball on the floor while looking for a teammate. X3, relishing a trap of 05, also releases from his set position to combine with X2 against 05. Right now, we hope that 05 can find a teammate as soon as possible, and that is what is also depicted in Figure 10-19, as 02 meets the pass from 05 in the area vacated by X3. 02 turns to pass to 04, also down the middle. 01 and 02 fill the outside lanes.

Besides the filling of the middle areas by players operating as post men, and the concurrent filling of the outside lanes, one other tactic is important for the Option Offense. Our player with the ball *wants* to see two opponents coming at him for the double-team. This should be regarded as a situation to be exploited. It means that a nearby section of the floor, usually in the middle, is going to be open. So, let them come, but get rid of the ball at the right time, without a dribble!

To review Figure 10-19: 03 has the ball, is threatened by the double-team of X1 and X2; passes back to 05 because his forward passing lanes are restricted, and moves on down the floor. 05, also threatened by the trapping duo of X2 and X3, alertly passes down to 02 in the middle area. 02 continues the high-low action down the middle seam as he passes to 04, who is creating a post position at about center court. 02 and 01 fill the outside lanes.

The 2-2-1 full-court zone press has been defeated, even with the unfavorable pass back to 05.

FORMATION SHIFTING

The Option Offense must never be surprised at a pressing team's sudden shift from one formation to another. Many coaches call this shifting response the *combination* method, and sometimes it may involve the conversion from man-man to zone, and vice versa. This points out the importance of having a press-breaker plan that doesn't require much, if any, adjustment. In Figure 10-20, the 2-2-1 zone press replies to our triangle-and-one by transferring into a kind of 1-2-1-1, which can be inferred from the diagram. Except for X5, it looks like a change to man-man; in reality, the defense is matching-up, as discussed in Chapter 6. X1 picks up 01 as he meets the in-bounds pass; X2 slides over to match-up with 3 (might even try to front him); 02 is taken by X3 as he vacates the weak side; and X4 takes 4. The only man without a guard is 05, coming around the weak side, although X5 is certainly looking him over as he makes his move. The truth is, X5 is frozen in place by our triangle-and-one movement. He cannot leave the court behind him unprotected by moving up into the action, and this illustrates the worth of our plan. Observe that 01 turns quickly to pass to 03 at the triangle corner (Figure 10-21). 05 is then totally open and unguarded for a pass from 03, and we are also hoping that 02 and 04 are making faking moves to get open for a pass. Here, we assume that 03 disregards 05 and turns to pass down to 02.

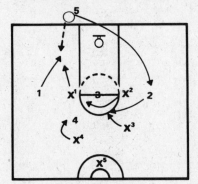

Figure 10-20. Shift to 1-2-1-1, with man-man features.

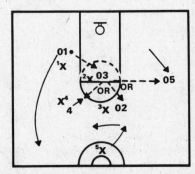

Figure 10-21. Passing options of 03.

Figure 10-22 brings this example to a conclusion. We overcome the attempt of the defense to shift its formation and mask its zonal technique of *matching-up* or *combining*. 02 turns, passes to 04 (high-low); 04 turns, finds 05 arriving at a lower post in the middle (more high-low), and passes down to him. 01 and 03 fill the outside lanes. This press is defeated.

MY 1-2-1-1 ZONE PRESS

In this discussion of zone presses and attacks against them, I will present my own 1-2-1-1, which sets as a three-quarter court press, and operates with sideline trapping areas. The design shown in Figure 10-23 was first used in my army coaching, with the designation of Chaser (X1), Left Front Trapper (X2), Right Front Trapper (X3), Interceptor (X4), and Rear Trapper (X5). The terminology serves to partially explain the responsibilities of each. There is a Permit Zone, within which there is no challenge of the ball or offensive player. On either side of the court are imaginary trap zones, also shown in Figure 10-23.

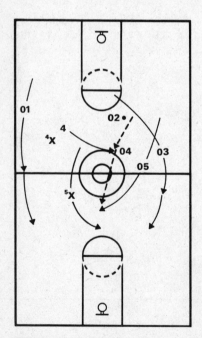

Figure 10-22. End of the pressure problem.

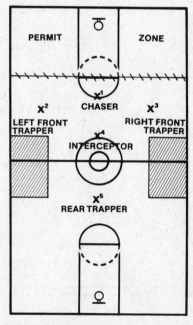

Figure 10-23. My 1-2-1-1 zone press.

As clearly as possible, Figure 10-24 points out the areas and limits of responsibility. The explanation which follows is quite thorough in clarification of what may appear to be a complicated diagram.

The chaser, X1, works both sides of the court, going to the ball. (Check the arrows pertinent to him). He goes to X2's primary side, and to X3's, as double-team harassment and coercion is applied. The objective is to force a lob pass or a desperation pass into the middle, for interception by X4, or to combine with either X2 or X3 in coercing a dribbler into the side-court trap areas. (Diagonal lines).

Notice the long arrows marked *Get Back!* They apply to X1, who releases from his double-teaming duties just at the instant the opponent enters the side-court trapping area with the ball. X1 has done his job, and now he races to front court, as the arrows indicate. This frees X5 so he can set the trap from the rear on either side, and combine with either X2 or X3 in the trapping action.

In addition to interceptor duties, X4 roams his area to go one-on-one against any man with the ball, or against any man who receives the

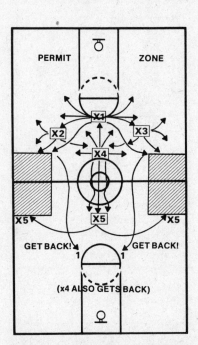

Figure 10-24. Areas of responsibility.

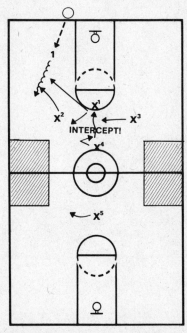

Figure 10-25. My 1-2-1-1 press in action.

ball. He also releases to get back to front court when the action leaves his areas of responsibility. He does not operate in the side-court trap areas. Notice from the arrows that X5 moves into the rear part of the trap zone on either side, just as X1 releases. X1 gets back to replace X5. This action is an important part of the 1-2-1-1. When X5 moves in to trap, there must be simultaneous replacement by X1. As mentioned before and shown in the diagram, X4 also gets back.

In Figure 10-25, X1 has challenged the dribbling 01 at the free throw line, followed immediately by teammate X2 for the double-team. X4 moves up, with hands high, in the interceptor zone. X3 moves laterally, with hands high, to the limit of his zone near the middle. X1 and X2 want 01 to become flustered into committing a turnover while dribbling, or making a poor pass. If they fail in that, they will encourage the dribbler into the side-court trap zone, all the time inviting and funneling him there. As the dribbler goes into the trap in Figure 10-26, X1 will release at the top just as X5 enters the trap zone at the rear. X5 and X2, therefore, are the trappers; if similar

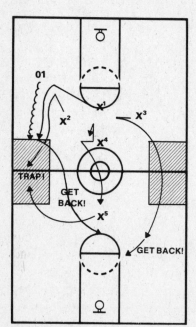

Figure 10-26. Action continues. X1 releases.

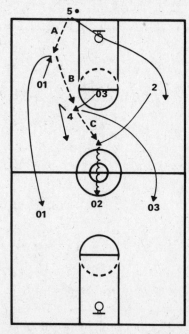

Figure 10-27. My triangle-and-one against my 1-2-1-1.

action takes place on the opposite side of the court, the trappers would be X3 and X5.

X4 also releases from his interceptor area and gets back for defensive balance, along with X1.

How would the triangle-and-one of the Option Offense fare against my own 1-2-1-1? Possibly we can answer by diagramming action in one example, such as Figure 10-27, with supporting explanation in Figure 10-28. The Option Offense sets up quickly in the usual press-breaker fashion because the opponent has, obviously, gone to the press. 5 passes in to 01, unchallenged (Pass A). 03 and 04 slide down, forming the triangle quickly and automatically, and the ball is passed to 03 (Pass B). 02 vacates the weak-side and heads for the middle seam. 05 replaces 02 in the weak-side area. High-low passing down the middle continues as the ball goes from 03 to 02 (Pass C), while 01 and 03 fill the outside lanes.

Figure 10-27 shows only the offensive action. The counteracting moves of the defense are not shown. I have diagrammed many defensive responses earlier, so the reader may apply these to Figure 10-27. Figures 10-24 and 10-26, in particular, should be rechecked, to relate their action to Figure 10-27.

Figure 10-28 is included to bring out more detail in the preceding diagram, and to help explain it. It shows the detail of the triangle formed by 01, 03, and 04, the move toward the middle by 02, and the pass from 03 to 02. The moves of 01 and 03 in filling the lanes are also repeated for clarification.

The triangle-and-one of the Option Offense is an effective way of meeting my own 1-2-1-1 zone press.

HALF-COURT ZONE PRESS

In preparing the Option Offense, you must consider that your team will be subjected to the half-court press. The 1-3-1 is typical, and maintains its popularity among coaches who like to operate the press in only the half-court area. It gains its effectiveness from surprise, because the signal for its use can be flashed suddenly from the bench. The idea behind this ball-hawking press is to force the offensive team out of its style of play, to effect a change of pace against a team using patterns, to harass, to force a turnover, to steal the ball, and to disrupt the pattern offense. Since the 1-3-1 is very popular in usage, it will be used as the example for our purposes here.

Figure 10-29 shows the 1-3-1 in one format as the ball is being brought down court. This initial set will have variations, and the point

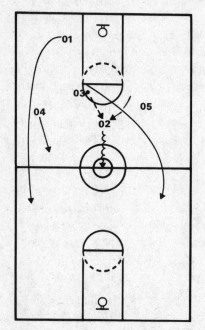

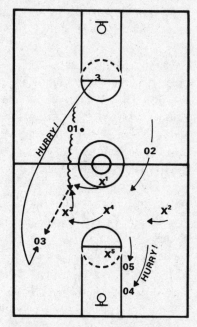

Figure 10-28. Details of Figure 10-27.

Figure 10-29. Option Offense meets the half-court press.

man, X1, will deviate in his approach to the dribbler as he nears center court. X1, the chaser, and X2 and X3, the wing men, are fast and aggressive. Areas of potential weakness are drawn in Figure 10-30 as shaded areas. They include the corners, which are unprotected initially; the right and left side wing areas, each of which become weakened when X2 or X3 vacate to go out to trap and double-team; at the top of the key when X4 releases to trap with X2 or X3; and in the area down the key, when X5 has to slide away, laterally, to protect the corner zones. With such an extensive territory of potential vulnerability to worry about, it is obvious that the 1-3-1 will have to do a lot of intelligent, aggressive sliding, shifting, and overlapping against the Option Offense.

The Option Offense goes into gear in Figure 10-29 against this particular half-court zone press as 01 brings the ball down court, un-challenged. Trapping harassment begins as the ball reaches center court. At this time, we want to avoid any passing back and forth between 01 and 02 as much as possible. Every cross-court pass is aimless and valueless unless there is a reason for it. For one thing, each time such a pass is made, the chaser (X1) has another chance at an interception. As the ball is coming down court, 03, 04, and 05 are getting into position quickly. The best countermeasure against this 1-3-1 is to get the ball into the operational areas quickly, using our regular offense. Certain, if not all, parts of Red, White, and Blue Series, will work against any zone press. In addition, the quarterback must not overlook the possibility of calling a Special Play, and I am particularly thinking of the play in Figure 8-3 (Chapter 8), which springs 03 open in the deep key area, and Figure 8-4, which gives 04 an open jump shot at the foul line. In Figure 10-29, 01 lures X1 and X3 to him (no panic, this should be considered an *opportunity* to pass to an open area), and passes down to 03 just before X1 and X3 become a trapping problem. This pass will go through because the area has been vacated. Look one way, pass another! Do not "telegraph" the pass!

It will be noticed in Figure 10-29 that X5 is having overloading problems as 04 and 05 start coming into the lane area. X4 would certainly slide over to defend against 03, and X2 will slide over to fill in the critical middle space left vacant by X4.

Figure 10-31 shows the beginning of the Red Series. It is repeated here to demonstrate its effectiveness in exploitation of the weak areas.

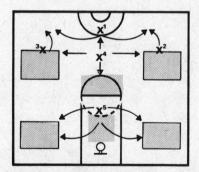

Figure 10-30. Potential weak areas in the half-court press.

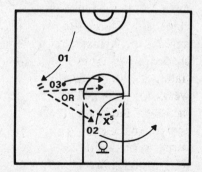

Figure 10-31. Exploitation of weak areas. Red Series.

03 hands back to 01 (vulnerable area) and cuts for the top of the key (vulnerable area). 02 has already been refused as he cut down the key, but he gives X5 something to think about. We will not go into a detailed account of options because I would be repeating other parts of the book, but I will make reference to them, briefly, in Figures 10-32 and 10-33. Figure 10-32 shows at least four passing possibilities as the

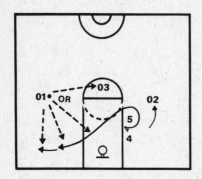

Figure 10-32. Passing options of 01.

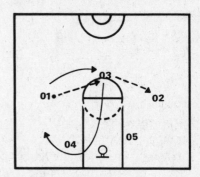

Figure 10-33. Option pass to 03. Mixmaster starts.

ball is handed back to 01, all of them pertinent to open areas in the 1-3-1 trapping process. In Figure 10-33, just one option is shown resulting from the pass from 01 to 03. 03 then swings a pass over to weak-side 02, who will have a jump shot in a potentially weak place. Since this is Mixmaster, 03 will cut down the key after his pass to 02, as shown. 01 is replacing him. In Figure 10-34, it is assumed that 02 does not have the open jump shot, so he reverses the ball back to 01 at the top of the key, and there is the natural overload creation by 03, 04, and 01 as a part of the Option Offense against a zone.

Figures 10-35 and 10-36 point out the use of the Blue Series against this half-court zone press. I will diagram only the opening part of the series. In Figure 10-35, 01, with the ball, has attracted X1 and X3 for the attempted trap. He sees 02 open, so he passes over to him, activating and keying the Blue Series. X4 and X2 would go to this new trap situation, and X3 and X1 would have to drop down. 02, with trapping problems coming, would go to the Blue Series. 04 pops out from behind 5 in Figure 10-36 to receive the pass. The development of this series, with its passes, movements, routes, and options, including those of Mixmaster, will not be repeated.

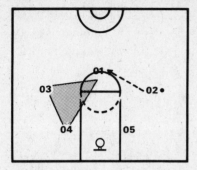

Figure 10-34. Natural overload triangle evolves.

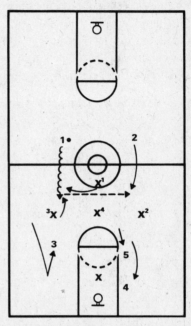

Figure 10-35. 01 passes over to 02 for Blue Series against the zone press.

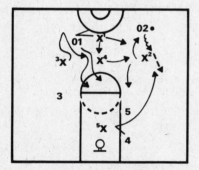

Figure 10-36. Blue begins.

SUMMARY

Here are some important points and basic principles to keep in mind. Your players should call them the "Big Ten":

1. Go to your positions quickly as your teammate goes to in-bound the ball.
2. Don't lose your poise. You have five seconds to in-bound the ball, and ten more to get it across the centerline.
3. It is better to pass than to dribble, especially against a zone press.
4. Meet the ball when receiving a pass.
5. Look ahead and pass ahead. Pass backward only if you have to.

6. Don't lob the ball. Don't "telegraph" your pass. Make short, snappy passes. Look one way, pass another.

7. Concentrate your passes, and the attacking axis, into the seam, down the middle.

8. The sides and wings are to be filled as the ball moves in high-low fashion down the seam.

9. All defenses have weak spots, including the presses.

10. When you beat the press, go to the basket for a good shot if it's there; otherwise, go to your regular pattern without interruption.

Chapter Eleven

Protecting the Lead

WHAT IS SLOW-DOWN?

There comes a time when the Option Offense will choose to slow down the action. Slow-down occupies a definite, important place in basketball tactics and strategy, and there are situations where its use is absolutely necessary.

To the professionals, slow-down involves only taking advantage of, and using, as much of the 24-second clock as possible; yet, they have their game situations in which the stretch-out of just this small segment of time, 24 seconds, without giving up the ball, is strategically important to the total picture. Their method seems simple; impose more restraint on shooting, as the team maneuvers in the normal pattern, and get the ball to a high-percentage shooting area as the clock runs down. Sometimes, just by a simple application of time arithmetic, the success of the shot is deemed relatively unimportant. The coach of a high school or college team, on the other hand, has an involved and complicated teaching job. Maintaining possession of the ball, in most cases far beyond a period of 24 seconds in a half-court area against a team that needs and wants the ball itself, is no simple chore.

For years, many high school and college coaches have strongly advocated the 30-second clock, without success.

Some of the situations or circumstances that call for slow-down should be described. Possibly we have had a big lead, but for various reasons it has been melting away as the game nears the end. There is a need to establish a different tempo. Time has become the dominant factor. The clock becomes the center of attention. We are five points ahead with two minutes to go. We are one point ahead and have called time-out with forty seconds to go. Our star player is hobbled with four personal fouls, and is in danger of fouling out of the close, hard-fought game, so we are trying to protect our lead, buying time, while he sits on the bench, waiting to go back in the critical closing moments. These, and any number of other conditions, can dictate the strategy of employing slow-down.

SLOW-DOWN OF THE OPTION OFFENSE

Some coaches state that there are three parts, or phases, within a slow-down strategy: ball control, semi-freeze, and freeze, each with a separate technique or objective. I suggest that ball control and semi-freeze can be merged into a single concept called *passing game*, which, added to *freeze*, simplifies the slow-down component of the Option Offense into just two parts.

The plan for *passing game* is simple. With or without a time-out, we merely make a minor adjustment in the set position of the Mixmaster (see Figure 11-1), adjust the tempo of the game, and run the modified Mixmaster. Players are cautioned to take only close-in, high-percentage shots. The under-basket lay up, resulting from sharp passing and movement, is most desirable. Quite simply, you don't want any surprises from an outside gunner in this situation, and you don't want to be embarrassed by having to leap from the bench screaming, "No, no!" when you see this player taking aim. We are willing to

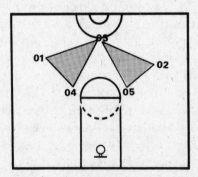

Figure 11-1. The set, and triangles.

be fouled by the other team while in our passing game, and we can tolerate giving up the ball, albeit reluctantly, if we have had a selective, hard-earned, sensible shot at the basket.

The plan for freeze is, likewise, quite simple. Put into effect most often after a time-out has been called, we use the same set as in passing game. In freeze, however, the team is concerned only with ball possession, and will shoot under no circumstance. Poise and self-restraint, gained through practice and teaching, really come to the front in this situation. Some coaches will not use the freeze because they never want to disrupt their offense which is designed to produce scoring opportunities. They figure that if the defense (opponent) discovers the non-shooting strategy, it will overplay, intercept passes, gamble, intimidate, and in general, upset the freeze. So, why create the problem in the first place, yourself? (They ask.)

FORMATION

As mentioned before, the Mixmaster will be used, with minor adjustment, for *both* the passing game and freeze. Inherent in the Mixmaster is the triangular concept, as mentioned in other places in this book. John Wooden once stated that basketball is a game of triangles. Figure 11-1 is drawn to illustrate the role of this geometric figure in the *protecting-a-lead* situation. Notice that the point man (in this case, 3) is the king-pin, just as in the Mixmaster. It will be further noted in Figure 11-1 that all five players have made the adjustment of moving farther out. The point man is out near the center circle, the wing men have moved out along the sides, and the double low post men are out on either side of the free throw line extended. From this adjusted set, the only new planned movement is the slide down the side of the key by 04 and 05. The rule is simple: Slide down your side of the key when the ball moves to the opposite side. Slide back up when the ball is being passed back around to your side.

It is obvious that one side of the court will be relatively open at all times, as 04 and 05 alternately release from their set positions to slide up and down the sides of the key.

THE ROLE OF THE DRIBBLER

Up to a few years ago, the coach could depend, to a major degree, on an expert dribbler to maintain possession of the ball while the clock ran down. His teammates would spread out, give him plenty of room in which to operate, and make themselves available if he got in trouble and had to pass. Nowadays, it is difficult, if not impossible, for the coach to have such dependence on dribbling as a time-waster or controller of the ball because of new rules which demand that forward areas be penetrated within time limits, and the 5-second limit in regard to the offensive-man versus defensive-man situation. Although the dribble is still an important part of ball possession, the accent must now be on movement of players and ball. And it had better be planned and practiced to a polished degree, because there is a tremendous requirement here in poise, discipline, and in the fundamentals of passing, dribbling, reception of the pass, and movement.

SLOW-DOWN BEGINS

In Figure 11-2, 03 passes over to 01, and cuts down the lane, following the same rule that applies in Mixmaster. It is entirely possible that 03 will be open to the give-and-go pass from 01, and he could have a clear dribbling path for the basket. In both passing game and freeze, such action is certainly encouraged. In freeze, the pass would be fine, and so would the dribble, but no shot would be taken. Such an option is not diagrammed, but it should be remembered as the first possibility. 01 passes the ball on to post man 04 in our example, 05 slides down the side of the key, and 03 goes down the key, to go around the screen of 05 down low. 02 has replaced 03 at the point.

ACTIONS BY POST MEN

In Figure 11-3, 04 sees 02 open at the point, so he gets the ball to him with an over-head, fan-pass. 02 reverses the ball to 03, who passes to 05 as he slides out to the free throw line. 02, of course, is cutting down the key, and goes opposite, around the screen of 04. 01 has replaced 02 at the point. No scoring options are shown. If the team was in passing game, it would be looking for the lay-up or the drive, all the time; if in freeze, control of the ball is the only objective. If 04 or 05 find it necessary to dribble out into an open area in order to pass off, they must be encouraged to do so. They will receive heavy pressure and intimidation, however, and will want to give up the ball to a

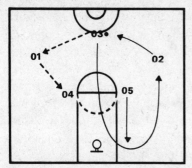

Figure 11-2. Movement begins.

Figure 11-3. From low to high.

teammate as quickly as possible. Also, they are told that the usual mechanics of post play go on when they receive the ball there. These procedures include turning, pivoting, facing the basket, looking down for an open man, dribble-driving down the key, dribbling out if no teammate is open for a pass, looking for a back door cutter, and so on. Except for the sliding movement up and down the side of the lane, these post play options are not diagrammed.

PERIMETER PASSING

Still more continuity and alternative in the same sequence is shown in Figures 11-4 and 11-5. Crisp, precise, perimeter passing is characteristic of Figure 11-4, where at least four passes take place. 05, in possession of the ball at the end of Figure 11-3, passes out to 03 (Pass A). 03 reverses the ball to the point, 01 (Pass B). 01 continues the reversal with his pass to the other wing, 02 (Pass C); then, as he is

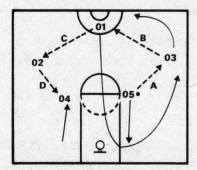

Figure 11-4. Perimeter passing.

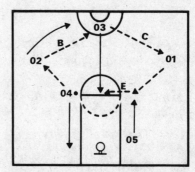

Figure 11-5. Perimeter passing, ball to cutter.

supposed to do when he passes off to the wing or when the ball goes down to the low post, 01 cuts down the key, and comes out opposite. Simultaneously, the ball has been passed down to 04 (Pass D). Notice that 05 slides down the key.

Perimeter passing such as this, with the threat of scoring options all the time, will cause the harassing defense to become desperate as they chase, trying to get possession of the ball. With all the defensive overplay, double-teaming, and scrambling going on, the offense can expect lay-up opportunities for back door and give-and-go almost every time the ball goes from the point to the wing, and from wing to low post or the cutting point man. (Unless, as in freeze, no shots are to be taken; then, we have only the movement and the passing.)

PASS TO CUTTER IN THE KEY

More concentrated passing is shown in Figure 11-5. 04 had the ball at the end of Figure 11-4, and 01 was cutting down the key. In Figure 11-5, he passes back out to 02, (Pass A); 02 reverses the ball to 03 at the point (Pass B); and 03 continues the perimeter reversal of the ball with his pass over to 01 (Pass C). 03 starts his cut down the key as 01 passes down to low post 05. This time, 03 is open, so 05 passes to him as he comes down the key. In passing game, he would have a lay-up. In a freeze situation, we go on to Figure 11-6, which shows him dribbling in, refusing the lay-up, and dribbling back out, around low post 04. Notice that there is no confusion in the continuity. 02 is already at the point, and the side is open for the dribble out by 03.

IMPROVISATION

Figures 11-7 and 11-8 intend to show that defensive harassment in a slow-down situation will become hectic, and in reacting to it, the team may have to improvise within the plan. The example in Figure 11-7, just one of the many probable developments, show 03 at the end of his dribble, passing out to point man, 02. The defense is really becoming aggressive and desperate, as 02 passes to wing man 01, then cuts down the key in usual fashion. 01 can't find an open man, and he is being overplayed himself, so he puts the ball on the floor, dribbling down the side. Nearing the corner, he turns and passes back out to 05, who is facing him.

Now, 05 is in trouble in Figure 11-8, to the extent of having to dribble out to the wing area, which is open. He gets rid of the ball just as soon as possible, by passing to 03 at the point. We want to discourage as much of this kind of ball-handling by 05 as possible, but if he has to, he must. In a simple, natural readjustment, within the philosophy of the Blue Series and the Mixmaster, 01 comes back out to the wing, and 05 goes back to his post position. For the moment, the defensive flurry has been handled by common-sense, solid application of basics (dribbling, passing, looking for the open man), and the offense is still in its pattern.

HIGH-LOW PASS IN SLOW-DOWN

To give even more meaning and significance to the slides of 04 and 05, Figure 11-9 shows a high-low cross-key pass from 04 to 05.

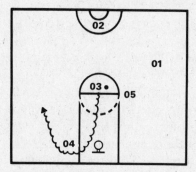

Figure 11-6. Freeze, dribble out.

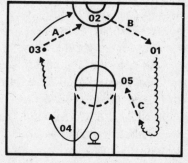

Figure 11-7. Perimeter pass, and improvise.

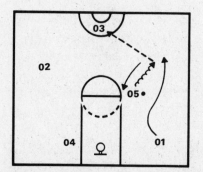

Figure 11-8. 05 in trouble, dribbles out.

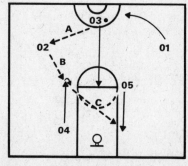

Figure 11-9. High-low pass option.

With all the double-teaming going on, 04 shouldn't be surprised at all to find 05 open under the basket as he turns to look down. This adds all the more dimension to the slow-down attack, whether it is passing game or freeze.

SUMMARY AND CLOSING NOTES

In the Option Offense, the ball control phase is called slow-down. It consists of *passing game* ("you will shoot only lay-ups, or from close-in"), and *freeze* ("you will shoot under no circumstance").

The objectives of slow-down vary according to the game situation, and are defined as follows: (1) to protect a lead, (2) to adjust the offense to a situation concerning *time*, in which one of our key players may be sitting on the bench, in foul trouble, (3) to force the defense out of their zone, and (4) to change the tempo of the game for any other tactical reason.

In passing game, the Option Offense does not want to give up the ball without scoring.

In freeze, we do not want to give up the ball.

In both passing game and freeze, the Mixmaster is the basic set, with only a minor adjustment.

As a strategy, slow-down is very important, and must be a part of the total Option Offense; but it has problems and negative aspects. One big problem is to know when to initiate passing game and/or freeze. Sometimes it can be done too early; sometimes, too late. You always leave yourself open to criticism. If you win, after resorting to slow-down, you have done a great job. If you lose, you should have done something else.

Some bad things can happen. In passing game, sometimes the team gets so interested in passing and moving that the scoring threat is not maintained. In freeze, there is a complete break in the scoring threat, and this may work negatively. Another aspect to consider is that the other team adjusts to the freeze by refusing to allow the waste of time, and commits fouls to interrupt the plan. Under pressure, our shooters may miss crucial free throw attempts, and the other team gets the ball without having lost much time, or putting forth much defensive effort.

The following specific points are important. The team can refer to them as the "Big Five":

1. Be careful in cross-court passing. Before actually passing, be sure a defensive man is not shooting the gap and flashing out to intercept. Anticipate such action, and pump or fake the pass before making it, as necessary.

2. The 15 to 20 foot distance between players still applies. If the Mixmaster, with adjustment, is applied properly, we do not worry about spreading out (admonition we hear so much about).

3. If the Mixmaster, with its adjustment, is applied properly in slow-down, we need not worry about floor balance. It is inherent in Mixmaster.

4. Be sure you and the team captain are in touch concerning time-out strategy during slow-down.

5. In freeze, we prefer *not* to be fouled. Get rid of the ball, and move. Do not invite a foul.

Chapter Twelve

Directing Special Drills

PURPOSE AND PLAN

Just as there are hundreds and thousands of coaches, so is there an unlimited multitude of basketball drills to sharpen individual skills and accomplish certain team objectives. Many drills become common property among coaches as they are passed on at coaches' clinics and in national publications. Others have been modified by addition and subtraction, as coaches constantly strive to make them meaningful and worthwhile in meeting their own particular needs. It has been said that there are no secrets in basketball. Undoubtedly, this is especially true for practice drills.

The drills that are diagrammed and described in this chapter have been selected as singularly relevant to the development of the Option Offense. Combined with the drills in Chapter 7, this material should contribute to the success of this offense.

Drills in this chapter pertain to both defense and offense. Some are very fundamental in dealing with such basics as pass-reception and footwork in starting, stopping and turning; some add to competitiveness, as the players receive a total score for their work; about a dozen drills, called "hard nose," stress the need for aggressiveness; and a few are intended to enhance shooting skills.

DESCRIPTION OF DRILLS

First to be presented are the hard nose drills. "He comes to play" is the way Leo Durocher described the competitive, aggressive baseball player who gives a little bit extra as he clearly wants to win. The same combativeness is needed in basketball, and you need as many players as possible who "come to play." Even more than baseball, basketball is an emotional, fast-moving game which calls for the spark of individual effort and enthusiasm.

ME AGAINST 'EM ALL

To toughen up our rebounders, there must be at least one drill that allows plenty of illegal body contact. In Figure 12-1 the team's rebounders (3's, 4's and 5's) are positioned around and under the basket. You are the shooter, and the metal insert is placed in the basket. Physical contact of grabbing, pushing, hacking and shoving is allowed, but no tackling. The rebounder may not dribble; he puts the ball up from where he gets it, and the first one to score four baskets is the winner. Since the insert will prevent the shot from actually being successful, you will decide and announce the scoring. Besides teaching our rebounders to be physical, this drill points out the importance of following through with the lay-up or close-in shot while being fouled, and not giving up just because of intimidation.

3 AGAINST 4

Three men are on the offense (0's); four men (X's) in a trapping, harassing, pressing defense which begins at the centerline and continues in the front court until the ball reaches an imaginary line across the top of the key. Along that line, one of the four defensemen quickly drops out along the side, and the play becomes three-against-three until a basket is made or the ball is turned over. This is a good chance to put the statisticians to work, with whatever records of a competitive nature you want to keep. Have the rest of the team organized and waiting along the sides, ready to step in.

HEAD HIM OFF

1, the dribbler, and X1, defense, start together, as shown. No fouling is permitted, although spirit and aggressiveness is applauded as X1 tries to head off the offensive 01. The players go one-on-one until a

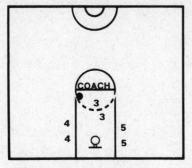

Figure 12-1. Me against 'em all. Rebounding.

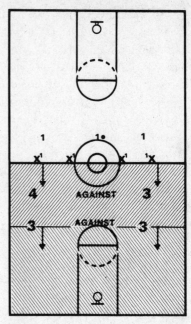

Figure 12-2. 3 against 4. Half-court press.

Figure 12-3. Head him off.

shot is taken by 01, or until the ball is given up by him. The two lines rotate. This is a drill for all team members, with you pairing them off as desired. If X1 makes 01 turn his back on the basket while maneuvering with his dribble out around the top of the key, he has done a good job of defense.

HARD NOSE DENY

You (passer) slap the ball to start the action, and count aloud to four if necessary (the maximum time allowed to get open), as 01 and 02 try to get free for a reception of the pass. Pass goes to first man to get open as X1 and X2 exert pressure. Back door is permissible, and encouraged, but 01 and 02 must restrict themselves to their respective side areas, from their baseline out to the free throw line extended. Head-faking and footwork are stressed. Offense and defense lines rotate. Have waiting lines ready. Statistician keeps records of this drill, according to your criteria. Legal body contact only.

A FIGHT AT THE HIGH POST

1 passes to high post 3, then follows his pass. He goes over the top of 3, forcing X1 to fight through and also go over the top to keep from getting rubbed off on 3. Action stops at the free throw line. Lots of spirit. Is X1 aggressive enough to refuse to be pinched out as 01 goes over the top? No shot, keep the drill moving. Vary the drill later by giving X1 the option of sliding through between his teammate, X3, and the high post, 3, as 01 goes over the top, but not until he has had a good taste of the first drill. His teammate, X3, must call out "slide through" or "come through." If he doesn't, make him run a lap, because the man behind the action always calls out switching and slide-through directions. Legal contact only.

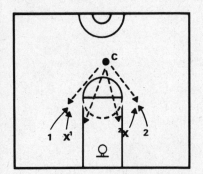

Figure 12-4. Hard nose deny.

Figure 12-5. A fight at the high post.

A FIGHT AT THE LOW POST

After passing down to the low post, 01 uses head-shoulder fake and footwork to try to get open for a return pass and jump shot. X1 tries to prevent the return pass; if he can't, he continues his aggressive defense, one-on-one against 01 until a shot is made or the ball is turned over. One side of the floor for maneuver only. Run the drill on the other low post side. Have 1 and X1 rotate.

NO PASS-IN

Man-man full court pressure, three-on-three, with X1's trying to deny the in-bounds pass. 01 may run along the end line. Action stops when the ball, if successfully thrown in, gets to mid-court. You set a

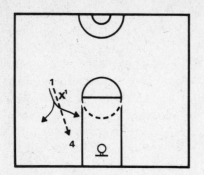

Figure 12-6. A fight at the low post.

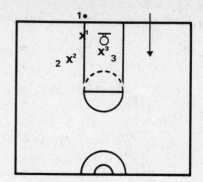

Figure 12-7. No pass-in.

rotation plan so that all get a chance to play at all positions in the drill, particularly 01. You want to be sure that all are ready before starting the drill. You want to encourage and commend aggressiveness and spirit of X1, X2 and X3. Drill ends if ball isn't passed in within five seconds, or if and when it is passed in successfully and reaches center court.

GET IT AND GO

You and your assistant stand at opposite free throw lines, and the drill starts when you each roll a ball mid-point between two players on their half-court, as shown. Fouling and illegal body contact are permitted until the ball is secured, then the drill is one-on-one with no intentional fouling permitted. As the diagram indicates, there will be a great deal of confined action around the center circle, especially as the players have to go one-on-one toward the opposite end. The drill intends to demonstrate that basketball action does become intense and restricted, and calls for aggressiveness. Statisticians keep records of the drill according to your needs.

FREE FOR ALL

Two teams of four players each (1's against 2's) are lined up on either side of the free throw lane, facing each other. Action starts when you, using as much deception as possible, roll the ball between the two lines, or dribble around the lines and lob the ball into the contested area. You must be sure that both teams are equally ready. Illegal body contact is permitted until the ball is secured, then the action becomes four-on-four, with no intentional fouling. Statistician keeps records; two points for initial recovery of basketball, two points for successful field goal, one point for successful free throw during four-on-four, one point for causing the other team to commit a turnover, one point for each rebound. As in all other games of this type, the team that rebounds defensively must move the ball back out beyond the top of the key before initiating its own offense. Action stops with successful field goal, resumes with the lineup along the lane.

HARD NOSE TWO-ON-TWO

Two 0's against two X's. You use deception as you circle around the four players with a dribble, stop, fake a throw-in among them, dribble some more, then suddenly lob or bounce-pass the ball in. Players may intentionally foul in securing the ball, then two-on-two

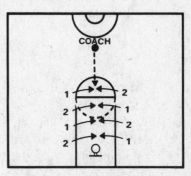

Figure 12-9. Free for all.

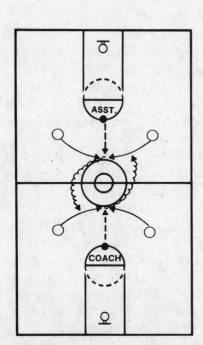

Figure 12-8. Get it and go.

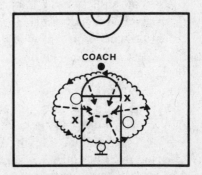

Figure 12-10. 2-on-2.

begins, with no intentional fouling. Some method of scorekeeping is suggested, similar to that in Figure 12-9.

HARD NOSE ALL THE WAY

This is an excellent conditioner as well as a drill for simulated dribbling against full-court pressure, and boxer stance, slide-stepping defense. Court has an imaginary line down the center, dividing it into two sides. Defensive man, X, versus offensive man, 0, on each side of the court at the starting end line. No basketball. 0 simulates dribble with zig-zags and change of pace, while X slide-steps in boxer stance, exerting pressure all the way. You make corrections because there will be a tendency to gloss over fundamentals in this drill. 0 changes direction by properly pushing off on either his right leg or left leg, in a kind of jab step. No running; this is zig-zag. The offensive man's head is up, he never turns his back on X, and he simulates a proper dribble. The idea is to make X work hard on defense! X and 0 change places. Waiting lines are ready at the end line.

BOXER STANCE AND SLIDE-STEP

The boxer stance with slide-step (or boxer step) method of individual defense is recommended to you, the Option Offense coach. It embodies those qualities of footwork, lateral movement, and body balance that are uniquely required of a defender in basketball, and of most other athletes. A baseball catcher, finding it necessary to move right or left behind the plate without losing body balance, uses the slide step principle because he does not want to cross his feet awkwardly. Of course, the slide step is a feature of footwork in boxing. In basketball, the individual on defense must not cross his feet as he moves laterally. If he does, the opponent with the ball can change direction and leave the awkward guard standing. If a defenseman moves to his right, his right foot should move right, and the left foot is brought alongside in a sliding move. If he moves to his left while guarding his man, the left foot moves left, and the right foot slides alongside. In moving forward or backward, one foot is kept ahead of the other, and the feet are shuffled in a sliding, skipping movement. Figure 12-12 shows a drill after the team has been introduced to the boxer stance and slide step. The team lines up facing you, arms-length apart, as shown. Players

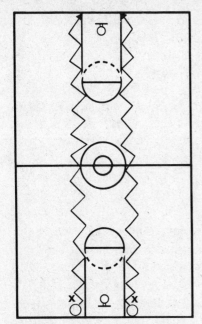

Figure 12-11. All the way.

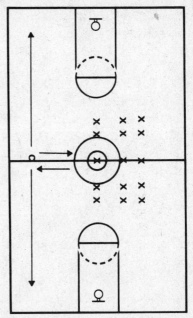

Figure 12-12. Boxer stance and slide-step.

assume the boxer stance. The knees are slightly bent, flexed; the butt is down, upper body rather straight, eyes straight ahead, feet spread slightly more than the width of the shoulders. There is a feeling for comfortable balance. The player is alert, ready to slide-step backward, sideward or forward. One arm is up, with the hand waving in the opponent's face; the other arm and hand is down, pawing at the dribble. The arms can be rotated in a wind-milling effect, as the guard moves with the man and ball. The wind-milling rotates the responsibilities of the arms and hands as the player moves, and also helps maintain body balance. The three lines slide-step laterally to their right, in unison with you, wind-milling and using the boxer stance all the way to the gym wall; then with you, back to their left, never crossing their legs, one foot always solid on the floor while the other slides or shuffles. Body balance is maintained. You return them to the original place, then move them straight backward, then forward. This is excellent conditioner, and it will be necessary to take a breather once in a while. You may want to cease your own personal exertion and stand in place, giving signals and shouting corrections. Corrections will have to be made all the time by you and your assistant—there is a

tendency for the players to get careless. A stand-out sign of carelessness or tiredness is the player's tendency to straighten up while moving, and this is poor basic technique. The butt is down, the upper back
straight, the knees flexed!

Teaching notes and reminders about the basic fundamentals and
skills for the individual player have been included in the description of
this drill as a service to you. The boxer stance, with slide-step, is the
defensive accompaniment to the total sum of the Option Offense, and
must be treated with that aspect in mind.

TORTURE COURSE

The "torture course" is as much an instrument for teaching the
boxer stance and slide-step as it is a physical conditioner. If competition is desired, use a stop-watch and statistician. There are three parts
to the drill, which makes it a real conditioner. Instructions:

1. (a) Two lines. Start at the end (base) line. Run to the free
       throw line extended. Stop, bend, touch floor, turn, run
       back to end line.
   (b) Run to center line extended, touch floor, turn, run back.
   (c) Run to other free throw line extended, touch floor, turn,
       run back.
   (d) Run to other end line, touch floor, turn, run back.

2. Repeat all the above, except each player has to return to the
   starting endline from each stop by running backwards. No
   turn.

3. This time, slide the lines. Face the sideline, to start. Boxer
   stance, slide step, do not cross the legs, wind-mill the arms.
   Stop at same designated place as in 1 and 2, above.

DEFENSING THE HIGH POST,
RIGHT AND LEFT SIDE

In both Figures 12-14 and 12-15, the drill ends when you pass the
ball, probably by bounce pass, into the high post. Up to that time you
have been teaching and correcting the skills of X, the defensive man.
You want X to overplay on the strong-side (side of the ball) of the high
post. You want him to be aggressive without fouling, and you teach X

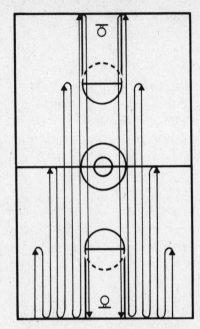

Figure 12-13. Torture course.

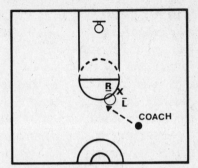

Figure 12-14. Defense the high post, right side.

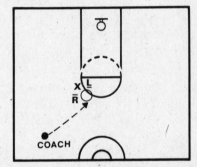

Figure 12-15. Defense the high post, left side.

to concede *nothing*. The left arm, symbolized as /L, is waving to the oblique as a distractor and to discourage the pass. The right arm, /R, is rigidly extended, like a bar, across the back of 0, the high post. This bar acts as a warning device if 0 suddenly moves to release for a back door lob pass from you. It cannot, however, be used to hold or deter 0 if he does move unexpectedly. Figure 12-14 is for right side action. Figure 12-15 is for left side action.

DROP AGAINST THE SCISSORS

Reference has already been made to the drop tactic against the offensive scissors in Chapter 5. It is included here as an important defensive drill to consider. By defensing an option of our own offense, we also get offensive experience in reacting to different methods, so this drill will serve two purposes. Either X1, X2, or X3 (doesn't matter

who) calls out "drop!" after the pass is made to the high post, and as
01 and 02 are crossing. 01 and 02 are simply picked up, without a
switch, by X1 and X2 as they come by on either side of high post 3.
You want the defensive men to communicate here. If "drop!" isn't
called out properly, laps should be run for discipline. The proper boxer
stance, slide-step, one arm up, one arm down (windmill), lateral
movement, and post-defensing technique as described before, are
items to evaluate during this drill.

SOME FUNDAMENTALS, REBOUNDING

Figures 12-17 through 12-20 illustrate footwork that is related to
defensive rebounding by X4 and X5. These special drills add to the
suggestions for rebounding and outlet passing work contained in Chapter 9 (Fast Break), and individual fundamentals that can not be taken
for granted or overlooked.

Some coaches, probably in the minority, recommend that the
outlet pass be made while the rebounder's body is turning on the way
down *before* the feet strike the floor. I do not agree with this idea
because most of you don't work with young men who have the excep-
tional coordination, agility and strength necessary for such acrobatics,
nor do I believe that such a movement is necessary for successful
defensive rebounding. I believe that if X4 and X5 are trained to go up
and come down with the ball as suggested in Chapter 9, and then use
the footwork shown here, the rebounding phase will be successful in
our Option Offense.

In Figure 12-17, the rebounder jack-knifes with the ball coming
down, his feet stomping the floor; he pivots to the right, almost in the
same motion, on the ball of his right foot; holds the ball securely in his
turn away from his opponent; and *swings* the left leg completely
around for the finale of his outlet pass. The swing with the left leg
takes the leg and foot first toward the end line, and then around; all the
time, only the side of the rebounding X4's body is being presented to
his opponent. This footwork, in other words, takes X4 *away* from the
opponent, who was boxed out, but can still interfere with, and be a
nuisance to, X4, if footwork training hasn't been emphasized.

Figure 12-18 shows one other technique which may be acceptable
to some. Here, the left foot acts as the pivot to the right, while the right
leg swings around and back, to face the new direction for the outlet

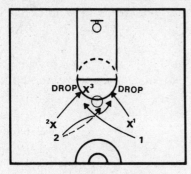

Figure 12-16. Drop.

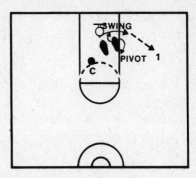

Figure 12-17. Rebounding, basic footwork.

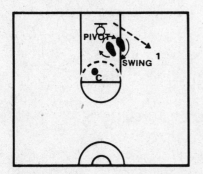

Figure 12-18. Another way of pivoting.

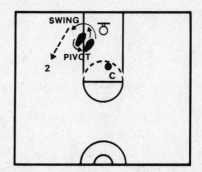

Figure 12-19. Rebound and outlet pass, other side.

pass. Some coaches prefer this; I do not. It seems to me that this method causes the ball to be unprotected as the rebounder turns *in* toward, instead of *away* from, his opponent.

For whichever method, Figures 12-17 or 12-18, you stand in the lane and throw the ball up in the basket, which has the metal insert attached. The drill includes the outlet pass to teammate 1. The work of 01's and 02's in getting open for the pass, meeting the pass, and receiving the pass is a part of Chapter 9.

Figure 12-19 shows the footwork action for X5 at the other defensive low post area, and Figure 12-20 is the alternative action.

OVER THE TOP

You pass the ball to 2 to start the action, although he has had

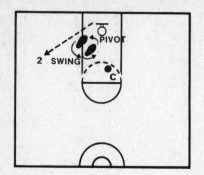

Figure 12-20. The other way, other side.

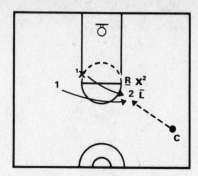

Figure 12-21. Over the top.

X2 to contend with. X2 has been overplaying 2 (strong-side), and adhering to the points already discussed pertinent to Figures 12-14 and 12-15. 01 is coming over the top of teammate 2 to receive a hand-off pass. X1 sees that 01 is going to allow some daylight as he moves around the screen of 2, so X1 decides to fight through. Pay particular attention to the boxer stance and slide-step of X1, and before that, the post-defensing techniques of X2. The action stops if X1 successfully fights over; if he doesn't, try again. 01 is instructed to give just a little daylight for purposes of the drill.

SLIDE THROUGH

Again, you pass to 2. 01 comes across the key, hoping to receive a hand-off pass and screen from 2. Seeing no daylight X1 calls "slide through" or "coming through," warning X2 to step back. X2 must close back up on 2 very quickly as X1 slides through, because 2 can refuse to pass to 01, turn, and jump-shoot from a high-percentage area if left unguarded. By sliding through, X1 retains responsibility for 01, and X2 for 02. You make corrections about boxer stance, slide step, the post-defending of X2, and the talking aggressiveness of X1 and X2.

SWITCH

In Figure 12-23, 01 has the ball for a dribble across the key and around the screen of 02. As 01 dribbles, X1 must communicate with

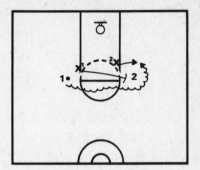

Figure 12-22. Slide through.   **Figure 12-23. Switch.**

teammate X2 about defense. Seeing no daylight, and knowing that he is going to come up solid against the screen of 02, he calls out "switch!" At the instant of the screen, X1 and X2 trade, or switch, responsibilities—X2 takes 01, and X1 takes 02. The coach must not tolerate any timidity in this situation. The call ("switch!") is loud and clear, and the switch, itself, is aggressively done. Either X2 or X1 may call, and I even teach that a truly-aggressive player may have to grab his partner and push him into the switch (exactly where he wants him to go).

DEFENSING THE SIDE-SCREEN

The two feet represent X3 in Figure 12-24. He is defending against 3, you pass to 3, and X3 is going to have to contend with a side screen from 02. X2, of course, comes along with 02. A good teaching technique is to have X3 pivot and turn as shown, opening up toward, and facing, the screener, 02. This causes congestion and traffic problems for 03 as he begins his left-hand dribble, enables X3 to avoid a complete screening, and makes possible an easier switch by X2 and X3. The illustrated footwork shows the left foot of X3 pivoting toward the key, and the right leg swinging right and back. X3, thus, faces the key and the screener, before the screen can set.

REBOUND AND OUTLET

Drill is for rebounding work for X5's and X4's, including outlet passing, and for the outlet receivers, X1 and X2. You shoot, with the

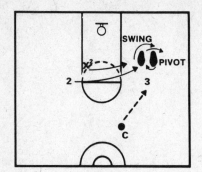

Figure 12-24. Defensing the side-screen.

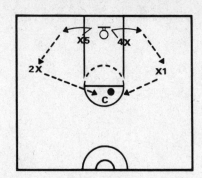

Figure 12-25. Rebound and outlet.

metal insert in place. X5 or X4 rebounds, turns, and outlet-passes to a receiver on his side. The receiver passes smartly back to you to continue the drill. Rebounding fundamentals and outlet passing are described in Chapter 9, as well as in this chapter.

PREVENT THE OUTLET PASS

Drill is for rebounding X4's and X5's, and outlet receivers X1 and X2. You are the shooter, with the metal insert in place in the basket. Player who does not get the rebound (X4 or X5), becomes the opponent just as the rebounder is coming down with the ball, and makes every aggressive attempt to prevent and smother the outlet pass. X1 or X2, depending on the rebounding side, moves fast on his side to receive the pass. Drill is valuable in that it teaches rebounders to expect a fight when they turn to pass.

FREE THROW REBOUNDING

Diagram shows how our team lines up when the opponent has a free throw attempt. X4 and X5 are in usual areas of operation, X1 and X2 are in outlet positions, and X3 is in the position which has the responsibility of blocking out the shooter in the lane in case he misses. X3 is being instructed in both blockout and check-and-go methods. In the former, he steps into the lane at the instant the ball makes contact with the rim, turns to square up in front of the shooter, faces the basket, brings his elbows out, his hands up, and denies the shooter any

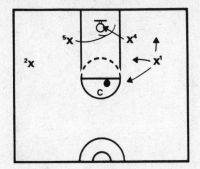

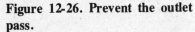

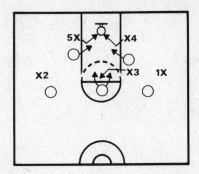

Figure 12-26. Prevent the outlet pass.

Figure 12-27. Free throw rebounding.

kind of a path to the basket. The check-and-go method calls for him to come out in the lane, make contact, pivot and turn, then go for the boards and the ball, without maintaining contact and denial.

FIVE UP

There will be interest and excitement in this drill. You stand at mid-court, along the side, and call out the progress of the drill. Team is divided into two teams. Teams stand in lines, starting at opposite free throw lines, and extending toward center court. First player in line for team #1 shoots free throw. If he makes it, you hold up one finger and call out "One up!" The first player in line for team #2 attempts a free throw. If he makes it, you make a fist, and call out "Even up!" Next player for team #1 shoots. If he misses, there is no change in the score, and the next player for team #2 makes his attempt. If this one is successful, the score is announced as "One up!" for team #2. Shooting and scoring continue in this manner until one team or the other reaches "Five up." The losing team runs laps. Shooters go to the end of their lines after each attempt. Managers act as retrievers.

SHOOT AND RUN

Team is divided into two groups, with each group at opposite foul lines, players lined up and extending toward the center line. There is no competition between teams. This is a competitive drill involving total points for the individual. Each shooter, as he comes up for his free

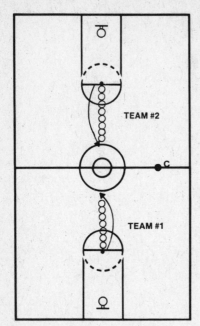

Figure 12-28. Five-up.

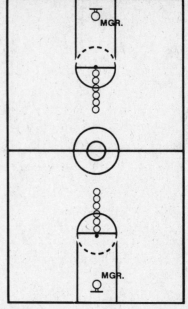

Figure 12-29. Shoot and run.

throw, is given a one-and-one (bonus) situation. If he misses the first, he immediately runs two laps, and comes back to the end of his line. If he makes his first free throw, but misses the second, he gets one point, runs one lap, and comes back to the rear of his line. If he makes both in succession, he gets two points and goes to the rear of his line. Statistician keeps record. Managers act as retrievers.

NOTES ABOUT INDIVIDUAL FOOTWORK

Watch the young player as he tries to put a move on his defensive man. Too many times you will see him take an illegal step, shuffle his feet into a violation, or just plain travel with the ball. This indicates a lack of preparation and work in individual one-on-one fundamentals. The player must be trained to realize that being able to maneuver and drive with the ball is an important basketball skill for attainment, the same as being able to shoot. In teaching individual footwork skills, you may do well to concentrate on the jab step, lead step, rocker step and cross-over step. There are others, but these four are basic, and from them you and your players may expand your efforts. Figures 12-30 through 12-33 will deal with the four.

JAB STEP SEQUENCE

The jab step is a kind of tentative half-step as it begins, usually in a right or left oblique direction. If jabbing to the right (Figure 12-30a), the right foot leads off; if jabbing to the left, the left foot leads off. The player is testing when he takes a jab step. The jab is accompanied by a head-shoulder fake, and the player protects the ball by carrying it securely at the hip of the jabbing leg. The opponent's response, or lack of it, will determine and precipitate further movement by our offensive player. If the opponent does not react quickly by shutting off the jab, the player would probably go on with a drive to the side by putting the ball on the floor with a right-hand dribble, (not shown). In assuming,

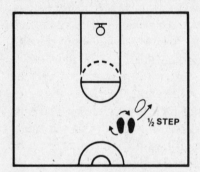

Figure 12-30a. Jab step starts.

Figure 12-30b. Back to original.

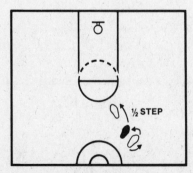

Figure 12-30c. Jab step left.

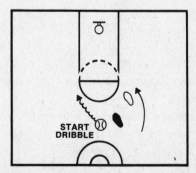

Figure 12-30d. Jab step success. Dribble-drive.

however, that the jab step was shut off, Figure 12-30b shows the jab foot and leg coming back to the original position, as the player decides to try a jab to the left. He does this in Figure 12-30c. The right foot pivots, the left takes a half-step, and the ball is brought back to the protection of the left hip. Sensing an advantage now, the player puts the ball on the floor with a left-hand dribble (Figure 12-30d) simultaneous with the step of the right foot (arrow in Figure 12-30d). Our player is driving for the basket, and a basic rule is being followed: the body of the dribbler is between the ball and the opponent.

LEAD STEP

The lead step differs from the jab step in that the player has made up his mind, and commits himself to an explosive move, a full step in the new direction after the head-shoulder fake. Maintaining body balance, as he must always do, the player first pivots both feet to the oblique direction, and in Figure 12-31a, steps full with the right foot. This establishes position, and fixes the opponent away from the basketball, so he starts the dribble-drive, right hand, right side. Simultaneously, there is a giant, driving step with the left foot and leg (numbered 2).

In Figure 12-31b, the player decided to go left with the lead step. The feet pivot in the new direction, there is a step with the left (numbered 1), and the ball is put on the floor for a left-hand dribble as the right leg follows with its step (numbered 2).

ROCKER STEP

In the rocker step, the idea is to get the opponent into a rocking

Figure 12-31a. Lead step right.

Figure 12-31b. Lead step left.

rhythm, during which he might yield to an outside shot or a drive. There are many ways to perform the rocker step, and our example is only one. Take a full step forward or to the side; if the opponent gives ground, he is responding to the rhythm, so take a jump shot with a quick release. If no shot is possible, recover to the original, take another step backward, and pull the ball back on the right hip (if "rocking" on the right side). This is the rocking motion, and it may be repeated in a similar way, along with head fakes, until the opponent is exploited by the rhythm. Figures 12-32a, b, and c, illustrate this, and a rule might be made: if the opponent moves forward with your motion, drive on him; if he gives ground, think about a jump shot! Figure 12-32d suggests that a quick change to rocker step left is successful, as

Figure 12-32a. Rocker step right.

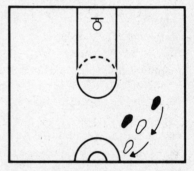

Figure 12-32b. Rocker rhythm.

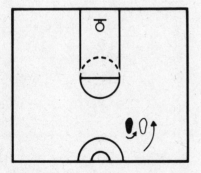

Figure 12-32c. Back to the start.

Figure 12-32d. Rocker step left, with drive.

the lead step is made with the left foot (numbered 1), the right leg slides in the new direction as the ball goes to the floor (numbered 2), and the left-hand dribble begins.

CROSS-OVER STEP

The cross-over is a move whereby the player steps across his body with the far foot and leg for his first step (Numbered 1, Figure 12-33a). This shunts the opponent to the outside, right at the beginning. The other foot (the right, in Figure 12-33a) pivots, then steps in the new direction, numbered 2. The right-hand dribble starts at this time, the outside foot and leg continue the drive (numbered 3), and the player has his drive going, with the opponent forced to an ineffective defensive position. Figure 12-33b is the identical technique to the left.

One suggestion must be made concerning an improvisation during the cross-over step, and you might consider adding it to your one-on-one special drills. The description does not require a diagram. Sometimes, the defensive opponent will try to overplay and shut off the dribble, especially at number 3 in Figure 12-33a and b. When this happens, the answer is a reverse dribble, which leaves the defensive man leaning toward the sideline, and takes the dribbler into the lane, an important half-step to the good. The reverse dribble is sometimes called the spin-off dribble, but it is the same thing as far as I am concerned. Regardless of the terminology, lots of intensive practice is required, to guarantee success.

The cross-over step, right or left, with reverse dribble held in reserve as an added threat, adds a great deal to the one-on-one repertoire.

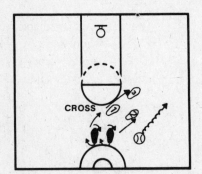 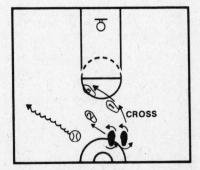

Figure 12-33a. Cross-over step, right.   **Figure 12-33b. Cross-over step, left.**

THE TRAPPER

In my opinion, too much credit is given, and too much attention paid, to what are called natural moves in basketball. If a player has great natural and exciting individual potential abilities in certain areas of basketball, they should be polished fundamentally in practices, and then channeled into the overall team strategy. Moves can be acquired through diligence and practice; not all are natural. Too many young men, ambitious for "play for pay" in professional basketball, are surprised to find that scouts turn away, more and more, from natural-ness, and are attracted to the basketball athlete who shows that he has worked at his basic skills and fundamentals. Natural moves draw "oohs" from spectators, but too often the personal acclaim detracts from the team effort and offensive plan.

Figure 12-34 shows a move that can be practiced until it pays off, and it needs only the usual amount of natural ability. In the White Series, 03 flashes out to the high post to receive the pass from 2, and the series unfolds from there. 03 can add dimension to this attack if he will always keep in mind the possibility of taking advantage of any carelessness or defensive lapse by X3. In Figure 12-34, 03 receives the pass, stops, plants both feet, pivots to the right on the foot nearest his defensive man, X3, traps X3 on his right hip, swings his left leg quickly around to the right as he pivots, puts the ball on the floor with a left-hand dribble, and drives as shown with some possible help from a screen by 5, also shown. We call this *The Trapper*.

THE SPINNER

Figure 12-35 shows the Spinner for special practice and inclusion as a part of the White Series. Like the Trapper it will appear to be free-lance and natural, but the basketball student will instantly recog-nize the practiced basic skills involved. Again, the idea is for 03 to get

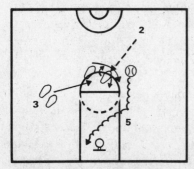

Figure 12-34. The Trapper.

Figure 12-35. The Spinner.

X3 on his inside hip, the hip nearest X3. This time, the reverse pivot is executed by the action of the left foot, while the right foot and leg swing around to the left. X3 is trapped on the left hip, the ball is put on the floor with a right-hand dribble, and 03 has the advantage for his one-on-one. If he has the natural grace and agility for a long step, and a float or hang in the air right here, so much the better. His move would be unstoppable.

TURN-AROUND JUMPER

In writing about, or discussing certain moves, it is easy for you to state that specific, needed skills are involved in a play or pattern, and take for granted that the reader or listener understands the technicalities and concepts without explanation. Worse still, we assume that the player understands a term, and has by some mysterious means acquired the skill connected with it, to the extent that it need only be diagrammed and put into effect.

A case in point would be the turn-around jump shot in Figure 12-36. Easy to say, sounds good, and looks good in a diagram, but the skill has to be explained, demonstrated, and practiced. For the drill, we need 1's and 4's. The action is mainly appropriate to the Red Series. 04 moves around an imaginary 5 and receives the swing pass from 1. Dribbling down, he is forced away from his lay-up, so he stops as shown, fakes left with the ball secured and protected, pivots on his left foot, turns to his right, swings to face the basket with one step, and goes high in the air for his turn-around jumper.

THE PUMP

Being completely overguarded, intimidated, and overplayed in Figure 12-37, 03 goes back door and receives a pumping pass from 1. This will teach X3 a lesson as the Option Offense runs the Red Series. Basics are involved. First of all, the passer, 1, must learn how to pump, and 03 must learn his footwork as he executes the V-cut. As 03 comes out for the pass, 1 pumps at him by pushing the ball straight outward from the chest, as if a two-handed chest pass is intended; then, in refusal, brings the ball back to the chest position, pulling it straight back, and finally, completes the deception by actually passing to 03 on a second push as 03 goes back door. On this second push, the passer

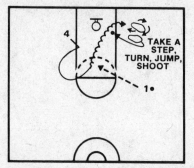

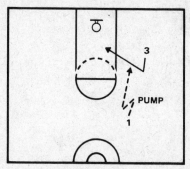

Figure 12-36. Turn around Jumper.

Figure 12-37. Pump.

may find more strength and velocity if he takes a step in the direction of the pass as it is delivered. 03's footwork must be practiced, with the objective of learning how to trap X3 behind the right leg, and freezing him in place for just the fraction of an instant. 03, of course, is head-faking and feinting as he comes out for the pass from 1. Suddenly, his left foot sets, pivots to the right smartly; simultaneously, there is a push-off from this same left foot and leg as the right foot steps abruptly in the new direction. This traps X3 temporarily, and 3 makes his power-drive for the basket as the ball is delivered.

FRONT-WHEEL DRIVE

Figure 12-38 demonstrates a move that 03 may decide to try as he receives the initiating pass from 1 in the Red Series. He runs forward, plants his feet just momentarily, and as he receives the pass, executes a cross-over with his left foot and leg. The right foot has pivoted, (numbered 1) as the left leg swings around (numbered 2). 03 may now dribble-drive with the left hand, and the ball is protected by the body.

REVERSE FRONT-WHEEL DRIVE

Figure 12-39 shows a reverse move by 03 when he receives the pass from 1 in the Red Series. The left foot begins the pivot to the left as the feet are planted. The right foot and leg swing across and over (numbered 1), simultaneous with the pivot of the left foot. The right foot takes a power step in the new direction (numbered 2), and numbers 3 and 4 show the steps that follow. The pass should be practiced as

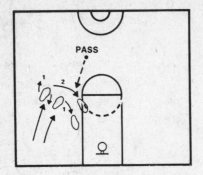

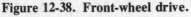

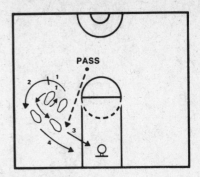

Figure 12-38. Front-wheel drive.   **Figure 12-39. Reverse front-wheel drive.**

a *pumping* pass, because as shown, it is not delivered until number 3 in the sequence.

BASICS AT START OF BLUE SERIES

The pass from 2 to 04 which starts the Blue Series, is an opportune time to discuss the technique of catching, or receiving, a pass, and having a drill pertinent to this basic fundamental. You must teach the technique of pass reception because your team cannot afford to fumble or blunder away passes in the Option Offense. Actually, any one of the initiating passes in Red, White, or Blue lend themselves very well to pass-catching drills.

As 04 steps out from behind 5 for the pass, his hands are carried about waist-high, and the arms are relaxed, not carried stiffly. As the ball is about to be received, the receiver must meet it, not wait for it, with his eyes on the ball all the way. When the hands move out to receive the ball, they give at contact in such a way that there is no shock of opposing forces. "He has soft hands" is a basketball coach's way of describing a player who is receiving the pass in proper fashion. Pushing out with the hands against the direction of the ball will cause fumbling. The fingers are spread, and the ball comes to rest in the finger and thumb areas, never in the palm or heel.

The players must be drilled in catching a high pass, and a low pass. The high pass is caught with the thumbs pointing toward each other. A low pass is received with the body bent down and the little fingers pointing downward as the two hands are opened to catch the low ball. There are also times when the receiver will have to accept the ball at his side; for example, as the receiver comes out, the defender may be overplaying on the receiver's right side, and the ball is therefore passed to the receiver's left side, away from the defensive man. In this case, our receiver may block the ball in its flight with his left hand, while the other hand (right) acts as a stabilizer in gathering the ball into the blocking hand. This method, similar in idea to that of a catcher or first-baseman snaring a baseball, must be practiced extensively.

The laws of learning, mentioned in Chapter 1, are in effect in pass-catching drills: *explanation, demonstration,* and *application.*

In keeping with the Blue Series, the receiver in Figure 12-40a has considered handing back the ball to 02 as he came by, then refused him. In Figure 12-40b, the left foot is pivoting, and the ball is carried high and securely, for the sake of protection. The pivoting is done in

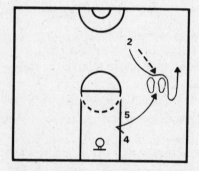

Figure 12-40a. Receiving a pass, Blue Series.

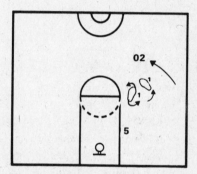

Figure 12-40b. Turning and protecting the ball.

the manner which turns the receiver away from his defensive man. The ball is received at about the free throw line extended, just to the side of the lane. The left foot pivots as shown (numbered 1); at the same time, the right foot and leg start the swing to the left (number 1). At number 1, the player is about half-way around in his turn, with the ball held high, and the side of the body presented to the defender. The left foot completes the pivot (Figure 12-40c), and the right foot and leg come alongside, completing the movement. The receiver may be open for his jump shot in Figure 12-40c, or he may be looking down at low post 5, or thinking about the other options of the Blue Series as described in Chapter 4.

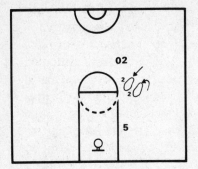

Figure 12-40c. Completed turn, look down.

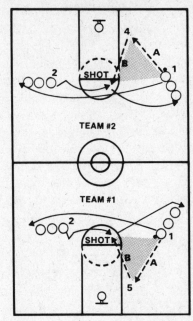

Figure 12-41. Shoot in the triangle.

SHOOT IN THE TRIANGLE

Assistant coach and manager supervise Team #1 (half the team) at one end, where 5 acts as low post. Coach and one manager work at the other end, Team #2, where 4 acts as low post. A statistician for each group keeps shooting records, as set up by the coach. 1's start the drill by passing down to low post. 02's come across the key to receive the over-head, fan-type pass from their low post teammates, and take the jump shot from the free throw line area. 4 and 5 practice offensive rebounding. 1's and 2's rotate. Groups change ends of the court. Coaches stress attention to skills of passing, pass reception, feinting without the ball, and jump shooting. *Elbow in*, and *follow through* are two mechanics of shooting that might be watched very closely.

QUICK RELEASE

Team is divided into two groups, with coach, manager and statistician at one end, and the assistant coach, another manager, and statistician at the other. Six shooting points are designated and marked around the perimeter. Drill begins at each end when the first shot is attempted from point 1. The shooter moves to the next higher point only if the shot is successful. Coach and assistant coach, with stop watches, time the action from point #1 to point #6 at their respective baskets. As point #6 is completed, the shooter will have for the record a total number of attempts and total elapsed time. Alertness, skills of shooting accuracy, and quick release are sharpened in this drill. Have the 4's and 5's act as retrievers as much as possible, because of the rebounding and outlet passing involved. They must work at equal pace for all shooters.

SHOOT AND RETRIEVE

Shooting accuracy in high-percentage areas; alertness and spirit in retrieving a shot; speed, technique and precision in passing; and proper reception of a pass are the elements to be sharpened in this drill. There is competition between two groups; half the team is at one end under the supervision of the coach, the other half at the other end, under the

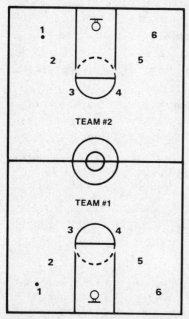

Figure 12-42. Quick release.

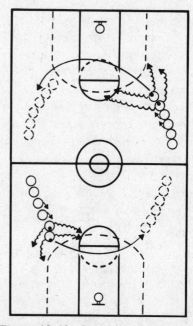

Figure 12-43. Shoot and retrieve.

assistant coach. Players line up as shown, with the first two players in each line having a ball. On signal, the first player in line at each end dribbles to the designated shooting perimeter, takes a shot, retrieves and passes out to the third man in line, who must meet and receive the pass properly. After retrieving and passing, the shooters form a line in proper order on the other side of the court to continue the drill. The second man in line (also with a basketball) is allowed to start his dribble just as the man ahead makes his shooting attempt. This second man retrieves, and passes out to the fourth man in line. As the lines run out on one side, they reform on the other, until one group achieves ten successful attempts. This group wins. Statisticians at each end keep records according to coach's needs. A poorly executed fundamental calls for a repeated effort, on the coach's order.

TRIANGLE PASSING

Figure 12-44 illustrates a drill that stresses the importance of the post player's responsibilities (alertness, peripheral awareness, pass reception, pivoting and turning, protecting the ball, and passing), and the responsibilities of the other players in alertness, passing, and pass reception. There is a 2-1-2 setup, with basketballs at 1 and 3. 1 starts the drill with a pass (make it a bounce pass, or over-head pass) to P at the top of the key. P pivots to the direction of the other man in this particular triangle, 4, and passes to him. Just as P pivots back to the original, 3 hits him with his pass, and P pivots toward 2, to pass to him. The third pass (pass C) in each triangle completes one sequence, and the drill continues. There is no rotation.

DOUBLE-POST DRILL

The post men (P) are at each side of the free throw line in Figure 12-45, with each the part of a three-man triangle on his side of the court. 1 and 3, with basketballs, are in the traditional offensive guard positions, and 2 and 4 are set in the corner areas, as shown. The two triangles operate separately. 01 passes to P, cuts inside and down the lane, asking for the give-and-go. P refuses him, pivots to his left rear, passes to 4 (Pass B), who passes out to the replacement at 1 (Pass C). 01 becomes 04, and 04 becomes 01. P remains in place. The same procedure of passing, cutting, and rotating takes place on the other side

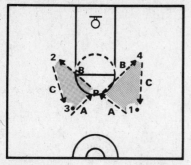

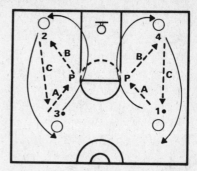

Figure 12-44. Triangle passing.   **Figure 12-45. Double-post drill.**

by 03, P, and 02. Over-head (fan-passing), or bounce passing is suggested. This closely resembles the *passing game* phase of the Option Offense when controlling the tempo of the game, or protecting the lead.

WORK FOR THE GOOD SHOT

The purpose of the drills in Figures 12-46 through 12-48 is to, generally, emphasize the importance of purposeful movement without the ball, passing, and patience in the Option Offense. In Figure 12-46, the drill is 3-on-3, with a time limit of, say, ten minutes. An imaginary line is designated beyond which no shots may be taken, because we want close-in attempts and lay-ups in this drill. Upon possession of the ball, both X's and 0's must pass at least ten, and no more than fifteen, times before a shot attempt is permitted. All three members of the offense call out the number of the pass as it occurs. No dribble is allowed unless the player is going on a drive for the basket. The group on defense, rebounding a missed attempt, has to pass the ball out beyond the limit line to start their offense, and the pass(es) count against the minimum of ten. Rebounding their own missed attempt, the offense does not have to do the same. Statisticians record whatever offensive and defensive information the coach wants to evaluate. Coach encourages post play, both high and low. A wasteful dribble is a turnover.

4-ON-4, COUNT THE PASSES

In this 4-on-4 drill, a minimum of fifteen passes must be made

Figire 12-46. Work for the good shot.

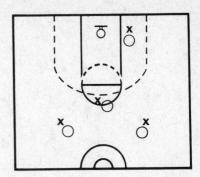

Figure 12-47. 4-on-4, count the passes.

before a shot can be taken. Beyond the maximum of twenty, the ball is turned over as a reward for good defense. All four players call out the number of the pass. No dribble is allowed, unless the player is going for the basket. A wasteful dribble is a turnover. Defensive team, rebounding, has to pass the ball out beyond the limit line before going on offense. Offensive team, rebounding its own missed attempt, has no such requirement. Statisticians record whatever information the coach wants to evaluate. Player movement is the objective!

THREE PASSES TO NUMBER THREE

Figure 12-48 shows a 5-on-5 drill which will add to the proficiency of the Mixmaster phase of the Option Offense. Other chapters contain the description of options emanating from the Mixmaster, so this drill is not intended to add to that. Its purpose is to point out the importance of movement without the ball, good cutting techniques, taking advantage of screens, passing, pass reception, and good shot selection, all within the purview of the Mixmaster. As in the Mixmaster, the point man (here, 03) passes to a wing man, cuts down the key, looks for the give-and-go, looks for the little pass from the post man, if applicable, and comes out on the opposite side, after finally, trying to hang his defensive man on the screen of his low-post teammate, 5. 02 replaced him at the point as the pass was made. Passes move from point to side, side to point, side down to low posts, low post to the cutter coming down the key, and low post out to the point. You designate a player by number who must receive the ball at least three times and no more than five before any one may attempt a shot. The down-the-key cutter is allowed to dribble if he receives a pass under the basket, and is not supposed to shoot. The offense must confine itself to general Mixmaster routes. 0's stay on offense, regardless of rebound recovery or good defense, for a designated time, then the X team plays offense for a time. Man-man and zone defense are alternated by the coach. Statisticians record necessary information. You change the number of the player who must receive the three passes, from time to time.

EXAMPLE OF PENETRATION BY A PRO

In order for you, and the player, to really appreciate the importance of penetration in the offense, some kind of a definition is necessary. Penetration is an individual tactic in basketball which requires the ability to, first, move the ball by dribble-driving toward the basket deep within the defense, and then, pass off to an open teammate for a close-in, high-percentage shot. The penetrator causes confusion, and creates his own offense as he sets up plays or shots around the basket; therefore, penetration cannot really be diagrammed formally, or programmed into a plan. It is one of the most valuable offensive traits a player, particularly an outside player, can have. Even though it comes from individual improvisation and imagination, it has a place in a rules-oriented, pattern offense.

Figure 12-49 illustrates one of the many penetrative actions by a play-maker in present-day professional basketball. This is one of the

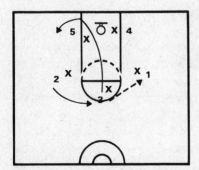

Figure 12-48. Three passes to number three.

Figure 12-49. Penetration by a pro.

simplest and least-complicated of his moves, and one that can be observed in every game in which he participates. To the average spectator, only individual imagination and skill is being required in this movement, which has the appearance of free-lance. The truth is, this dribble-drive deep into the defense, culminating in a pass to an unguarded teammate, has been practiced over and over, and plays an important role in the offensive plan. The individual with the facility for making it a part of the offense is a highly prized player. Besides skills, this player needs all his *courage* as he dares to run the gauntlet. A burly and prideful professional defense around the basket is very sensitive to this kind of daring and audacity! Many times, the penetrator is, literally, dribbling for his life, especially if he is repeating an earlier foray. A lot of vengeful head-hunting will be going on!

The Option Offense has a high regard for penetration, and emulates its utilization by the professionals. The example in Figure 12-49 can be used as a drill at any level.

PENETRATION, RED SERIES

The drill in Figure 12-50 is within the domain of the Red Series. It could be an excellent option at the very beginning of the series, but was not suggested in Chapters 1 and 2. 01 passes to 3, follows his pass, and receives the hand-back. Facing the basket from his side position, 01 decides to penetrate. Possibly using the lead step, cross-over, or other individual skill, he starts his dribble, goes under the basket and across the key, and suddenly, dumps the ball out to an open man, 03, who has cut to the top of the key in his usual Red Series route. The jump shot is taken by 03. As stated before, the penetration action must, by necessity, be drawn simply in a diagram, but in reality there might be evasive dribbling, reverse dribbling, or dribbling around a screen; and at the time of the pass, the penetrator would be jumping and twisting in the air to face his teammates, who are trying to get open for the pass. Also not shown could be another type of pass, the *drop-back*, in which the dribbler spots his receiver behind or to the side, so the passing hand is brought up and behind the head, the passer goes in the air, and the pass comes from behind the head. Still another method of passing during penetration is becoming very effective, and must be noted here. It is the *wrap around*, which usually occurs very close-in, around the basket, when the dribbler draws an additional defender to him, one guarding the dribbler's teammate. So he goes in the air, fakes a little shovel-like pass with the ball in the left hand, transfers the ball to his right hand, and swings his right hand and arm around the body of this defensive man in a *wrapping* effect as he jumps the little pass to this teammate for the close-in shot. None of these actions can be diagrammed, but they must be practiced.

DOWN THE MIDDLE AND PASS OUT

The 01's and 02's must be trained to exploit any defensive lapse in the middle, by dribble-driving and penetrating down the key, then passing out to an open man. Figure 12-51 illustrates this kind of free-lance and imagination we want in the Option Offense. Our driver must be aware of the peripheral presence of teammates such as 02 and 03 in the diagram; and they must move to get open. Somewhere in the lane, within the 3-second limit, our driver must stop, turn, jump, and twist in the air to jump-pass back out to an open man, or he will make a drop-back pass as he dribbles down the key, without stopping.

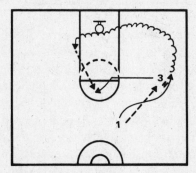

Figure 12-50. Penetration, Red Series.

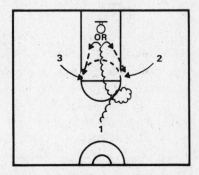

Figure 12-51. Down the middle and pass out.

MOVE OR RUN A LAP

Movement without the ball is the feature of the drill in Figure 12-52. Half-court 3-on-3 competition is involved, with the coach, manager, and statistician at one end, and the assistant coach, manager, and statistician at the other. The 0's are on offense for eight minutes (one quarter), then the X's get the ball for eight minutes. Any member

of the three-man offensive team caught *not moving* while his team is
working for a shot, must drop out and run a lap. This creates an
outnumbering situation against his team while he is running, so it is
best that he runs his lap in a hurry. Movement is defined in this drill as
purposeful. Only the two without the ball are subject to the penalty.
Statisticians keep score. Players will like this drill, but coaches won't
be popular because of the judgment calls on movement. Do not suspend play when penalizing; just call out the player's name, he immediately runs for the sidelines to run his lap, and then returns to the
game while it is in progress.

FAST BREAK

Three fast-break drills are drawn in Figures 12-53 through 12-55.
Figure 12-53 begins as 5 makes an outlet pass to 2. He has rebounded
the manager's missed free throw attempt (the metal insert is in place in
the basket). 03 and 01 cross, and reference should now be made to

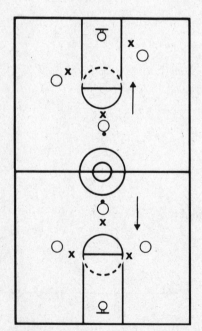

**Figure 12-52. Move, or run a
lap.**

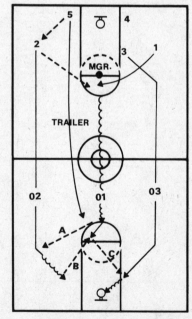

**Figure 12-53. Fast break, missed
free throw.**

Chapter 9, because the fast break procedure of the Option Offense will not be repeated here. The lanes are filled as shown. For purposes of this drill, 01 passes off to 02 at about the free throw line extended; 02 takes a dribble, assumes he is shut off by the defense, and makes a drop-back return pass to 01. 01 reverses a quick pass over to the driving 03, who goes on in for the lay-up. 05, the rebounder, is the trailer. It would be customary to have two defensive men in the drill against 1, 2, and 3, but for this particular one we are trying to polish the fundamentals of the movement, and we can always insert the two defensive men later.

FAST BREAK, PASS TO THE TRAILER

In Figure 12-54, the opponent has scored, so 04 steps out as quickly as possible, and passes in to 1. 1 looks for the center man, 02, passes to him, and the lanes are filled as shown. We illustrate the importance of the trailer in this drill as 02 dribbles all the way,

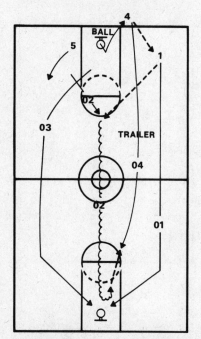

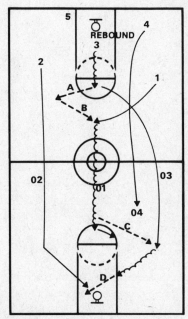

Figure 12-54. Fast break, pass to the trailer.

Figure 12-55. Another fast break.

reverse-turns, jumps high, and dumps the ball back out to the trailer, 04, who will certainly free-lance from then on.

ANOTHER FAST BREAK

We realize that not all rebounds will be the property of 4 and 5, so we have to train 3 as a possible rebounder and outlet-passer. In Figure 12-55, he passes out to either 01 or 02 (02 here), crosses with the opposite man, and goes on to fill a lane. 02 fills the other outside lane after getting the ball to the center man, 01. 01 dribbles in, passes off to the cutter, 03, who passes under-basket to the driving 02. While we do not encourage Pass D (a cross-key pass doesn't always get through the defense), we have to realize that there will be instances where the pass will get through.

It is suggested that the five men in each diagram (Figures 12-53 through 12-55) go down and back with the same drill, and that a waiting line of five men be ready to take over and run the drill upon the return of the first five. There are many variations and ideas in conducting fast break drills, so we will leave additional ramifications up to you.

COUNTY FAIR

A *County Fair*, made up of stations, one at each basket in the gym, is an excellent way to add interest to special drills. It also saves time and consolidates some of the programming. A County Fair is interesting to players because it furnishes a break from the usual drills, and creates a feeling of competition. The one here consists of six stations (six baskets), with the equipment, personnel, and procedures listed and described for each. No diagrams are drawn for Stations #1, #3, and #5. A model score card is included.

STATION #1. LEFT HAND, RIGHT HAND.

Equipment, personnel: Stopwatch. Basketball. One scorer.
Procedure: Player presents his scorecard as he comes to the station. To start, player faces the basket, just to the left side. Standing and jumping, he lays the ball up left-handed; rebounds the ball if it misses, or pulls it out of the net if it goes in, and moves in the air to jump

and shoot right-handed on that side of the basket. Traveling violation not permitted. Continues left side, right side. Tries to make as many jumping lay-ups as possible in time limit. Player moves to next station.

STATION #2. SHOOT AGAINST TIME.

Equipment, personnel: Stopwatch. Basketball. One scorer. One rebounder.

Procedure: Players present their scorecards, Two players are necessary. One is the shooter, being scored, the other is the rebounder, who works quickly. Perimeter for shooting is shown in diagram. Shoot, move to new place on perimeter, receive pass from rebounder, jumpshoot again. Procedure continues until time is up. Change places. Scorer records points on scorecards. Shooter goes to new station.

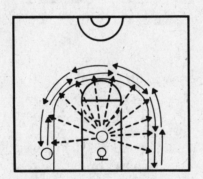

Station #2. Shoot against time.

STATION #3. MAKE YOUR FREE THROWS.

Equipment, personnel: Basketball. One scorer.

Procedure: Player presents scorecard. Shoots 15 free throws. Scorer records points on scorecard. Player goes to new station.

STATION #4. PITCH AND CATCH.

Equipment, personnel: Watch or stopwatch. Basketball. Scorer.

Procedure: Player presents scorecard. As shown in the diagram, from area #1, close to the basket, player tosses ball high and across the board so that it can be caught before striking the floor in area #2. From area #2, repeat the action so the ball may be caught in area #1 before it touches the floor (Criss-cross). Scorer records points on scoreboard. Player goes to new station.

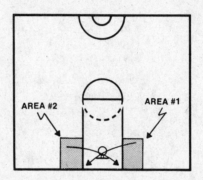

Station #4. Pitch & catch.

STATION #5. ONE-ON-ONE

Equipment, personnel: Stopwatch or watch. Basketball. Manager. Two scorers (one for each player).

Procedure: Two previously matched players go one-on-one. Manager controls action. Match has time limit as shown on scorecard (four minutes). Jump ball starts action. Turnover by man on offense gives defensive man the ball and one point. Free throws awarded for all fouling violations. If successful with free throw, player retains offensive possession. If he rebounds own shot, offensive man stays on offense at the point of rebounding, and he can shoot again from this point; but defensive man must dribble out to starting point to go on offense if he has rebounded the opponent's shot. Scorers record points. Players move on to new station.

STATION #6. MAKE IT AND GO ON.

Equipment personnel: Stopwatch or watch. Two basketballs. Two rebounders. One scorer.

Procedure: One ball with shooter at position #8, one ball with
another shooter at position #1. One rebounder with
each shooter. Start together, #8 goes clockwise, #1
goes counterclockwise. Must sink the field goal at
one position before going to next. Scorer records
points. Players move on to new station.

Station #6. Make it and go on.

SCORE CARD
BASKETBALL COUNTY FAIR

NAME _____

Station #1. Left hand, right hand.
Time: one minute
One point for each successful   POINTS:_____

Station #2. Shoot against time.
Time: two minutes
Two points for each successful   POINTS:_____

Station #3. Make your free throws
Shoot fifteen
One point for each successful   POINTS:_____

Station #4. Pitch and catch.
Time: one minute
One point for each successful catch   POINTS:_____

Station #5. One-on-one.
Time: four minutes
Points as recorded under procedure   POINTS:_____

Station #6. Make it and go.
            Time: 1½ minutes, or successful shots at
            all 8 positions, whichever first
            Two points each successful shot at each
            position, up to 1½ minutes   POINTS:_____

                                        GRAND TOTAL:_____

SUMMARY

The special drills in this chapter are appropriate and applicable to a specific objective: promoting proficiency in the Option Offense. It has been stated that this offense requires a high degree of proficiency in basketball fundamentals, intelligence, poise, restraint, and aggressiveness. The drills were selected and programmed with these requirements in mind. From the beginnings of basic footwork through graduation into fast break, these drills should prove beneficial to the players who will experience them, and they will be a valuable part of your overall plan. By the way, you are reminded that practice sessions seem to go more smoothly and efficiently when they are carefully planned. To promulgate this planning, a Daily Practice Programming Worksheet is included at the end of the chapter. It is tightly constructed, self-explanatory, fits a clipboard, and is highly recommended as a teaching aid to the busy Option Offense coach.

DAILY PRACTICE PROGRAMMING WORKSHEET

| Skills: | Drill # | Drill # | Skills: |

Names: Time:_____ min.   Time:_____ min.   Names:

_____ (in charge)   _____ (in charge)

Description: _____   Description: _____

Comments, reminders: Comments, reminders:

Chapter Thirteen

Preparing the Offense

For the Game

OBJECTIVE

In this chapter, the team is ready to play a game of basketball. All the planning by you, and hard work by your players during the daily practice sessions; all the concentration on perfection of Option Offense fundamentals and skill; all the comment, censure, criticism, flattery and praise; and, most understandably, all the pride and hopes of both you and your team for a winning game next day, culminate here, the day before the game.

As described and suggested here, the team puts it all together. The objective now, is to reach a desired peak of proficiency and efficiency through a rehearsal of the offensive techniques and strategies of the Option Offense. Time is devoted to this review as a part of the practice session on the day preceding every game.

GENERAL PLAN

Material in this chapter is in two parts. The first consists of dialogue, or scenario, as the entire team is put through its paces during part of a practice session, reviewing and running through the major option possibilities for the next day, with your narration and supervision coming from your position along the mid-court line.

The second part describes and illustrates the pre-game warm-up drills that will also be rehearsed.

Your word-for-word planning and preparation for the first part is absolutely necessary, if the drill is to be successful and meaningful. The players, recognizing the preparation and sensing its value, will respond with enthusiasm. There is no waste of time, no standing around; the team's execution of the practice drill will be impressive because it does not have to contend with a defense; and most importantly, this review of options ends on a positive note, with a happy coach, and a confident team that appears to be ready to use the Option Offense next day.

PROCEDURE FOR OPTION OFFENSE REVIEW

For the review of the offenses, you station yourself at mid-court with a copy of the Red, White, and Blue Dialogues, and the Special Plays (all presented in this chapter) on your clipboard. The starting five has one end of the court, the second five the other. They are in the set formation of the Option Offense (quarterback, driver, stack, and wing men). There are no defensive players. Any extra players (beyond the ten) are standing along the sidelines, observing, and ready to come in as replacements. In the narration, you never have to raise your voice. The gym is quiet, the players attentive; by now, they fully comprehend your verbalization. They have been hearing the language of the offense for days and weeks. This is polish time!

You read the dialogue for the first option quickly, ("Red. 1 to 3 to 2 as he cuts. Drive, lay-up, by 2") and point to the starting five. They execute, while the players on the second five, at the other end, watch; then you point to them, and say, "You do it." You continue the drill in this manner, running through the Red, White, and Blue Series, and the Special Play situations. Corrections are made, but you expect that the constructive criticism will be kept to a minimum. The team knows the offense. You do expect, also, leadership from 01, your quarterback. There is a manager at each baseline to retrieve basketballs as necessary, and to provide additional leadership. The assistant coach is mainly concerned with the performance of the second five. The estimated time requirement is thirty-five minutes. It is impossible to cover every single option and offensive alternative, so the dialogues do not attempt to do that. As a matter of fact, different coaches in different situations will undoubtedly adjust and convert the dialogues to fit their own needs for a particular game. For example, if the opponent features a zone defense, you may want to concentrate on the Blue Series, the Mixmaster, and certainly, those options and strategies that are applicable to attacking a zone defense.

For simplicity, Red, White, and Blue practice options are separated; your verbatim dialogue is on one side of the chart; and there is a column for your notes and reminders.

RED DIALOGUE (Day before the game)	COACH'S REMINDERS
1. "1 to 3 to 2 as he cuts. Drive, lay-up, 2."	Figures 2-1. 7-1
2. "1 to 3, hand-back to 1, 1 goes on with dribble, down the side. Free-lance, penetrate."	Figures 2-6. 5-2. 5-3. 7-5.
3. "1 to 3, hand-back to 1, to 4 as he cuts across the key."	Figures 2-2. 6-10
4. "1 to 3, hand-back to 1, to 5 as second man through."	Figure 2-3
5. "1 to 3, hand-back to 1, reverse to 3 at top of the key for jump shot."	Figure 2-4
6. "1 to 3, hand-back to 1, to 4 down at the low post. 4 to 3 as he cuts down the key."	Figure 2-7. To vary, have 4 work for a shot, also pass back out to 1 for jumper.
7. "1 to 3, hand-back to 1, reverse to 3 at top of the key. Mixmaster starts. 3 over to 2 at the wing."	Figures 1-15. 7-14. Make sure 3 cuts down the key after his pass to wing.
8. "1 to 3, hand-back to 1, reverse to 3 at top of the key. Mixmaster. 5 passes, including at least one down to low post. Shoot on count of five."	Figures 2-7 through 2-15. 2-22. 2-23. 6-13. 6-14. Make them use low post screens when they cut down-key and around the low posts. Team counts, aloud.
9. "1 to 3, hand-back to 1, reverse to 3 at top of the key. Mixmaster. Seven passes, including at least two down to either low post. Shoot on seventh."	Figures 2-7 through 2-15. 2-22. 2-23. 6-13. 6-14. 6-18. 6-19. 6-30. 6-31. Team counts.
10. "1 to 3, hand-back to 1, reverse to 3 at top of the key. Mixmaster. Nine passes, including at least one pick-and-roll at low post. Shoot on ninth."	Figures 2-7 through 2-23. Team counts passes.

WHITE DIALOGUE	COACH'S REMINDERS
1. "1 to 2 to 3 at top of key, back door to 1"	Figure 3-1. Timing.
2. "1 to 2 to 3 at top of key, back to 2 for free-lance and jump shot on his side."	Figures 3-9. 5-15. 7-20. Dribble in, or use stack as a screen.
3. "1 to 2 to 3, 3 keeps, goes to his right, free-lance, jump shot."	Trapper. 3-11. 12-34.
4. "1 to 2 to 3, 3 stops, keeps, turns to his left, free-lance."	Spinner. 3-12. 12-35
5. "2 dribbles down court, keeps dribbling as 3 comes out from high post to screen. 2 dribbles on by. Roll by 3. Jump shot by 2."	Figure 3-10. Discourages defensive sag. To vary, have 2 pass to 3 on the roll, or penetrate and pass out.
6. "1 to 2 to 3, 3 turns, looks down, passes high-low to 4."	Figure 3-2. Make sure 1 and 2 run their routes, even though they know they will be refused.
7. "1 to 2 to 3, 3 turns, looks down, passes high-low to 5 as second man through.	Figure 3-3. 1, 2, and 4 run good routes!
8. "1 to 2 to 3. 1 and 2 scissors off the high post. Hand-back to 1."	Figure 3-13. Vary by passing to 2, as he comes by.
9. "1 to 2 to 3. High post scissors. 3 turns, looks down, passes high-low to 4."	Figures 3-14. 3-15. 5-28. 1 and 2 run usual routes!
10. "1 to 2 to 3. High post scissors. 3 turns, looks down, passes high-low to 5 as second man through."	Figures 3-15. 5-28. 1, 2, and 4 run usual routes. Vary with jump shot by 3, after refusing everybody.
11. "1 to 2 to 3. 3 refuses everybody. Start Mixmaster. 3 over to 1. Jump shot."	Figures 6-13, 6-19
12. "1 to 2 to 3. 3 refuses everybody. Mixmaster starts. Five passes, including at least one down to either low post. Shoot on fifth."	Sequence of 1-7 through 1-10, into Mixmaster. Any options of Mixmaster, including 3-4 through 3-7, and 7-34 through 7-40. Team counts.
13. "1 to 2 to 3. 3 refuses everybody. Mixmaster starts. Seven passes, including at least two down to either post. Shoot on seventh."	Sequence of 1-7 through 1-10, into Mixmaster. Any options of Mixmaster. Team counts.

BLUE DIALOGUE	COACH'S REMINDERS
1. "1 to 2 to 4 as he pops out of the stack. 4 turns, takes jump shot."	Figures 4-1. 6-25. Check signals, 5's screen for 4, and rebounding.

2. "1 to 2 to 4, hand-back to 2 as he goes by. 2 dribbles, free-lances."	Figures 4-2. 6-22. 6-26. 6-34. 6-38. 7-10. 4 clears, cuts through key to his low post.
3. "1 to 2 to 4, reverse ball to 1 at top of key for jump shot."	Figures 4-3. 6-40. Make sure 2, 4, and 5 run their routes.
4. "1 to 2 to 4, reverse to 1 at top of the key, over to 3 for jump shot."	Figures 4-3. 6-23. 6-41.
5. "1 to 2 to 4, reverse to 1, right back to 4 as he goes over the top of 5."	Figures 4-3. 6-41. 7-32. Timing. Screen by 5. 2 runs his route. 5 is second man through.
6. "1 to 2 to 4, 4 holds as 5 sets pick. Pick and roll by 5 as 4 dribbles by."	Figures 4-4. 4-5. 5-16. 5-17. 6-40. Have 4 go in, then vary by passing off to 5 on his roll.
7. "1 to 2 to 4, down to 5 at low post."	Figures 4-6 through 4-8. Have 4 turn, pass down, without hesitation, various types of passes. 5 works for shot, also passes back out.
8. "1 to 2 to 4, hand-back to 2. 2 reverses ball to 1 at top of key and cuts over 5. 1 passes to 2 for lay-up."	Reverse-shuffle. Figure 4-10. Make sure 4 clears quickly after handing back, goes to low post. 5 is second man through.
9. "1 to 2 to 4, hand-back to 2, 2 reverses ball to 1, who passes over to 3. 3 to 2 for lay-up."	Figure 4-10. 4 clears ahead of 2's cut, and goes to low post. This is complete shuffle from one side to other. Make sure 5 goes as second man through.
10. "1 to 2 to 4, hand-back to 2. 2 reverses ball to 1, who refuses 2 and passes to 5 as second man through."	Figure 4-10. 5 is actually third man through, because 4 has already cleared, and 2 has cut.
11. "1 to 2 to 4, hand-back to 2. 2 reverses ball to 1, over to 3, down to 4 at the low post. 4 works for shot."	Figure 4-11. Vary. 4 can pass to cutter coming down the key; back to 3 for jump shot; or back out to new point man at the top of the key.

12. "1 to 2 to 4, reverse ball to 1 at top of the key. 1 refuses everybody. Go to Mixmaster. Five passes, including one to low post. Shoot on five."	Any Mixmaster option. Make the minor adjustment if practicing against zone. Sequence of 1-11 through 1-13 into Mixmaster.
13. "Repeat the Blue moves into Mixmaster. Seven passes, including two to low post. Shoot on seventh."	Any Mixmaster options, including the Mixmaster backdoor (4-13 through 4-16). Minor adjustment for zone. Have them do 9 passes, shoot on ninth.
14. "1 and 2, bring the ball into the front court. Run the 'blast'."	Figure 6-42. Everybody run good routes. Blast is designed for 2's jumper, but he can free-lance and hit open man.

PROGRAMMED PLAYS DIALOGUE	COACH'S REMINDERS
1. "Play #1"	Figure 8-7. Stress speed and aggressiveness of 4 and 5 as they get across the key to set a new stack in the play. 1 is on his own to get around the stack. Discuss, run options.
2. "Play #2"	Figure 8-2. 2 is on his own to get open around the stack.
3. "Play #3"	Figure 8-3. 3 gets the shot, but look for options, especially in practice, when players release and "cheat" on defense. New stack by 4, 5. 3 is on his own to get open.
4. "Play #4"	Figure 8-4. 4 gets the shot. He must fake, feint, as he comes out of stack.
5. "Under-basket play"	Figures 8-9 through 8-14. 3 slaps ball for start. Options.
6. "Out-of-bounds, side"	Figures 8-15 through 8-27. 3 slaps ball for start. Lots of options. Try both sides of the court, going for the basket at each end.

BALL CONTROL DIALOGUE	COACH'S REMINDERS
1. "Passing game. Lay-up only. Anybody can score, after 12 passes. Count 'em. Pass and move. Don't get fouled!"	Stress any necessary points between Figures 11-1 and 11-9.
2. "Freeze game. You will not shoot. Pass and move. Don't get fouled. 1 and 2, watch the clock. Call time-out in 2½ minutes"	Set up other freeze situations. Install the game clock for this practice. Stress necessary points between Figures 11-1 and 11-9.

PURPOSE OF PRE-GAME WARM-UPS

The rehearsal of pre-game warm-up drills requires twenty minutes of practice time, which is the usual amount of time given to a team for warm-up before a game. The rehearsal ensures that the team will know exactly how to utilize the pre-game time to best advantage. We want drills of planned exercise that (1) will bring the team to a desired peak of attitude and exertion that will carry over into the game, (2) will require bending, stretching, jumping, and other muscular movement which is *planned* to lessen the risk of injury in the game (by the same token, unplanned warm-ups, in other sports as well as basketball, have been known to *cause* muscular injuries *before* a game), (3) will be of tactical value in furnishing passing, moving and shooting situations that bear resemblance to the options and plays of the offense, (4) will enhance the appearance, demeanor, and efficiency of the team.

A team that warms up in a business-like, planned manner, without confusion, adds a great deal to its own feeling of optimism, confidence, and well-being; this attitude is important, right along with the physical exertion.

The five warm-up drills of Figures 13-1 through 13-5 are suggested because they bear relationship, directly and indirectly, to the Option Offense. In running through these warm-ups just before the game, the team is being reminded of pertinent parts of their offense (without revealing too much of it) right up to the opening whistle. In addition, those characteristics of sharp passing, pivoting, dribbling, rebounding, and shooting that go hand-in-hand with the necessary stretching, bending, and loosening of muscles, are prominently inherent in the five drills.

WARM-UP DRILL FOR REBOUNDERS AND PASSERS

The warm-up in Figure 13-1 separates the 3's, 4's, and 5's (our biggest players) from the 1's and 2's, with the two groups running their respective drills at the same time. The 1's and 2's form a circle for *continuous pass and re-place.* For continuity in the passing circle, there must be an extra man (as shown), at the start, behind the man who starts the drill with his pass. The passer runs *outside* the circle to replace. Passes are of passer's choice.

The 3's, 4's, and 5's separate from the 1's and 2's as they come out of the dressing room and on to the court. The 01's and 02's go on with their passing drill along the side. The 03's, 04's and 05's run a circle around the foul lane first; then, without pause, the lead man (who is carrying a ball), jumps and puts the ball up on the board to the right of the basket, and the loosening-up drill begins as the other running players, following in line behind, rebound, leap, and put the ball back up on the board, away from the basket. The ball is put up on the board to the cadence of "run, jump, catch, control, put it up." This jumping, rebounding-type drill ends after two minutes, when the man who put the ball up in the first place puts it in the basket. The passing drill for O1's and O2's ends at the same time and the team reforms as a full unit to go on to the next drill.

WARM-UP FOR THE BACK DOOR

The warm-up drill in Figure 13-2 is pertinent to the back door

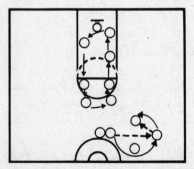

Figure 13-1. Drill for rebounders and passers.

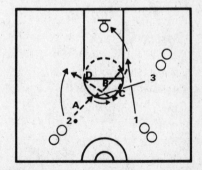

Figure 13-2. Warm-up for the back door.

option of the White Series. There are four passes, as shown (A, B, C, D), with the choice of free-lance (jump shoot or drive) for 02 at the end of Pass D. 2 has passed to 03 (as in the White Series) at the high post, as 01 goes back door. 03 turns to pass to 01, then faces him to meet the return pass (C). 03 then passes over to 02 (Pass D). 01 rebounds and passes out to the starting line. For rotation, 01 becomes 02, 02 becomes 03, 03 becomes 01. All players participate. Timing is important. Two balls can be used to speed up the action. This is an excellent precision drill, which embodies many of the fundamentals that need to be a part of pre-game preparation.

WARM-UP FOR DRIBBLERS, TALKERS, AND SWITCHERS

Two lines, each with a basketball and comprising the entire team, are formed for the drill in Figure 13-3. Heads-up dribbling with both right and left hand against a defensive opponent (who doesn't work too aggressively), and an under-basket lay-up, are the features. There is also a defensive aspect. To remind our players that they must talk on defense, X1 and X2 call "switch," and trade dribbler-opponents just as they near the basket. Dribblers become X1 and X2 in the rotation. To the on-looker, this warm-up will reflect all the hard work in fundamentals: (1) the dribbler stays low, (2) he keeps his head up, eyes off the ball, (3) he changes his dribbling hands in his reverse dribble in the corner, and as necessary otherwise, in keeping the ball to the farthest possible point *away* from the defensive man, (4) the player dribbles with speed, but under control, and (5) after working so hard to get under the basket, the dribbler shows *no* carelessness with his lay-up. It goes in the basket!

WARM-UP FOR PASSERS AND MOVERS

Figure 13-4 represents an impressive, worth-while warm-up. The passes are crisp, the player-movement alert and purposeful. It is restricted Mixmaster, with dribbling and shooting disallowed. The players have heard the coach's threats over and over in practice: "All I want to hear is the squeal of your shoes!" Many coaches wouldn't want to reveal this, or any other part, of the Option Offense to the opponent during warm-ups, but I call this *planned arrogance*, and let them have a preview!

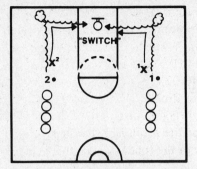

Figure 13-3. Warm-up for dribblers, talkers, and switchers.

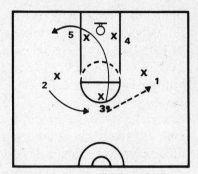

Figure 13-4. Warm-up for passers and movers.

The starting five operates for three minutes offensively, moving and passing in probable routes of Mixmaster against the second five, then changes over to defense for two minutes. Any extra players, beyond ten, may step in as replacements on *defense* at any time, so there is a minimum of inactivity. The ball must be passed down to the low post men by the wing men, as well as from point to wing. The point man always cuts down the key after the pass to the wing, and when the ball goes from wing to low post. While not passive, the defense does not anticipate and overplay. This warm-up will cause a bit of sweat, and also reminds the team of the importance of planned movement for the game ahead. Only the pass to begin the drill is shown in Figure 13-4. Chapters 2 through 6 are references for descriptions of Mixmaster movement, all of which applies to this drill.

WARM-UP FOR PASSERS AND SHOOTERS

Figure 13-5 illustrates the importance that is attached to the following aspects: (1) the pass of penetration from wing to low post, (2) the mobility and movement requirement of wing men to get open for a return pass, (3) the action of low post men, (4) the high-percentage jump shot, and (5) rebounding.

The first men in the two lines at the wings have a basketball, and start the drill with simultaneous passes (of passer's choice) to their respective low post men. 01 then cuts, as shown, to receive the fan-type pass from the *opposite* low post man; at the same time, 02 is cutting to receive a similar pass from *his opposite* low post man. Both 01 and 02 take their jump shots. There is blocking out and rebounding

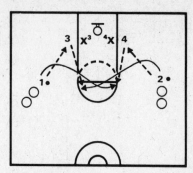

**Figure 13-5. Warm-up for pass-
ers and shooters.**

action by X3, X4, 03, and 04, with the successful rebounders throwing
the two balls back out to the lines. They also rotate their duties, but
stay at the low post area. They get their shots, occasionally, by refusing to pass back out to the cutters.

The precision and timing, pass penetration, jump pass from low
post men to cutters, success of the close-in jump shot, intensity of
rebounding, and the rotation movement make this an appropriate and
impressive warm-up drill for our team.

SUMMARY

As explained, the final preparation for the game next day is programmed in two parts. First, the team reviews the offensive option
framework by means of your prepared dialogue. This reminds each
player of his place, and importance in the Option Offense, and irons
out any questions and problems that may exist. Confidence in the
offense is one of the main products of this part.

In regard to the second part, it is believed that selected and well-
executed warm-up drills are important to the team in its mental and
physical preparation for the game. The five planned drills shown in
Figures 13-1 through 13-5 require the attentiveness, precision, and
physical movement that will get the team ready to play. Pre-game
warm-ups should be timed and rehearsed in practice, should be programmed to reflect game situations, and should, in our case, bear the
stamp of the Option Offense. I believe that the team should put its best
foot forward at this time. If any of the Option Offense is revealed to an
opponent during warm-ups before a game (the White Series back door
of 13-2, the Mixmaster of 13-4, the low post action of 13-5), he is
challenged to do something about it when the game starts!

Index